D1551366

Sacred Custodians of the Earth?

Sacred Custodians of the Earth?

Women, Spirituality and the Environment

Edited by Alaine Low and Soraya Tremayne

Berghahn Books
New York • Oxford

First published in 2001 by **Berghahn Books**

www.berghahnbooks.com

© 2001 Alaine Low and Soraya Tremayne

Library of Congress Cataloging-in-Publication Data

Sacred custodians of the earth? : women, spirituality, and the
environment / edited by Alaine Low and Soraya Tremayne.
p. cm.
Includes bibliographical references and index.
ISBN 1-57181-467-1 (alk. paper) -- ISBN 1-57181-316-0 (alk. paper)
(pbk. : acid-free paper)
1. Ecofeminism--Religious aspects--Congresses. 2. Human ecology--
Religious aspects--Congresses. 3. Women and religion--Congresses.
I. Low, Alaine M. II. Tremayne, Soraya.

HQ1233.S135 2001
305.42--dc21   2001035409

British Library Cataloguing in Publication Data

A catalogue record for this book is available from the British
Library.

Printed in the United States on acid-free paper

ISBN 1-57181-467-1 hardback
ISBN 1-57181-316-0 paperback

Contents

PART III – THE GREAT RELIGIONS

PART IV – NEW TRENDS

Preface

This volume is the result of a two-day international workshop organized by the editors at the Centre for Cross-Cultural Research on Women at Queen Elizabeth House, University of Oxford, in June 1996.

The book explores connections between spirituality and the environment, and the role of women within this context. The choice of the title is a response to the new feminist movements which link women with spirituality and the sacred, and which are having an increasing influence on environmental thinking and planning. It is also in tune with the rapidly growing interest over the past three decades in environmental issues on a global scale (Brundtland Report, 1987), women's issues (UN Decade of Women) and the emphasis being placed on the importance of the role played by women in the use and protection of natural resources. Literature on women and their relationship with the environment is abundant, and this has been analysed from different perspectives in various disciplines by specialists from the developed and developing world. The convenors therefore set the premise of the workshop at a different level, namely to explore some of the major spiritual, religious and philosophical views and beliefs concerning women and the environment. The participants questioned how these belief systems affect behaviour, and whether they can be put to use to create an awareness among people of the need to protect, preserve and enhance the environment. Central to the discussion was the consideration of how women are viewed in various spiritual and religious ideologies in relation to the environment and the community, and whether in reality they occupy the place accorded to them by post-modernist thinking, as well as by many policy-makers and planners. The contributors aimed to explore whether women were 'innately' connected to nature because of their responsibility in the daily management of natural resources, and whether women manage and exploit the environment more sensitively than men. We also set out to assess whether any practical lessons can be learnt from these ideologies which could be incorporated in the education of their adherents in approaches to environmental conservation. The idea of a spiritual link and sense of sacredness needs to be tested against the everyday realities of life.

The workshop brought together thirteen speakers from different disciplines including social anthropologists, historians, theologians, and academics in the field of development studies. The papers were wide-ranging, stretching in time from ancient Greece to the present, and in space across many regions of the world. The contributors approached the issues from the point of view of their own discipline, each retaining the three major themes of spirituality/sacredness, environment and women, whilst searching for the practical dimension of issues at the heart of the debate. We are aware that this volume is by no means comprehensive as far as all major religions are concerned.

The book is divided into four sections. The first part provides an overview and background to the subject and a critique of 'ecofeminism'. In Part II, five chapters are case studies of what one might term 'The Sacred'. This group includes the classical world as well as contemporary 'traditional' societies. The classical world's influence on western civilization and Christianity is widely recognized. The third section on the Great Religions begins with Christianity and is followed by Islam – both religions of 'the Book'. The last three chapters in this part cover great Eastern religions/philosophies: Hinduism, Theravada Buddhism and the Chinese worldview. The latter considers the attraction of Chinese tradition in the West and the concept of holism. The final chapter on Modern Paganism also addresses the concept of 'wholeness' and it reflects some of the new trends in environmental thinking and philosophies.

The workshop was generously sponsored by the Environment Policy Division of the Department for International Development (DFID). The Commonwealth Foundation also made a contribution. The editors wish to thank both donors. We would like to acknowledge Sarah White's invaluable contribution to the workshop as the rapporteur. The introduction draws widely on her report which was prepared for DFID. We are indebted to Brenda Thornton, Camillia Fawzi El-Solh and Jane Khatib-Chahidi for their advice and comments. Orbis books kindly granted permission to quote from H. Assmann. We are also grateful to those specialists who chaired the workshop sessions, made a valuable contribution to discussions, and subsequently commented on the papers.

Alaine Low and Soraya Tremayne

Contributors

Tahera Aftab is editor of the *Pakistan Journal of Women's Studies* and Director of Women's Studies at the University of Karachi, where she is Professor of History. She is currently teaching in the Department of Religion at Gettysburg College, Pennsylvania. Her research interest is in Islam, women and environment.

Sandra Bell is Lecturer in Anthropology at the University of Durham. She has worked on the development of Buddhism in Britain and America and is co-editor of *The Anthropology of Friendship: Community Beyond Kinship* and the forthcoming volume *Celibacy, Culture and Society: The Anthropology of Celibacy*.

Cecile Jackson is Dean of the School of Development Studies, University of East Anglia. Her research interests centre on gender and environmental change. She has worked in Nigeria, Zimbabwe and India, and held an ESRC Global Environmental Change Fellowship for conceptual work on gender and environment in developing countries. She is joint-editor of *Feminist Visions of Development: Gender Analysis and Policy*.

Monica Janowski is Lecturer at the Natural Resources Institute, University of Greenwich. She has published on the Kelabit of Sarawak, is currently co-editing a book on Food and Kinship in South-East Asia, and is completing an Occasional Paper: *Mining the Forest: A Material Ethnography of the Kelabit of Sarawak*.

Elena Kingdon has an MSc. in Social Anthropology from the London School of Economics. She is an independent researcher with experience in East Africa. Her main interests are in anthropology, religion, and conservation. Her publications include *Caught Between the Two Worlds: Moral Problems Relating to Conservation in South West Uganda*.

Alaine Low is an historian and an Associate Lecturer at the Open University in Third World Development. Her research interests lie in Latin America and the former British Empire. She is the Associate Editor of the five-volumed *Oxford History of the British Empire*.

Stewart McFarlane is Director of the Centre for Asian Studies at Liverpool Hope University College and Director of Ki Health and Security. He is a teacher of Chinese martial arts and author of *Complete Book of Tai Chi*. In 1998 he wrote, and presented, the BBC World Service series *Shadow Boxing on the Way to Nirvana*.

Vijaya Rettakudi Nagarajan is lecturer at the Department of Religious Studies, University of California at Berkeley. Her research interests are in Hinduism, women and environment. She has carried out extensive fieldwork in India.

Anne Primavesi, formerly Research Fellow in Environmental Theology at the University of Bristol, is currently a Fellow of the Centre for the Interdisciplinary Study of Religion at Birkbeck College, London. Her publications include *From Apocalypse* to *Genesis: Ecology, Feminism and Christianity* and *Sacred Gaia: Holistic Theology and Earth System Science*.

Terence Ranger was former Rhodes Professor of Race Relations at the University of Oxford. He has taught at the Universities of Rhodesia and Dar es Salaam, UCLA and Manchester. He is currently at the Institute of Development Studies at the University of Zimbabwe. His most recent book is *Voices From the Rocks: Nature, Culture and History in the Matopos*.

Amy Simes completed her Ph.D. in Religious Studies at Nottingham University. Her thesis was on contemporary Pagan groups in the East Midlands. She is working on contemporary Paganism in the United States where she is the Director of the Center for International Education at Frostburg State University in Maryland.

Veronica Strang is Senior Lecturer in Social Anthropology at the University of Wales, Lampeter. Her research interest is in cultural construction of environmental beliefs and values. She is the author of *Uncommon Ground: Cultural Landscapes and Environmental Values*.

Soraya Tremayne is the Coordinating Director of Fertility and Reproduction Studies Group, Institute of Social and Cultural Anthropology, Oxford, and formerly Acting Director of the Centre for Cross-Cultural Research on Women at Queen Elizabeth House, University of Oxford. With David Parkin she is co-editor of the series Fertility, Reproductive Health and Sexuality. She has worked in Iran, Romania and Malaysia.

Piers Vitebsky is Head of Social Sciences at the Scott Polar Research Institute, Cambridge. He works among the shifting cultivators in tribal India and reindeer herders in Siberia, especially where psychology and theology meet in shamanism. His books include *Dialogue with the Dead: The Discussion of Mortality Among the Sora of Eastern India*.

Sally Wolfe is a counsellor and intercultural therapist. She is Training Day Convenor for the Race and Cultural Education division of the British Association for Counselling. She has been engaged in assessing the suitability of Western counselling models to meet the needs of indigenous people in Siberia.

1

Introduction

Alaine Low and Soraya Tremayne

Myths, rituals and spiritual beliefs and practices in different traditions include many references to measures taken by humans to conquer, appease, maintain or create a harmonious relationship with nature. These beliefs and practices are articulated in ways as various and as numerous as the societies themselves. To nurture and protect their relationship with their environment, societies have developed a number of belief systems which manifest themselves in the worship of gods, objects, monotheistic religions, and, as the contributors to this collection demonstrate, more recently a return to paganism, and revivals of shamanism and witchcraft. Anthropological literature is abundant in demonstrating that 'rituals, practices, beliefs and spiritual values are often adaptive responses (not consciously) to the ecological environment'.[1] The concern for the environment is not, therefore, a phenomenon restricted to the last part of the twentieth century, but awareness of the global scale of the problem is obviously new.

People in the West are increasingly disillusioned by what they commonly perceive as the failure of rational and scientific explanations of their relationship with the natural world and this has led to a search for new ways of understanding. At the same time, late twentieth-century dissatisfaction with the inability of traditional, organized religions to provide a more harmonious way of life, has led to a search for alternative ideologies for spiritual fulfilment. The dualistic approach of Western culture in separating mind and body, male and female, spirit and matter, culture and nature, and placing the former above the latter is questioned. In the West popular interest in the spiritual values of 'traditional' societies, and in Eastern philosophies and religions, has been based upon the assumption

1

that these provide a more holistic worldview and are more environment-friendly than Western ideologies. Among the popular assumptions is the idea that women are in some way closer to Earth/Nature, more in tune with feelings and emotions, and more 'spiritual' than men. The 'Mother Earth' and 'Mother Goddess' figures are often invoked, and many believe that there is an innate relationship between women and the Earth, and that women are indeed the 'custodians' of the Earth. It is time to examine these assumptions. On a more practical level, and running parallel with the debate about women and nature, there has been a shift in attitude to the role of women in the management and conservation of resources, as is demonstrated in recent development project work. When the two areas are considered together the implication might seem to be a rise in women's status and also an increase in their responsibility for sustained development. Is there a correlation between the two?

This collection of essays explores connections between spirituality and the environment, and women's role within this context. The contributors challenge directly and indirectly the idea that women are the exclusive custodians of the Earth. Most of the ethnographic material presented here suggests that no transcendental links exist between women and nature, and in the case of those societies where women appear 'closer' to nature than men, this is considered to be as much a cultural construct as a natural one. The idea of a special relationship with nature inherent to women is contested. The overall conclusion is that each culture and community is unique in its relationship with the environment, and that often even shared spiritual views take on a different meaning and interpretation in different cultural contexts. It is suggested that those who advocate that women universally play a sacred role in their relationship with nature have neglected an important dimension, which has been addressed by anthropologists specializing in gender studies, namely that of perception of self and of others as a cultural construct.[2] As Humphrey writes, 'the idea of what women are or should be in any particular society is not totally, or even primarily, natural or given; rather it is culturally determined. In other words the notion of "women" is symbolic or ideological too.'[3]

Background to Current Movements and Ideologies

Significant interest and debate on the issue of women and their relationship with nature dates from the early 1970s with the work of Ester Boserup.[4] Research and publication of case studies on poor women highlighted the need to 'end subordination on the basis of gender, race, ethnicity and class', and to check the degradation of the environment. In 1984 Development Alternatives with Women for a New Era (DAWN) was launched as a Third World initiative. Its main purpose was to mobilize public opinion and to create a global support network for 'equitable development'.[5] What is generally understood by the term 'development' has itself changed dramatically over the last forty years, and its definition has followed a process which can be summarized 'as economic growth, as modernization, as distributive justice and as socio-economic transformation'.[6] As a result of a shift in development thinking, women began 'to be viewed as *the* most valuable resource, and not just as victims but as major local assets to be harnessed in the interest of better environmental management'.[7] Various streams of thought about women, the environment and development emerged stressing different aspects of women's role in managing the environment. These had a cultural dimension. Cultural environmentalists view women's position as essentially closer to nature than men's because of the traditional sexual division of labour that has involved them in agricultural work and child-bearing and rearing. In general women are depicted as 'naturally' privileged environmental managers who over generations have accumulated specific knowledge that is different from, and more appropriate than, that of men.

One recent perspective which has made an important contribution to environmental thinking is 'ecofeminism', described by Braidotti as 'the feminist position most explicitly concerned with environmental destruction'. Ecofeminism is closely associated with the French feminist Françoise d'Eaubonne who considers the two most immediate threats to human survival to be 'overpopulation' and 'destruction of our resources'. This she blames on the 'Male System'.[8] In d'Eaubonne's view the only solution would be women's destruction of this male power. Then 'the planet in the feminine gender would become green again for all'.[9] The term 'ecofeminism' now refers to a significant stream within the feminist movement, containing a range of theoretical positions which rest on the assumption that there are critical connections between human beings' domination of nature and the domination of women by men.

Literature on environmental issues flourished in the late 1970s and 1980s and the work of feminist environmentalists such as Mies and Shiva, Merchant, and Griffin had a great impact on the thinking about the role of women and the environment, and the link with the concept of sustainable development.[10] Most of these writers proposed alternatives to Western development models. Shiva, the Indian physicist, philosopher and feminist, in her book *Staying Alive*, influenced to a great extent the debate on the limitations of the Western models of sustainable development involving women in poorer countries.[11] This theme of Women, the Environment and Development (WED) was widely adopted by the Western Non-Governmental Organizations (NGOs). Ecofeminism in the First World then became a new social movement consisting not only of women but also men and groups such as the Women's Environmental Network (WEN) in Britain, and the Women's Pentagon Action in the United States. Ecofeminism is by no means a monolithic movement and includes contradictory strands drawn, in part, from divisions within feminism.

The philosopher, Alison Jaggar, categorizes four types of feminism: liberal, Marxist, radical, and socialist. All have their bearing on ecofeminism.[12] Liberal feminism (sometimes described as 'equal rights' feminism) is seen as the least able to address ecology because it tends to be a white, middle-class movement; radical or cultural feminism accepts a simple association of women with nature and sees this as emancipatory. These radicals, however, have come in for criticism for ignoring race and class issues in the domination of women. 'Social Ecofeminism', on the other hand, is influenced by Marxism and is based on the recognition of the social construction of gender; the emphasis being on developing conceptual tools for analysing ecological and social change.[13]

In addition to ecofeminism, other ideologies and movements concerning the environment emerged in the 1970s. Concern for the environment spilled over into more radical thinking about the natural world itself and the newer concept of ecology gained acceptance. Ecology is defined as 'the scientific study of all organisms as they interact with each other'.[14] Arne Naess, the Norwegian philosopher, introduced and developed the concept of 'Deep Ecology' which is not a man-centred ideology but affords the same respect and meaning to all nature as to humans. It is concerned with holism. Deep Ecologists are critical of mere environmentalist reforms. Many find their inspiration in traditional societies and Eastern cultures in which they perceive interdependence between Nature and Culture. Deep Ecology's critique of Western culture centres on its anthropocentrism, and the placing of humans in a superior position over other elements of nature. Some Deep Ecology thinkers criticize the Judeo-Christian religions and their anthropocentric worldviews. In this collection Cecile Jackson, Anne Primavesi and Stewart McFarlane consider aspects of Deep Ecology.

The concept of 'Social Ecology', which developed slightly earlier than that of Deep Ecology, was a response to the perceived ecological crisis. It is concerned with structures of domination, and links social and ecological issues. In common with Deep Ecologists, 'Social Ecologists' seek the roots of their thinking in indigenous cultures.[15] They also draw upon a variety of 'emancipatory' traditions including utopian socialism and Liberation Theology's concern with justice.

Spirituality and the Sacred

Central to this volume is the consideration of whether religious norms and beliefs lead to ethical behaviour and respect for nature, and whether non-Western religions really do avoid 'unhealthy dualism'. The latter is seen by some as the root of the oppression of both women and nature, and as being responsible for the separation of the sacred and profane, male and female, and spiritual and material. If spirituality is understood to permeate life then it could be a force for right action. In central Africa sins of incest and murder are seen to anger the gods and so rains are withheld. In other words good management of nature depends upon correct management of society.[16]

Concern with spirituality appears frequently in feminist writings on the environment. Shiva and Mies argue that sacredness is an inseparable part of everyday life and that the link between 'the ecological relevance of the emphasis on "spirituality" lies in the discovery of the sacredness of life, according to which life on earth can be preserved only if people again begin to perceive all life forms as sacred and respect them as such. Deep Ecology as a world-view has been described as profoundly religious.'[17] The quality of sacredness is in everyday life, in our work, in the things that surround us, in our immanence. And from time to time there should be celebrations of this sacredness in rituals, in dance and song.'[18] 'Sacredness' is also linked to conservation because it 'encompasses the intrinsic value of diversity; it also denotes a relationship of the part to the whole – a relationship that recognizes and preserves integrity.'[19]

The concept of 'sacred' is explicit in the title of this book, and 'spirituality' remains implicit throughout, on the assumption that an intimate knowledge of the environment is often articulated in terms of the sacred and entails 'spirituality'. As Sarah White writes, 'The recurring theme in the case studies in this collection is that changing views of nature are related to changing forms of social organisation',[20] but that the sacred remains embedded in essence regardless of the changing form. In this collection authors focus on the role of shrines 'where heaven and earth meet' and, in some instances, on sacred books. The long history of 'negotiation' between human societies and their environment stretches back to ancient Greece and beyond. Elena Kingdon describes the sacred groves and taboos on damaging trees and polluting springs and angering the gods. Terence Ranger writes of a sacred shrine which can accommodate various 'meanings' and messages subject to the will of the priestess. The search by people in the West to understand the spiritual dimension of the 'ecological' beliefs of non-Westerners is also, according to Vijaya Nagarajan, 'centred on their religious notions of respect and even worship of natural landscapes such as rivers, mountains, forests and even earth itself'.[21] Matthew Schoffeleers writing on territorial cults in central Africa describes them as profoundly ecological and providing a coherent worldview.[22] New Paganism is a modern attempt to reintroduce that 'spiritual attitude', and to 'revalue the deeper connection between humankind and nature by combining ancient myths with religious ritual. Paganism is specifically concerned with emphasizing the sacredness of the feminine, or perhaps with its 're-sacralising.'[23]

The oneness of the spiritual with the social and material in 'traditional' cultures is confirmed in several of the case studies, which maintain that spiritual beliefs provide organizational principles for social and economic practices. This is exemplified in Artemis in her role as the protector of all young life, human and animal, and as the patroness of the hunters;[24] Australian Aborigines' beliefs about 'spirit children' located in the landscape;[25] spirits in the Siberian forest 'which abhor excess noise or waste, and the fire which speaks if you know how to listen;'[26] and the creation of the 'kolam' every morning by which Hindu women in south India become aware of the earth goddess and create a sense of sacred space in the domestic household or in public rituals.[27]

The way in which societies express their sense of interdependence with their environment is often expressed through their interaction with the spirits. These vary, and have a degree of flexibility depending on the context. For example, for the Australian Aborigines 'nature is sentient, responding differently according to who fishes, or the status of one who dies. The powers of the persons in society are importantly indexed to their power over the environment'.[28] Initially in Zimbabwe the action of a woman taking power as keeper of the most senior shrine in Matopos was met with hostility, but the fact that the best rains ever coincided with her installation, strengthened her position. 'At the same time the spirits warn of the limits to human power. For example, in Zimbabwe the Europeans have given single names to sacred rocks, but the Africans are more circumspect. They say the rocks have many faces, and in some cases they proscribe the human hubris of seeking to encompass the rocks by walking all around them.'[29]

A dominant theme in this collection is the 'everydayness' of the sacred, and how deeply infused the sacred is with the practical. The inseparable links between humans, their environment, and spirituality is reflected in the practical aspects of daily life in various forms. Humans seem to share their habitat with spirits for a variety of purposes. They can seek relaxation in the locations where spirits live; they can use the forest as a source of livelihood but at the same time respect the fact that it is also the home of the spirits; or they can mediate between the 'wild' and the 'civilized', and transform nature to make it fit for humans. In central Africa territorial cults are concerned with man's role as 'a transformer of and a recipient of his natural environment'.[30] In many communities people consider their environment as 'created' solely for human use. Even among Buddhists, as Elizabeth Harris's interviews with Buddhist monks demonstrate, activist monks in Thailand link conservation action with maintaining the environment on which the livelihood of the villagers depends. In her words, 'they were not so much interested in the environment for its own sake but for the good of the villagers'.[31]

The pervasive nature of the spiritual/religious instructions which codify secular ways of life are common. These codes are often embedded in myths, legends and stories, and depending on the context in which they are told, they can be re-invented to fit the realities of life. Stories told by the old Australian Aboriginal women to the young provide instructions for hunting, gathering, cooking, and storing food. Religious leaders at territorial shrines in central Africa gave instructions on issues such as the choice of crops, fire management, conservation of fish and migration of people.[32]

Islam, although diverse in its application in different cultural contexts both in time and space,[33] is pervasive in its detailed instructions for the everyday behaviour of its adherents.[34] In Confucian cosmology the 'order of things' is set out not only at a spiritual level but also in daily practice. Most Pagans consider themselves as '24 hours a day' Pagans, as Amy Simes puts it, meaning that their ideology is reflected in their daily practice.

Interestingly the link between the sacred and the practical is reflected in a post-Brundtland shift in environmental studies towards a more spiritual version of ecology; 'a kind of pantheism in which moral and practical cues are taken from the environment'.[35] The interpretation of spiritual beliefs and their practical application, however, remain the subject of debate between specialists themselves. Ian Harris expresses doubts as to whether the Buddhist doctrinal views of nature can provide the kind of foundation 'from which environmental concerns can easily be developed, in the way that some other religions, notably the Semitic religions of Judaism, Christianity and Islam do'.[36] He also argues that everything is subject to decay, and so in essence and theory, therefore, Buddhism cannot uphold an environmentalist ethic.[37] In discussing the Christian view of loss, Martin Palmer concludes that a 'vital Christian feminist perspective on Christianity and ecology is that suffering and loss exist; suffering and loss are a natural part of life and suffering is not itself life-destroying'.[38] Conservationists, on the other hand, might argue that decay and loss do not necessarily exclude the idea of sustainability.

Gender

Ursula King argues that women in many religions stand high at an ideological level but occupy a low status in everyday life, and that a distinction should be made between the 'religious place given to women in the world of religious imagination and that accorded to them in the actual world of religious life. These two often stand in an inverse relationship to each other and remain poles apart.'[39] She also refers to women who occupy an important religious position such as shamans, witches, healers, nuns, mystics and ascetics as women who are 'revered as women apart' and are 'recruited from among women who eschew established female social roles'.[40]

The chapters in this volume confirm that although women are widely excluded from direct contact with the 'sacred' at an institutional level, their involvement with the practical aspects of the 'sacred' is evident in various forms, and testifies to their centrality and importance to everyday spiritual rituals. The importance of the role played by women in funerary rituals and agricultural events, whilst being excluded from major positions of power in ancient Greece, is discussed by Kingdon.[41] As King writes, 'women have always been deeply involved in religious belief and practice, but they have rarely held significant institutional roles'. She argues that the more institutionalized the religions have become the more women have been excluded from power. In her view women's marginalization is partly the result of a move away from the prophetic, oracular aspects of religion, where they served as seers, visionaries and priestesses, and the denial of higher education to women.[42] Tahera Aftab also dwells on the 'de-linking' of women from power in Islam through their lack of access to education and other resources. In central Africa there seems to be clear evidence that in matrilineal and uxorilocal societies women held very influential positions. The arrival of patrilineal peoples certainly weakened women's positions but, as Ranger shows, this by no means meant that they were, or are, excluded entirely from priestly activities. Elsewhere the centrality of women's role, although restricted in the spiritual cycle of life, may well be important in the economic sphere. For example, in the case of Theravada Buddhist monks in Thailand, women's participation in the day-to-day feeding of monks and their other contributions to monastic resources, is essential, and generally the 'Sangha' relies for its continuing existence on women's productive capacities, as well as their reproductive function in producing male children.[43]

There is much in this collection on gender complementarity in relation to the environment, but this does not necessarily mean equality. Ultimately, it is the complex combination of social, political and historical factors which determines the balance of gender relationships. Social relations are dynamic, flexible, and subject to change, and the ideologies which serve as the basis for these relations undergo major reinterpretations in different cultural contexts. The actions, role and status of men and women vary not only in different cultures, but also within the same culture. In describing gender relations in Mende rice farming in Sierra Leone, Melissa Leach looks at 'the *use* of the environment as a context through which cultural constructions of both environment and gender are created and recreated', and argues that 'social relations should not be viewed as static but as fluid and negotiable, able to be created and re-created through performance, event and action'.[44] It is not surprising, therefore, that the idea of a unique custodianship by women of nature is questioned by most contributors. Piers Vitebsky argues that 'there is nothing inherent in the nature of women to be custodians of the earth'.[45] Indeed in his case men are the custodians. Stewart McFarlane points to the relativity of the concept of gender itself, which can change its nature depending on the time and place in Confucian cosmology. What can be female in one context can become male in another. The Chinese worldview does not privilege women in relation to nature and the environment, and one interpretation of the ying/yang way of thinking is that it avoids polarizing the genders. Women can be yang in quality and men can be ying in quality depending on the context. Monica Janowski's example of the Kelabit on the need for both (female) rice and (male) wild foods is another illustration that custodianship of the environment is not uniquely in the hands of women.[46] The concept of equality or even its necessity, is rejected by several of the contributors as a totally alien Western notion. They maintain that 'power is essentially inscribed in gender relations and that notions of complementarity often provide key mechanisms which these sustain'.[47] The issue of duties rather than rights is the determining factor in the balance of the relationship.[48]

Those ideologies described in this collection which closely identify women with Nature and men with Culture, also place men in a superior position vis-à-vis women. These deny that women play any significant role that would make them the guardians of Earth. Nature itself is often viewed as a phenomenon which needs to be tamed, and conquering it and building upon the landscape can only be a man's achievement. Recognition is given, however, to women for their role as mediators between the spiritual elements and humans. The Hellenic worldview of male and female, and the belief that women were identified with Nature while men were identified with Culture, places women in a subordinate position. 'All evils that beset mankind were released from Pandora's jar (symbol of the womb).'[49] Nevertheless the existence of exclusive female festivals and cults in Greco-Roman civilizations, and other 'women's mysteries', points to the link between men and women's complementary roles since many of the female rituals and festivals relate to men's agricultural work. Women were also essential to the performance of key rituals that ensured human and land fertility.

The question of the custodianship of the Earth is challenged altogether by Primavesi, who raises the issue of the 'order of things' within Christianity in the context of women's relationship with the Earth. She refutes the idea of custodianship of the Earth by humans altogether, finding it arrogant. In her view the hierarchical order of things within Christianity, and its practical application in matters such as custodianship 'have no existence except in the grid created by theological language'. She argues that in Christianity the principle of ranking beings in relation to God, the Supreme Being, has to a large extent determined the Western cultural perceptions of human identity as distinct from the identity of Nature/Earth, as well as what it means to be female rather than male; 'in the order of things' women are subordinate to men.[50] This focus on patriarchy and hierarchy expresses a view shared by many Christian feminist theologians.[51] Some theologians have hopes for what has been termed a post-patriarchal theology.[52]

The balance of the relationship between men and women is shown to vary considerably across communities. Among the Australian Aboriginal cultures, gender roles are clearly defined and men and women have different responsibilities, but it should not be assumed that one is subordinate to the other. For example the less visible public role of women does not necessarily place them in a secondary position to men in what is a fundamentally gerontocratic society. As Veronica Strang argues, it is the older women who are foremost in expressing concern for the land and preserving their traditions. Buddhism and Christianity on the other hand seem to uphold the view that women are inherently subordinate,[53] while Aftab maintains that the teaching of Islam is that men and women are equal, and that it is not the text but its interpretation which has placed women in a subordinate position.[54] This misrepresentation of text and subsequent subordination of women in Islam is viewed as a historical process which has reduced women to a vehicle of procreation; 'the axis around which woman's history as myth or religion is organized'.[55] In contrast, the conscious aim of the modern Pagans, as explained by Simes, is to correct the imbalance of gender relations created by the patriarchal systems in the West; for the modern Pagan the reunification of male and female, nature and culture, are the way forward.[56]

The flexibility of spiritual ideologies with regard to gender relations is taken up by the contributors from different angles. While several chapters discuss the obvious complementarity between genders, others draw attention to the finer points of negotiation between the 'text' and practice in patriarchal systems, whereby women are accorded certain privileges in exchange for their support in strengthening and sustaining the fabric of the society. In ancient Greece, for example, the partnership between women's rituals and men's work incorporated women into the state cosmologically, socially and politically. This throws doubts on the misogynous ideology evident in the work of Greek poets and philosophers.[57] By supporting Buddhist monks materially, women can accumulate merit, but not on equal terms.[58] Islam offers 'paradise at a mother's feet' to women in exchange for bringing up suitable children. McFarlane, on the other hand, argues that in Confucian cosmology the relationship between man and woman lacks dynamism and is problematic, and women are placed in the private sphere of home and are subordinate to men.[59]

Women's sexuality in some spiritual belief systems, especially those which favour patriarchal systems, can be the cause of their exclusion from rituals and from being viewed as equal to men. These patriarchal ideologies emphasize the inherent distinctiveness of males and females and maintain that the power of sexuality, if unregulated, can destroy society. While this view might exclude women from being custodians of the Earth on the grounds of being polluting and 'essentially' different,[60] it does not exempt them from providing the labour required to sustain the life of the community. As Sandra Bell shows Theravada Buddhists exclude women from the 'Sangha' of monks on the basis of their female sexuality. At the same time women are associated with the natural environment and the usually fearsome forces of nature, locating them in opposition to men who come to stand for the reassuring and civilizing forces of Culture.[61] In Islam women are considered as irrational and emotional and their sexuality, which is a threat to the order of society, must be controlled by men.[62]

Modernity

The impact of modernity, whether positive or negative, in the context of environment and gender relations, has generated a variety of responses from the communities it has affected. Some societies have reacted to modernity by apparent adaptation to the new while maintaining their own values. Others have responded by reviving their semi-forgotten traditions to confront their political regimes, the incoming rulers, or more recently the 'well-meaning' developers. In some cases there has been resistance to change and a

reinforcement of cultural identity. In several of the instances discussed in this volume modernity has led to dispossession and fragmentation. Among the reindeer herders, the reforms of the Soviet
regime in the collectivization of agriculture shattered community
and family structures. Nomadism as 'a way of life', which included
the entire family, changed to 'production nomadism' with men
alone working together as 'workmates' as in a factory. It is men,
rather than women, who are now closer to the environment. The
relationship between parents and children, especially in their education, has been changed radically. In Vitebsky's words 'parents
view the situation as a kind of theft, whereby the young people
were taken out of the community and taught different ways and
values'.[63] This was also the experience of the Australian Aborigines
where children were taken to boarding schools and even permanently removed from their native environment.[64]

Several of the case studies reveal an unusual and unpredictable
outcome arising from the impact of modernity on gender relations.
'Common modernity is seen to serve male gender interests over
female, with men being privileged through land rights, access to
new technologies, access to employment in the formal sector and
so on.'[65] This seems to be contradicted by Piers Vitebsky and
Veronica Strang who argue that women may be more able to take
advantage of the opportunities that modernity has to offer. For
example women are seen as agents of change among the reindeer
herders of Siberia. When uprooted from their traditional way of
life, they have adjusted to the new conditions more easily than
their men. In the Australian Aboriginal community those women
who had become concubines to the white settlers used their position to mediate between their own group and white society, and to
secure certain privileges for their communities through their con-
tacts. Their men, on the other hand, in the face of the change and
the inability to confront colonialism, resorted to alcohol and drugs,
a not unfamiliar occurrence among other communities who are
affected by the impact of modernization. Native American Pueblo
women describe their men as follows: 'Pueblo men are people who
women take care of.'[66]

Modernity has also generated resourcefulness and adaptation.
In some cases a distinct lack of sentimentality is demonstrated
which reveals that the spiritual dimension of the relationship
between people and their environment may have to be negotiated
in the context of strategic choices for survival. As van den Breemer
puts it 'a reasonable inference is that, despite religious ideas and

norms oriented towards maintenance of an ecological equilibrium, certain processes have influenced people to ignore them'.[67] Women of the Siberian reindeer-herding communities, in their new situation of village life, are losing their non-verbal communication skills in favour of verbal language. The understanding of nature through silence is lost, and values concerning the natural wilderness are downgraded and associated with men. The kolam rice drawings in which Tamil women invoke the earth goddess, Bhudevi, are increasingly coloured with garish bazaar-bought powder, or even made in stick-on transfers. Near the Matopos Hills in Zimbabwe, farmers growing food crops follow the instruction of the shrine, but those growing cash crops follow those of technical demonstrators. The message is clear that what feeds the spirit and what feeds the body must be separated but preserved. 'The relationship between humanity and environment might be elaborated in spiritual terms, but it also has a hard-edged economic and political aspect.'[68]

The revival of traditional beliefs and practices as the result of social stresses caused, in part, by the process of 'modernization' is manifested in the rise of the politicization of belief in occult forces which remain deeply rooted in many societies.[69] The revival of the 'messianic grassroots movements "from below" is one form of social conflict resolution which uses magic and witchcraft accusations as means to fight the "evil" in this world by establishing "cults of counter-violence"'.[70] Other examples include the revival of shamanism in Siberia as an opposing force to the dictates of the Soviet regime,[71] and the revival of religious fundamentalism (especially in Islam) in several parts of the world stemming from the perceived threat that modernity has brought to traditional patriarchal systems.[72]

The impact of arbitrary political decisions has been seen to affect women's status in relation to their environment and to their relationship with men. The imposition of the communist ideology in collectivizing farming in the former USSR seriously affected the family structure and resulted in a change in gender relations. Among the reindeer herders in Siberia women are no longer controlled by their own men, but by administrators in the villages. Men, on the other hand, from being the heroic hunters in a shamanic cosmology, have been reduced to 'wilderness proletarians'.[73] The passing of control of the shrines from women to men as a result of incoming rulers, and the 'masculinization' of eco-religion is elaborated on by Ranger, who also points to the increasing use of magic and witchcraft as instruments for political resistance.[74] The Western colonization of the East and the Antipodes is held responsible for denying women's specific needs by Aftab and Strang. Like Shiva they argue that colonialism created conditions which favoured men's rights over those of women, and which reinforced the patriarchal systems in which male domination over natural resources involved the domination of women and excluded them as partners. Lorna Devaraja, a historian specializing in Kandyan (Sri Lankan) law, strongly defends Buddhism against the charge that it subordinates women[75] and holds British colonization of Kandy responsible for women losing their rights to land and for the dissolution of marriages. Schoffeleers writes that modernity in central Africa 'sounded the death knoll for territorial cults'.[76] Bureaucratic government separates chiefs from cults; land alienation and wage labour separated sections of the people from ecological activity and community responsibility.

Belief and Action

The spiritual beliefs which act as guidelines to the interaction between people and the environment are interpreted at several levels in this book. First, as White puts it, 'there is a consensus among the contributors that *no* major religion can uncontroversially claim to be progressive on environmental and gender relations. There is often wide divergence between the tenets of any religion and the folk beliefs in which it is embodied, let alone the actual practice of its adherents.'[77] Second, even those Eastern philosophies and religions which appear to advocate holistic notions of interdependence or an inherent respect for nature and the environment, have been exposed to ruthless exploitation by political leaders or abused by the poor who fight for survival. Third, the general belief that 'traditional' societies respect nature reflects a romantic and, at times, naïve view. The perception of nature in these societies is not necessarily one of harmony and peace. Beliefs and practices surrounding the relationship between people and their environment in many instances are formed around conquering nature rather than a harmonious relationship with it. Nature is too frequently viewed as 'hostile' and 'threatening' and its fearsome and unknown elements should therefore be tamed. The forest monks in Thailand who can reside in the dangerous and wild forests inhabited by uncivilized tribal peoples, dangerous animals and malevolent

15

spirits, can only do so as exceptionally pure beings.[78] In Christian England up to the eighteenth century nature had been treated as essentially 'an appendage to human handiwork which had to be tamed to serve mankind's purposes'.[79] In Hinduism, it is indeed difficult to untangle the ecological from non-ecological when it is embedded within other cultural practices, and the perception of the natural world as sacred does not necessarily lead to a more 'environmental' or ecological attitude towards nature, 'nature may be sacred and yet it is ill treated.'[80] On the other hand, the new idealization of nature reflected by some in the West is encapsulated in new Paganism. In the words of Harvey, Paganism is the religion of 'those who honour the earth'.[81] Modern Pagans are characterized by 'living their religion' and Paganism is often 'referred to as a lifestyle rather than a religious practice'.[82]

Conclusion

The contributors are unanimous in their view that understanding the relationship between women and the Earth should go beyond practical day-to-day ecological issues, and note that spiritual ideologies cannot be abstracted from their cultural contexts. Culture is dynamic, and people have an active role in reconstituting the traditions they inherit. These traditions vary crucially with economic and political circumstances. Poverty, political insecurity, economic systems and population pressure all play a part in the way that people refigure their sense of the world and their interaction with the environment. There is also consensus among the authors that women may or may not be the custodians, or the sole custodians of the earth; but the notion of women as *sacred* custodians and as having an *innate* relationship with the earth is strongly challenged.

Global generalization on the issue of women's supposed 'special relationship' with the Earth can lead to changes in the relationship between the genders, and in many instances to destruction and fragmentation of communities without solving environmental problems. It appears that modernization or 'development' generate a number of unexpected, and not necessarily positive, reactions in the communities studied. The issue of gender complementarity (not equality) and the mutual dependence of the sexes is strongly stressed in several chapters.[83] Recognizing men's equal responsibility in the sustainable development process in this respect is crucial.

The importance of Christian feminist theologians in opening up new questions about the nature of God and the world, which are intimately linked to issues of environmental concern, should be recognized.[84] Likewise women are aiming to enter Buddhist religious institutions. At the same time, female spiritual leaders in new churches in Africa, and elsewhere, are providing a new impetus and dynamism. The work of female activists such as Wangari Maathai, in the tree-planting schemes in Kenya, are well known. All, in their different ways, are catalysts for change. Ultimately, however, sound environmental management projects can only succeed if they have a local focus and stem from the practicalities of everyday life. Accepting planning frameworks as universally applicable means a disregard for local knowledge. Local priorities often override global concepts and issues such as 'rights' and 'social justice'. Furthermore, the environmental priorities themselves may not necessarily match those of social justice. For example the issue of global warming in the face of abject poverty tends to become devoid of meaning. So 'the response of local people to the challenges of the globalization and the market economy must not be assumed to be positive in either gender or environmental terms'.[85] 'While the world is bemoaning its ecological woes and is trying to construct a viable ideology, Africa is divesting herself of the one she so long possessed', writes Schoffeleers in the introduction to a collection of essays on central Africa published in the late 1970s.[86] Though the best way may be to nurture the environmental ethic by including relevant spiritual teaching and values in educational programmes, this presents a special challenge. 'To find allies within the religions of the world in the common task of protecting the earth means to oppose the global forces which make the task of raising awareness about the environment so difficult.'[87] Furthermore, planners and policy-makers need to recognize that, although each spiritual ideology may provide resources for an environmental consciousness, it will often be an uphill struggle to build on these and use them as tools to change practices.

Finally there is a passing mention in this collection of an issue which deserves greater recognition, namely that of generational differences. Children are increasingly seen as a valuable resource for future sustainable development in the long term and for educating the older generation in the short term. Children, regardless of their gender, are the key resource in achieving truly sustainable development which must incorporate a new relationship between humans and their environment.

Notes

1 See G. Schlee, 'Ritual Topography and Ecological Use: The Gabbra of the Kenyan/Ethiopian Borderlands', in *Bush Base: Forest Farm, Culture, Environment and Development*, eds E. Croll and D. Parkin (London: Routledge, 1992), p. 120.
2 See S. Ardener, ed., *Perceiving Women* (London: J. M. Dent and Son Ltd, 1975).
3 C. Humphrey, 'Women and Ideology in Hierarchical Societies in East Asia', in *Persons and Powers of Women in Diverse Cultures*, ed. S. Ardener (New York and Oxford: Berg Publishers Ltd., 1992), p. 173.
4 E. Boserup, *Women's Role in Economic Development* (New York: St. Martin's Press, 1970).
5 R. Braidotti, E. Charkiewicz, S. Hausler, S. Wieringa, eds, *Women, the Environment and Sustainable Development: Towards a Theoretical Synthesis* (London: Zed Books in association with INSTRAW, 1994), p. 117.
6 Croll and Parkin, eds, *Bush Base*, p. 5.
7 I. Dankleman and J. Davidson, *Women and Environment in the Third World: Alliance for the Future* (London: Earthscan Publication Ltd in association with IUCN, 1988).
8 D'Eaubonne 1980 (orig. 1974), cited in Braidotti *et al*, eds, *Women, the Environment*, p. 66.
9 Ibid, p. 236.
10 M. Mies and V. Shiva, *Ecofeminism* (London: Zed Books, 1993); C. Merchant, *The Death of Nature: Women, Nature, Ecology and the Scientific Revolution* (London: Harper and Row, 1982); S. Griffin, *Women and Nature: The Roaring Inside Her* (San Francisco: Harper and Row, 1979).
11 V. Shiva, *Staying Alive: Women, Ecology and Development* (London: Zed Books, 1989). Shiva writes of 'development' as a new project of Western patriarchy, see her 'Development, Ecology, and Women', in *Readings in Ecology and Feminist Theology*, eds. M. H. MacKinnon and M. McIntyre (Kansas City: Sheed & Ward, 1995), pp. 160–71.
12 As many as 7 varieties of feminism have been distinguished, see M. A. Hinsdale, 'Ecology, Feminism, and Theology', in *Readings in Ecology*, eds MacKinnon and McIntyre, pp. 196–207, esp. p. 197 n.8 and pp. 198–201.
13 Braidotti *et al*, eds, *Women, the Environment*; N. Sturgeon, *Ecofeminist Natures: Race, Gender, Feminist Theory and Political Action* (New York: Routledge, 1997) give a full description of these developments. See also Hinsdale, 'Ecology, Feminism, and Theology', in *Readings in Ecology*, eds. MacKinnon and M. McIntyre for a critique of social feminism.
14 C. J. Krebs, *Ecology: The Experimental Analysis of Distribution and Abundance* [3rd edn] cited in J. L. Chapman and M. J. Reiss, *Ecology, Principles and Application* (Cambridge, Cambridge University Press, 1992), p. 3.
15 For a discussion of Social Ecology see Braidotti, *et al.* eds, *Women, the Environment*, p. 155.
16 J. M. Schoffeleers, ed., *Guardians of the Land: Essays in Central African Territorial Cults* (Gwelo, Zimbabwe: Mambo Press, 1979), p. 5.
17 J. B. Cobb, Jr., 'Ecology, Science, Religion: Toward A Postmodern Worldview', in *Readings in Ecology*, eds MacKinnon and McIntyre, pp. 234–48 esp. p. 240.
18 Mies and Shiva, *Ecofeminism*, pp. 17–18.
19 Ibid.
20 S. White, unpublished Rapporteur's report on the workshop discussion, p. 3.

21 See below, chap. by Vijaya Rettakudi Nagarajan.
22 Schoffeleers, ed., *Guardians*, p. 5.
23 Anderson and Hopkins cited below in chap. by Amy Simes.
24 See below, chap. by Elena Kingdon.
25 See below, chap. by Veronica Strang.
26 See Vitebsky in *Bush Base*, eds Croll and Parkin, p. 228.
27 See below, chap. by Nagarajan.
28 Strang, cited by White, Rapporteur's report, p. 4.
29 Ranger cited in ibid., p. 3.
30 Schoffeleers, ed., *Guardians*, p. 8.
31 Personal communication from Dr Elizabeth Harris.
32 Schoffeleers, ed., *Guardians*, pp. 3–4.
33 C. Fawzi El-Solh and J. Mabro, eds, *Muslim Women's Choices: Religious Belief and Social Reality* (Providence/Oxford: Berg Publishers Ltd., 1994).
34 M. Afkhami and E. Friedl, eds, *In the Eye of the Storm, Women in the Post-Revolutionary Iran* (London: New York: I. B. Tauris Publishers, 1994), p. 6.
35 Croll and Parkin, eds, *Bush Base*, pp. 7–8.
36 I. Harris cited below, see chap. by Sandra Bell.
37 On the other hand see E. Harris, *What Buddhists Believe* (Oxford: Oneworld, 1998), p. 123, where it is pointed out that in the West ecological awareness and Buddhism frequently go together.
38 M. Palmer, unpublished paper, 'Women as Sacred Custodians of the Earth', presented at Workshop, Oxford, June 1996.
39 U. King, ed., *Religion and Gender* (Cambridge, Mass., and Oxford: Blackwell, 1995), p. 16.
40 Ibid.
41 See below, chap. by Kingdon.
42 U. King, *Women and Spirituality: Voices of Protest and Promise* (Basingstoke: Macmillan, 1993), pp. 32, 39. But see also S. Sered, *Women of the Sacred Groves: Divine Priestesses of Okinawa* (New York, Oxford: Oxford University Press, 1999), for women 'priestesses'.
43 See below, chap. by Bell.
44 M. Leach, 'Women's Crops in Women's Spaces: Gender Relations in Mende Rice Farming', in *Bush Base*, eds. Croll and Parkin, pp. 76–96, esp. pp. 76 and 77.
45 See below, chap. by Piers Vitebsky.
46 See below, chap. by Monica Janowski.
47 White, Rapporteur's report, p. 7.
48 For more detail on the contextual nature of gender complementarity see Croll and Parkin, eds, *Bush Base*, esp. p. 19.
49 See below, chap. by Kingdon.
50 See below, chap. by Anne Primavesi.
51 For a brief overview of Christian feminist thought see C. Deane-Drummond, *A Handbook in Theology and Ecology* (London: SCM Press Ltd, 1996), chap. 4.
52 For an interesting discussion see J. McDaniel, 'Six Characteristics of a Postpatriarchal Christianity', in *Readings in Ecology*, eds MacKinnon and McIntyre, chap. 24.
53 See below, chaps by Bell and Primavesi. All the great religions have been judged 'riddled with patriarchy', see I. Geraras, interviewed by M. J. Ress 'Ecofeminism and Pantheism' in *Readings in Ecology*, eds MacKinnon and McIntyre, chap. 17; p. 213.

19

54 See below, chap. by Tahera Aftab.
55 A. and E. Friedl, eds, *In the Eye of the Storm*, citing Y. Yazbeck Haddad and E. B. Findly, eds, *Women, Religion and Social Change* (Albany: State University of New York Press, 1985).
56 See below, chap. by Simes.
57 See below, chap. by Kingdon.
58 See below, chap. by Bell.
59 See below, chap. by Stewart McFarlane.
60 See below, chap. by Cecile Jackson.
61 See below, chap. by Bell.
62 Afkhami and Friedl, eds, *In the Eye of the Storm*, see also Jackson below.
63 See below, chap. by Vitebsky.
64 See below, chap. by Strang.
65 White, Rapporteur's report, p. 4.
66 R. Swentzell, on Native American people in unpublished workshop paper for 'Women as Scared Custodians of the Earth', Oxford, June 1996.
67 J. P. M. van den Breemer, 'Ideas and Usage: Environment in Aouan Society, Ivory Coast', in *Bush Base*, eds. Croll and Parkin, pp. 97–109, esp. p. 97.
68 White, Rapporteur's report, p. 6.
69 D. Kohnert, 'Magic and Witchcraft: Implications for Democratization and Poverty Alleviating Aid in Africa', *World Development*, 24 (8), 1966, pp. 1347–55, esp. 1347–8.
70 K. Wilson, 'Cults of Violence and Counter-Violence in Mozambique', *Journal of Southern African Studies*, 18 (3), 1992, pp. 527–82.
71 P. Vitebsky, 'Landscape and Self-determination Among the Eveny: The Political Environment of Siberian Reindeer Herders Today', in *Bush Base*, eds Croll and Parkin, pp. 223–46.
72 F. Mernissi, *Beyond the Veil: Male-Female Dynamics in a Muslim Society* (Cambridge, Mass: Shenkman Publishing Company, Inc., 1975).
73 See below, chap. by Vitebsky.
74 See below, chap. by Terence Ranger.
75 Harris, *What Buddhists Believe*, p. 137.
76 Schoffeleers, ed., *Guardians*, p. 43.
77 White, Rapporteur's report, p. 9.
78 See below, chap. by Bell.
79 D. E. Allen, *Naturalist in Britain: A Social History* (London: Pelican Books, 1978), p. 27.
80 See below, chap. by Nagarajan.
81 Cited in chap. by Simes.
82 Ibid.
83 See, for example those by Janowski and Strang.
84 See MacKinnon and McIntyre. eds. *Readings in Ecology*.
85 White, Rapporteur's report, p. 10.
86 Schoffeleers, ed., *Guardians*, p. 43.
87 Personal communication, Dr Elizabeth Harris.

Part I

The Current Debate

2

Gender, Nature and Trouble with Anti-Dualism

Cecile Jackson

Non-Western religious traditions are seen in Western environmental discourses as free of the nature-culture dualism which is believed to underpin the oppression of both women and nature in Western history and thought, and the absence of which is thought to engender positive and sustainable relations between peoples and their environments in many non-Western societies. This chapter questions these assumptions and argues that the relationships between belief and action are contingent since religious beliefs do not determine environmental relations in either a direct or a necessarily significant way; and that subaltern spirituality has a complex relationship with dominant religious traditions. Tropes of nature may be implicated in both the subordination and the resistances of women.

What is radical in Western environmentalism is almost by definition non-anthropocentric, i.e. non-human-centred or bioethical, although as Tim Hayward has argued there is considerable confusion over these terms, and a need to distinguish anthropocentrism, speciesism and human chauvinism.[1] Green theorists who differ in many other ways, see anthropocentrism as symptomatic of dualistic thought which divides nature from human culture and devalues the former, and many environmentalists share a concern to overcome this hierarchical dualism and to envisage, and practice, non-exploitative relations with nature.

In this chapter I am concerned with the gender politics of discursive efforts to overcome anthropocentrism, and of attendant claims that eastern and indigenous religions decentre dominant species (humanity), and genders (men). I do this, first, through a critical consideration of two possible approaches to dissolving the dualistic split between nature and culture, naturalizing humanity on the one hand and humanizing nature on the other. Next I enquire into what reverence for nature means in specific cultural contexts and how it connects to environmental action, before concluding that a sacralized nature cannot be equated with modern environmental sensibilities, and that religious beliefs do not simply determine environmental actions but are both discursive resources and constraints in the social and political relations of environmental change.

Anti-dualism

Green social and political theorists have criticized the Western humanist heritage which seeks a unified view of humanity as part of nature.[2] Deep Ecology[3] emphasizes a merger of humanity with nature, ecofeminism suggests an ethic of care,[4] and both oppose the setting apart of humanity from the rest of nature. Western humanism is said to be built upon a systematic devaluation of the non-human world that follows from its emphasis on what is special about humans, and on inter-human relations. The non-human world 'has attracted attention only in so far as it is instrumentally valuable to human actors, whether as a material resource or as some other means to human self-realisation'.[5] By contrast, 'Deep Ecologists see their philosophical principle of "biocentrism" (as opposed to anthropocentrism) realized in eastern religious traditions and . . . by "primal" indigenous people in non-Western settings who, through their material and spiritual practices, subordinate themselves to the integrity of the biotic universe they inhabit.'[6]

Feminist opposition to dualism also emphasizes what Val Plumwood sees as the systemic connections of dominance and subordination in concepts of nature-culture, female-male, reproduction-production, matter-reason.[7] The anti-dualism in ecofeminism[8] has strengthened recently. For example, at the 4th UN Conference on Women in Beijing in 1995 Vandana Shiva called for 'a democracy amongst species'.

Finally, southern populists have also constructed national and ethnic environmental attitudes as biocentric in opposition to the anthropocentrism, human-centredness, of Western relations with nature.[9] For India, Chaitanya, for example, promotes Hinduism as ecoreligion, and claims that 'the natural order . . . is the source of all values'.[10] 'Tribal' religions in India are celebrated for what is understood as an expression of oneness with nature, as Mahapatra states, 'The Khondh . . . always feels a mysterious sense of union with the earth',[11] or 'The Santal is . . . in the lap of nature and natural phenomena inspire in him [sic] a sense of wonder, awe and reverence.'[12]

Radical environmentalists,[13] from a range of standpoints, have remarkably consistent views on the character of non-Western religions and their generally higher green credentials. Since the influential paper of Lyn White[14] identified Christianity as an important foundation of the destructive and exploitative relations with nature in the West, and notwithstanding dissenting voices such as Murray Bookchin[15] and Janet Biehl,[16] environmentalists have generally idealized non-Western religions in terms of the absence of a nature-culture dualism. Otherwise distinct strands of environmentalism agree that the dualistic split between culture and nature is an important foundation for destructive relations of humans to nature. The contrasts made with Western cultures and religions most commonly turn on two elements: non-Western and indigenous religions are held to integrate humanity and nature holistically, and to value nature for its own sake rather than instrumentally, as 'resources'.

The anti-dualist position seems to me questionable, however, on a number of accounts. The polarized concepts of nature-culture, and female-male, are held to be much more coherent and consistent in Western history and thought than is justified,[17] the gender correlates of the nature-culture opposition are vastly more complex than anti-dualist theorists suggest,[18] and the identification of a monolithic power within the dominant term of dualistic pairs erases agency, resistance, the dependence of the powerful on the 'weak', and offers no conceptualization of social and historical change in structures of thought and their meanings. In so far as anti-dualism fails to examine the relationship between cultural representations of categories and concepts and the actions and behaviours of people, it is therefore an inadequate and possibly misleading approach to understanding gendered environmental relations, or indeed the significance of religious beliefs in relations of humanity with nature. Non-dualist readings of religious texts are plentiful;[19] squaring them with social action is much more problematic.[20]

If the significance of dualistic thought for environmental

destruction has possibly been exaggerated, there has also been a rather amnesiac tendency to equate an anti-dualist continuism with progressive politics. This is despite the European experience with fascism and the well-known vegetarianism and concern for animal feelings amongst the Nazis, who passed laws on the slaughter of animals, and the protection of wildlife, banned vivisection, and threatened to put those who mistreated animals into concentration camps. 'Animals were to be protected for their own sake rather than as appendages to the human moral and material condition.'[21] Hitler was a vegetarian and hated hunting, and he and other senior Nazis were devoted to their pets. Arluke and Sax conclude that 'the Nazis abolished moral distinctions between animals and people by viewing people as animals. The result was that animals could be considered "higher" than some people.'[22] In contemporary Britain too, animal rights protestors, over the export of veal calves, for example, frequently referred to the meat industry as equivalent to the Holocaust. Ideologies of nature combined with racism and romanticism can be fascist.

Nature was also successfully invoked by Hitler in his promises to repeal women's suffrage and constitutional equality and to promote instead the image of women as mothers and bearers of culture, through for example the setting up of a Women's Bureau oriented towards supporting women's reproductive roles.[23] Nazi women too argued that women possessed special natural characteristics which, if emancipated, would be of great social service. The history of continuist politics in the West should at least alert environmentalists to the possible political interests within the nature talk of other cultures.

Dissolving the boundaries between humanity and nature might be approached in a number of ways but here I consider only two – by naturalizing humanity or by humanizing nature, and I now look at each of these alternatives with a view to their gender implications.[24]

Naturalizing Humanity: Naturalizing Women

An emphasis on humans as animals, with natural needs, a species identity and a species way of life, and on social differentiation *between* species, potentially shifts the focus away from issues of social justice *within* the species. Furthermore the project of naturalizing humanity takes place within a history in which women's bodies and animal natures have been used to legitimize repressive ideologies. Although women are by no means universally associated with nature as many dualist accounts (including cultural ecofeminism) would have it, the naturalization of humanity invokes religious ideologies, a number of which have portrayed women as inferior on the basis of their physicality, their immanence, by contrast to male spirituality and transcendence. Consider this extract from a Jain guidebook to nirvana, for example:

> Infatuation, aversion, fear, disgust and various kinds of deceit (*maya*), are ineradicable from the minds of women, . . . [and] for women, therefore, there is no nirvana . . . In the womb, between the breasts, in their navel and loins, a subtle emanation of life is continuously taking place. How then can they be fit for self-control?[25]

The sexual appetites of women, their lack of control and of morality, are also used to legitimate Islamic exclusions of women,[26] and indeed in the debates around the ordination of women in the Catholic church, women's animal bodies are played against their eligibility on the grounds of the Nuptial Mystery.[27]

Naturalizing humanity also involves attempts to define human nature and female nature, another endeavour fraught with political risks for gender justice. In Britain statements about female nature are readily made by people like the self-declared 'scientific racist', Chris Brand, who relatively recently announced that 'anti-racism is coming to the end of the road . . . and the next menace to be tackled is feminism: "Of course, no two feminists agree with one another, although we expect this from girls, don't we? But what is wrong is that feminism denies human nature."'[28] Somewhat less confrontationally, Social Darwinist Kingley Browne also argues against the idea of a single human nature, in favour of distinctive male and female human natures. Thus social policy should assume sexual difference, and see gender differentials in career success as biologically based and not inequitable, and recognize that encouraging men to become homemakers is doomed to failure.[29]

Definitive and universal accounts of female human nature are certainly problematic. Those displayed in both Western and non-Western religious texts and practices commonly exclude women from full personhood by denying their spirituality, and envisaging them as polluting and anomalous. For the Theravada Buddhism of Sri Lanka and Thailand, Sandra Bell[30] shows how the exclusion of women from the Sangha of monks, on the basis of concepts of dangerous female sexuality and pollution, entails their exclusion from the attainment of sacred power. These exclusions reflect a fear of women as threatening the human social order and as wielding the powerful destructiveness of pollution. The moral inferiority of women is linked here, as in versions of Islam, with ideas about women's natures and bodies. Whilst Buddhist women no doubt struggle, in various ways, to subvert essentializing discourses such as these, it has to be asked how the texts and practices of such religions can possibly be formulated as either ecological or non-patriarchal?

Confidence about what is female nature, and indeed about the close links between women and nature, is characteristic not only of religious traditions but also radical green thinking. Many male Deep Ecologists are avowed adherents of ecofeminism[31] and share the ecofeminist certainty that 'The masculine mode of consciousness is one of intellect, reason, linearity; the feminine mode is analogy, intuition, feelings and emotions'.[32] Ecofeminists from Vandana Shiva to Hilka Pietila speak of women's natures and women's attitudes in deeply essentializing voices, and of 'womens culture' as a source of philosophical guidelines for sustainable development. The critique of ecofeminist essentialism[33] does not need repetition here, except to say that the differences between women, of culture, class, ethnicity, and age, at least, and the continual historical formulation and reformulation of gender relations invalidate attempts to define 'the feminine', let alone 'women' (rarely distinguished and usually collapsed in ecofeminist writing) as universal categories with transhistorical meanings.

Hilka Pietila, like many ecofeminists, links women's nature to their bodies thus, 'The menstrual cycle follows the stages of the moon . . . Women feel themselves as a part of the eternal cycle of birth, growth, maturation and death which flows through them, not outside them. In this way women experience nature as a process uniting all living things'.[34] The suggestion that women can have a pre-social, and 'natural' experience of menstruation, entirely separated from the negative social meanings attached to menstrual blood in many cultures, and unmediated by culture, shows how 'naturalizing humanity' risks the erasure of relations of social inequality in human society. This is not to deny that woman may have counter-discourses around menstruation, or that elements of pollution beliefs cannot be turned to explicit or implicit feminist purposes, but that these too are social processes in which embodied subjectivities of women are in constant formation, and the body incapable of determining a universal woman's nature, free of cultural and social influence.

The ecofeminist and Deep Ecologist acceptance of women as closer to, and in a special relationship with, nature is also mystified through the religious *bricolage* of ecofeminists who invent their own ecoreligions through adapting elements of what are thought to be non-patriarchal green religious traditions, in particular of Native Americans, witchcraft, and goddess imagery,[35] and inventing rituals. Essentialism as a charge has no doubt been overused, and Diane Fuss is surely right to object to the essentialism/difference debate as a 'dangerously sedimented opposition in feminist thought',[36] and to point out the shadows of essentialism in the majority of concepts used in academic discourses. She suggests that the relevant questions to ask are: what motivates the deployment of essentialism and what are its effects? What motivates the deployment of ecofeminist sex essentialism (political mobilization) may not be what motivates Deep Ecological sex essentialism (a desire for a simpler world where men are men, and women are . . . different?), and these in turn differ from the motivations in religious sex essentialisms (sacred exclusion?), but the effects are remarkably similar. Once women and nature are universally coupled, ecoreligions can be assumed to express women's, interests since what is good for nature must therefore be good for women too, and a religion which leads to conservationist practices must benefit women since their interests are coterminous with those of nature. At a stroke the feminist critique of patriarchal religions, now validated by ecology, vanishes. A gender sensibility suggests grounds for concern that women's bodies will serve as the bridgehead for the recovery of the species character of humanity, in ways that may not be consistent with their gender interests.

Humanizing Nature: Feminizing Nature

An alternative means of challenging dualism is the humanization of nature, i.e. the dissolution of the nature-culture distinction through the complete absorption of nature into the cultural. Objections to the humanization of nature have been raised from within environmentalism; there is a tension in the ways in which radical environmentalists seem to both condone the extension of human qualities on to nature, since it suggests a kinship of humanity with nature, and also to object to anthropomorphism as implying anthropocentrism. Ted Benton regards Marx's view of the conflict between humans and nature being overcome through the complete absorption of nature, practically and cognitively, into human society (i.e. the 'humanization of nature'), such that no separation from nature is perceived, as 'a quite fantastic species narcissism'.[37] He asks, 'If we can only be at home in the world, be properly, humanly connected with the world only on the basis of a thorough-going transformation of it in line with our intentions, then what space is left for a valuing of nature in virtue of its intrinsic qualities?'[38] I return to the intrinsic valuation of nature in the following section, but here consider the character and gender implications of anthropomorphist absorptions of nature by human society.

First I discuss alternative interpretations of anthropomorphism, and then I examine how gender relations are projected onto nature and whether anthropomorphism indicates non-instrumental relations with nature. The anthropomorphizing of nature, by projecting human qualities onto non-human life, for example in the frequently quoted words of Chief Smohalla, 'You ask me to plough the ground: shall I take a knife and tear my mother's bosom',[39] is the source of much of the confidence that religions, such as those of Native Americans are ecological, since they suggest a non-instrumental caring, an inclusion of nature in humanity, an extension of human rights to other animals and life. But it is not clear that anthropomorphism can be taken so literally.

Environmentalists can see cultures that regard nature as having intentionality as ones which thereby dissolve the boundaries between humans and nature, and also implicitly confer rights and respect on non-human nature. For Dickens the tendency to see nature in this way is constructed as a feature of human nature,[40] and indeed anthropomorphism has generally been seen as intuitive because it is so widespread. But Pascal Boyer[41] reviews cross-cultural research on spontaneous ontologies in child development, and finds that from a very early age infants distinguish the animate and the inanimate, and understand both intentionality and the distinctions and connections between states of affairs and mental representations. These intuitive principles are under-determined by experience, and thus also by culture. 'A general conclusion from [these studies] is that there is no such thing as a categorical "confusion" or spontaneous over-extension in the child's ontology. Live things are not artefacts, persons and plants are not the same, events and abstract objects are different . . .

[A]nimism and anthropomorphism cannot be constructed as "intuitive"'.

Boyer's approach is to distinguish the different kinds of projections whereby, say, mountains are alive, spirits have agency, human social organization is projected onto animals and intentionality conferred on nature. He concludes that religious representations derive from a combination of a background of intuitive expectations together with counter-intuitive assumptions that make them therefore 'attention grabbing' and the focus of cognitive investment. 'Anthropomorphism, then, is "natural" and widespread mainly because it is counter-intuitive';[42] it does not derive from human nature, nor can it be taken simplistically to speak of non-instrumentalism in human-nature relations.

Setting aside the question of why humans anthropomorphize nature, is it the case that anthropomorphism indicates non-dualist and non-instrumentalist approaches to nature? From an anthropological perspective, work such as that of Bird-David (1994)[43] on the different ways in which hunter-gatherers metaphorize human-nature relatedness, e.g. either on adult-child relations, or procreational relatedness or sexual relatedness, suggests that these derive from projections of human social relational experience. For the Cree, hunting is metaphorized as sexual intercourse between hunter and prey, and the actions associated with this sometimes interpreted as a 'conservation ethic' but Bird-David suggests a conservationist outcome is unintended. Kung Bushmen's social organization allows namesakes to claim each other's kinship position and resources, and the projection of this onto nature, such that groups of people become paired with namesakes in nature (eland, giraffe, rain), allows humans access to their (super)natural namesake's kinship relations and power resources, for use in healing. This is arguably about strategic alliances, access to resources and self-interest rather than a respect for nature independent of human interests.[44]

The content of anthropomorphism also clearly involves gender projections. For example, amongst some Western environmentalists the use of Gaia imagery anthropomorphizes the earth, sex-types it as female, and conceives of humanity as a male protector, and the earth as passive and female. Thus in James Lovelock's reference to the pleasure of an 'instinctive comparison of the smooth rounded hills with the contours of a woman's breasts'[45] is an assumption of a heterosexual male humanity. Anthropomorphism seems likely to bear the hallmark of gender relations of the

31

human cultures engaged in the project of absorbing nature in this manner.

Anthropomorphic projections of human social organization onto animal life, and peopling the world with gods and goddesses,[46] imposes the human onto nature, and since human social organization rarely values men and women equally it is not surprising to - find reflections of this in religious representations. Donna Haraway[47] has famously shown the projection of human gender - relations onto other primates in Western science, and Mary Douglas[48] and others have demonstrated how the rules and categories which are dominant in social life, in particular rules of marriage, are imprinted upon nature in the cosmologies of the Lele (Congo) and other peoples. The symbolic significance of various animals can only be understood in relation to Lele gender relations of exogamy and the importance of women's reproductive capacities in a context of demographic vulnerability.

Cultural ecofeminists have taken a positive view of anthropomorphism and sought an anthropomorphized spirituality through their goddess revivalism, and Earth worship, which is assumed to reliably indicate what are loosely referred to as matriarchal societies. For example Kheel writes: 'matriarchal societies of the prehistoric world . . . regarded all parts of nature as interconnected aspects of a nurturing whole, the sacred Mother Earth.'[49] The absence of goddess imagery is conversely linked with a desacralized nature; thus for Baring and Cashford god as Spirit arose around 2000 BC, the goddess thenceforth was associated with Nature, and for the last 4000 years the goddess (and her values of 'spontaneity, feeling, instinct and intuition') has been lost, except for in 'primitive' societies. Society gradually withdrew from nature and replaced the goddess with the god, and moved from identity with nature to dissociation from it.[50]

But although human social organization is projected upon nature through anthropomorphism, this is not a direct reflection in the sense that the worship of a goddess therefore equals 'matriarchy', whatever that might mean. Just as the presence of queens suggests little about the condition and position of ordinary women, so the worship of goddesses cannot be taken necessarily as indicating a powerful position for women relative to men, or, as Baring and Cashford have it, when matriarchy gave way to patriarchy men took over from women, and gods from goddesses.[51]

Cultures where goddesses have been prominent have hardly been matricentric,[52] and cosmologies have no direct correspondence with social relations and realities. Furthermore, ecofeminist interpretation of goddesses selectively emphasizes harmony and nurturance, and goddess worship is assumed to 'mitigate barbarism',[53] although a widely known aspect of goddess cultures is that 'human sacrifice is everywhere characteristic of the worship of the Goddess'.[54] The earth goddess is violent and bloody as much as sensitive and nurturing, in contrast to Baring and Cashford's goddesses who are not violent, unless 'degenerate'; and who, with a characteristically Western sensibility, 'explain' human sacrifice as 'the earliest collective expression of what has come in this century to be called 'psychosis'.[55]

The dehumanizing of sacrificial victims in acts of goddess worship indicates the difficulty with constructing goddess-worshipping societies as preferable social forms, for either a feminist or an environmentalist agenda. Goddess worship in ancient Egypt involved the mass burials of hundreds of Egyptian women, and in the *meriah* (human) sacrifices common amongst the Khonds of India until the early decades of the nineteenth century, people were traded for seasonal sacrifice, through flaying alive, by peasant communities in worship of their earth goddess.[56] Eco-populist Mahapatra,[57] however, appreciatively relates the songs sung on the occasion of the *meriah* sacrifice, and both glorifies the ritual as showing the connectedness of tribal communities to the earth, and dehumanizes the human victim, by referring to him or her as 'it'.[58] As Campbell denies the suffering of the Egyptian women buried alive,[59] so too does Mahapatra become an apologist for Khond human sacrifice.

Anthropomorphism is, however, effective in environmental mobilization. The political manipulation of anthropomorphism has been analysed by Baviskar in her work on the Narmada Bachao Andolan (Movement to Save the Narmada) and its public relations:

At a meeting . . . an active and influential supporter of the Andolan from Delhi gave a speech in which the audience were told that, as adivasis, they were 'mother earth's children' and that the dam would tear them – the children – from their mother's breast. As a rule, adivasis never use this metaphor, preferring more prosaic descriptions of the threat to their land and livestock. However, this speech evidently made an impact because, later on, a man from Anjanvara, [the tribal village where Baviskar lived] who is active in the Andolan and who had never before expressed himself thus, repeated this statement to a television interviewer as if it were his own. His tactic was well-chosen; another film-maker who had earlier taped an interview with this adivasi and had only heard of land being drowned, came to know of this, more colourful response. So he went back to the adivasi to rerecord the interview, this time ensuring that he had the mother-child metaphor on tape.[60]

The political objection to the misrepresentation of non-Western religions and eco-cosmologies are clearly put in this study which reveals the extent to which supporters of the movement are derived from the landlord class (of Patidars) from the plains rather than the tribal Bhilala of the hills, who are, however, showcased by movement activists to tap into the romantic projections of the urban elite and public opinion. Activists misrepresent tribal religion as inherently conservationist, and local resistance towards displacement as an indigenous critique of development, for political aims in which however 'intellectuals end up creating caricatures',[61] tribal voices are appropriated, and, I would argue, issues of social justice obscured.

Thus anthropomorphism cannot be seen as intuitive; it projects human gender relations onto nature and neither reliably indicates non-instrumental relations with nature nor is incompatible with patriarchy, the dehumanization of certain social groups and social violence. The previous two sections have suggested a sceptical view of assumptions that non-Western religions are either non-dualist or socially just. Next I would like to consider what reverence for nature means and how it connects to environmental actions.

The Intrinsic Value of Nature

When claims are made about indigenous peoples having religions which value nature for its own sake, it is not always clear exactly what kinds of indigenous societies are the reference points, however it is particularly hunter-gatherers who are claimed to have attitudes of sacramental equality towards animals, whilst agriculturalists express opposition and control of nature.[62] In his study of the 'animal estate' in Malawi, Morris shows that animals are simultaneously conceived of in 'contradictory' ways, as fundamentally hostile to humanity, as resources and, through the identification of animals with spirits of the dead and human fertility, as 'a crucial part in the ongoing cyclic processes of life and social reproduction'.[63] Sacramental egalitarianism and opposition and control co-exist. 'Respect for nature' here, for example, in the sexual abstinence of hunting rituals, expresses fear of mystical animal power. This kind of 'respect for nature' is rather different from that expressed by Deep Ecologists. Similarly, a woman breast-feeding a young animal (pigs in Papua New Guinea, deer in south India) is easily read in terms of selfless concern for the survival of the animal, forgetting that it will be killed and eaten later.

A core assumption is that ecoreligions embody ancient ecological wisdom and generate protective and positive environmental behaviours, and it is this that the next section addresses. When Vanucci writes that 'In traditional thought in India . . . everything is sacred',[64] he reads rituals involving trees and the garlanding of domestic animals as associating man holistically with nature; sacred forests are said to have resulted from Hindu ecoreligious protection,[65] and tribal 'worship of nature'[66] thought of as equivalent to what we now call biosphere reserves. Similarly, the Munda myth of origin, which refers to the smoke of the Asurs furnaces, is taken to be an ancient and prophetic protest against environmental pollution,[67] and Xaxa[68] suggests that when the Oraons incorporate nature into rituals and customs, e.g. in animal totems, the consumption prohibition for that animal can be read as a form of wildlife protection. Finally, Vatsyayan[69] maintains that the emphasis on purification in the Vedas is an ecological position, and the pollution prescriptions which uphold the caste system are represented as ecological awareness of pollution in the modern sense.

But a sacralized nature cannot be readily equated with a modern ecological understanding. Thus for Bhilalas, of Gujerat, 'the natural and the supernatural are sometimes indistinguishable. Hills, trees and stones are imbued with spiritual power and actively intervene in people's lives,[70] but that this does not generate anything akin to conservationism. Indeed:

> By establishing a religious connection with their environment and acknowledging its power to affect their fortunes, people also 'naturalise' their own existence, explaining and, at the same time, claiming for themselves their physical world. Appropriation, explanation and legitimation occur simultaneously.[71]

Baviskar finds in the Bhilala that whilst respectful relations with nature are evident in ritual, they also see the natural resources at their command as indestructible – 'the earth a cornucopia and the forest limitless',[72] and describes her experience of accompanying a woman on a fuelwood collecting expedition thus: 'I had imagined Binda collecting wood, gathering up fallen deadwood and lopping branches off trees. But this is killing, for the living green wood is hacked away to get at the fuel above.'[73] The idea of nature being both sacred and limitless is not necessarily contradictory and indeed appears in a number of studies dealing with environmental cosmologies.[74]

There is an immense cultural distance that separates traditional religious conceptions of the environment from modern ecological knowledge,[75] and it is historically distorting and anachronistic to seek to clothe such conceptions in ecological authenticity. There is also something of a contradiction in the ecofeminist claim that it is women who are the repositories of environmental wisdom, when they are marginalized in the tribal and Hindu belief systems which are simultaneously claimed to embody such wisdom. But it might be argued that even though the concepts of traditional belief systems are not equivalent to those of Western ecology, they confer cultural attitudes of protectiveness towards nature and therefore predispose towards less exploitative environmental behaviours. One thus comes back to the question of whether, and how, religious beliefs actually do affect the environmental behaviour of individual men and women?

Religious Beliefs and Environmental Behaviour

The idea that 'indigenous societies', rarely specified with much precision and usually assumed to be geographically and culturally isolated, do not damage their environments unless forced to by capitalism and modernity is widespread but not very robust. Buddhism and Taoism are religions of peasant societies which have not been 'a spiritual bulwark against pollution, erosion, deforestation and environmental wreckage',[76] and amongst foraging peoples, the potlatch of Native Americans such as the Haida looks rather like conspicuous consumption, the Plains Indians have destroyed forests and buffalo herds, Mbuti pygmies fire forests to drive out game, and forest destruction and hunting to extinction have not been confined to modern times or capitalism.

The mismatch between religious injunctions on nature and the actual behaviour of those who subscribe to such beliefs is extensively documented. Japanese Buddhist monks who perform funeral ceremonies for whales, apologising to the spirit of the whale, have thereby legitimized whaling.[77] Nepali Buddhists may not kill but do eat meat, and allow male yak calves to starve to death in order to maintain the milk herd,[78] and Thai Buddhist ideology, as it is understood and practised locally, actually subordinates all nature to culture, and offers men a means of asserting authority over female descent groups and control their fertility.[79]

Ecological interpretations of world religions fail to consider the gender and class critiques of religious texts and traditions. For example, Martin Palmer suggests that Hindu and Buddhist worldviews in which time is cyclical offer a better understanding of nature, and refers to Hindu beliefs in reincarnation as evidence. However the connection of this to the caste system and the subordination of women is not mentioned.[80] Palmer says of Hinduism, 'If the divine is present in all life, then the taking of life will disturb the chain of being, the wheel of *samsara*, and will affect the life of the person who has taken the life. This is the law of *karma*.'[81] Yet these beliefs co-exist with female infanticide. Hindu 'reverence for life' has safeguarded neither women's rights nor the environment.

In the light of this, one needs to ask two questions: firstly, how significant or insignificant are religious beliefs to environmental actions, and secondly, how *are* beliefs and actions connected? The first point to make here is that the management of natural resources predominantly reflects the gendered socio-political relations and history within which religious ideologies are nested, and beliefs do not entail particular forms of environmental management outside of a material and social context. Nature may be sacralized by peoples who simultaneously follow 'unsustainable' livelihood practices. In an analysis of the *kolam*, women's ritual art decorating the ground in front of the house in rice flour or coloured powders in Tamil Nadu, Vijaya Nagarajan, describes how such performances by women as a ritual of worship of the earth goddess, Bhudevi, in the early morning are, later in the day, the space upon which household waste is tipped. What is sacralized in the *kolam* becomes readily desacralized. Similarly, the Ganges is sacred, yet those who regard it as holy also subject it to extensive pollution. Nagarajan suggests that:

> it could be the very belief of a cosmological relationship that prevents the seeing of the . . . Ganga, or Bhudevi, as needing protection from human beings . . . [I]t is at times the very act of sacralisation that prevents the seeing of the necessity of conservation, in the Western sense.[82]

Nagarajan develops the idea of 'intermittent sacrality', as that which can be, as in the *kolam*, hosted by women – and then dehosted by them. She illustrates the ethnocentrism of radical environmental representations of the embedded ecological ideas of other cultures, which cannot serve the purposes to which they are frequently put, and her work also shows the fruitfulness of an approach which examines the disjunctions between beliefs, rituals and action.

A gendered political ecology of belief deployed towards understanding the connections and disconnections between belief and environmental behaviours also requires a recognition of the plurality in religious constellations faced by local peoples. Religious beliefs are portrayed in Western environmentalism as singular and universal in their command of allegiance, rather than plural, competing, and partial in their influence and their social constituencies. Furthermore, silences on local hierarchies and power relations, which include religious actors and institutions, are necessary to these misrepresentations. Three questions suggest themselves as a starting point for a gendered political ecology of belief; which social groups possess authority to formulate the vocabulary of religious belief?; in whose interests are metaphors of nature deployed?; how is nature talk used in resource struggles by men and women?

A gendered political ecology of religions seems likely to produce a significantly different image of human-nature relations than that currently found in ecocentric environmentalism. Examples of such an approach, briefly, are in the work of David Maxwell[83] in Zimbabwe and Janice Boddy[84] in the Sudan.

David Maxwell, in his study of the social history of the Hwesa in north-eastern Zimbabwe, tells a story of religious pluralism and the politics of nature in the religious rivalries of land cults and mediums, spirit possession cults, and latterly Christian missionaries (who also sacralized landscape) in a colonial and post-colonial context.[85] In his analysis male gerontocratic elites control the ancestor cults, and thus rain and fertility, and exclude women. Although mediums oppose modernization on ostensibly spiritual grounds, these are as much to do with the threat to their positions and local patriarchy. Women's experience has been one of exclusion from 'traditional' ecoreligion, including land cults, resistance through spirit possession and growing allegiance to the Christian churches offering opportunities, through the Catholic emphasis on Mary and other female saints, and in the Pentecostal case through opposition to Shona spirits as demons and displays of female power in church, to subvert male authority and re-invent gender identities.

Janice Boddy's work in the Sudan shows the subtle and some-times contradictory ways in which women relate to spirit posses-sion cults, *zar*, in northern Sudan, which exist alongside Islam. The religious beliefs and practices of women reflect the experi-enced tensions of ideal and actual womanhood, and obliquely offer discourses of resistance and self-recognition. *Zar* is revealed by Boddy as neither just 'letting off steam', nor as a serious challenge to the gender order, but as satire and social commentary. These occur through social inversions such as the behaviour of women during possession and the matriliny of the spirit world, a relativiz-ing perspective from the 'other' social world of the spirits, a nam-ing of the implicit alternatives held in tension with dominant gender ideologies, and an opportunity for the culturally over-deter-mined female person to see herself momentarily as an individual.[86]

Here religious belief neither determines action, nor is it irrele-vant: it presents actors with choices. It is socially constructed by both dominant and muted social groups and experiences, it is dynamic and changing in content (e.g. the changing cast of spirit characters). It offers women explanations for failure to live up to the social ideals of womanhood, especially regarding fertility and marital success. The active engagement of women in formulating religious meanings and in resistance to exclusion is also seen in Karin Kapadia's research with Brahmin women in south India, who, for example, secretly learn the sacred texts which are denied them by their polluted status as women, and privately assert their spiritual worth.[87] Subalterns speak in many ways, but their voices are not found in the sacred texts of world religions, written on the whole by educated elites, or indeed in the official belief systems of male-dominated religious ideologies, however ecological they appear.

Conclusions

Contrasts between Western dualist, and non-Western continuist, attitudes to nature as revealed in religious beliefs are questionable because there are credible arguments for an inherent dualism and instrumentalism in a great many non-Western religions, and the dissolution of dualism through either naturalizing humanity or humanizing nature carry old and new dangers for women which challenge any necessary compatibility of continuism with femin-ism, or environmentalism with social justice. The central role of women's bodies in how human religious expression socializes nature and enforces social rules and boundaries, and the flickering struggles by women to reformulate their positions in these cosmologies, both in dominant and subordinate religious institutions, suggests, for me, another allegiance. Before we re-invent ourselves as a species like any other, in 'a democracy amongst species' we need to offer a full humanity to women.

Notes

The author acknowledges the support of the ESRC Global Environmental Change programme, through a Research Fellowship held during the period in which this chapter was written.

1 Anthrocentrism is human-centredness, speciesism is the 'arbitrary discrimination on the basis of species' and human chauvinism is the specification of species 'differences in ways that invariably favour humans', see T. Hayward and J. O'Neill, eds, *Justice, Property and the Environment: Social and Legal Perspectives* (Aldershot: Ashgate, 1997); pp. 50–54; a disposition to exclude. Hayward suggests that anthropocentrism is a misleading term since human-centredness implies a spurious concern for the well-being of all humans, it fails to distinguish legitimate and illegitimate human interests, and is in some aspects unavoidable.
2 P. Dickens, *Society and Nature: Towards a Green Social Theory* (Brighton: Harvester Wheatsheaf, 1992); P. Dickens, *Reconstructing Nature: Alienation, Emancipation and the Division of Labour* (London: Routledge, 1996); and T. Benton, *Natural Relations: Ecology, Animal Rights and Social Justice* (London and New York: Verso, 1993); R. Eckersley, *Environmentalism and Political Theory: Toward an Ecocentric Approach* (London: UCL Press, 1992).
3 A. Naess, 'Deep Ecology', in *Key Concepts in Critical Theory: Ecology*, ed. C. Merchant (New Jersey: Humanities Press, 1994), pp. 125–39.
4 F. Matthews, 'Ecofeminism and Deep Ecology', in *Key Concepts*, ed. Merchant, pp. 235–47.
5 Eckersley, *Environmentalism and Political Theory*.
6 A. Baviskar, *In the Belly of the River: Tribal Conflicts over Development in the Narmada Valley* (Delhi: Oxford University Press, 1995), p. 46.
7 V. Plumwood, *Feminism and the Mastery of Nature* (London: Routledge, 1993).
8 C. Merchant, *The Death of Nature: Women, Ecology and the Scientific Revolution* (London: Wildwood House, 1980); V. Shiva, *Staying Alive: Women, Ecology and Development* (London: Zed Books, 1989); Plumwood, *Feminism and the Mastery of Nature*.
9 P. Pedersen, 'Nature, Religion and Cultural Identity: The Religious Environmentalist Paradigm', in *Asian Perceptions of Nature: A Critical Approach*, eds O. Bruun and A. Kalland (London: Curzon Press, 1995), pp. 258–76.
10 K. Chaitanya, 'The Earth as Sacred Environs', in *Indigenous Vision: Peoples' of India Attitudes to the Environment*, ed. G. Sen (New Delhi: Sage, 1992) pp. 35–48 esp. p. 43.

11 S. Mahapatra, 'Invocation. Rites of Propitiation in Tribal Societies', in ibid., p. 66.

12 Ibid., p. 70.

13 In drawing out themes from the explosion of radical environmentalist discourses, I have tried to focus on issues around which there is a certain consensus, but I acknowledge that particular authors may object to the inevitable levelling of ideas which occurs in such a process, and I do not pretend to do justice to the distinct approaches and inflections of emphasis in the branches of these literatures. The grouping of major world religions together with more localized religious traditions may also raise objections, but this only corresponds to their collapse in popular environmentalism, the assumptions of which are the focus of attention here.

14 L. White, Jr., 'The Historic Roots of Our Ecological Crisis', *Science*, 155, March 1967.

15 M. Bookchin, *The Ecology of Freedom: The Emergence and Disappearance of Hierarchy* (Palo Alto: Cheshire Books, 1982).

16 J. Biehl, *Finding Our Way: Rethinking Ecofeminist Politics* (Montreal: Black Rose, 1991).

17 K. Soper, *What is Nature? Culture, Politics and the Non-Human* (Oxford: Blackwell, 1995).

18 C. P. MacCormack, 'Nature, Culture and Gender: A Critique', in *Nature, Culture and Gender*, eds C. P. MacCormack and M. Strathern (Cambridge: Cambridge University Press, 1980), pp. 1–24.

19 E.g., J. R. Engel and J. G. Engel, eds, *Ethics of Environment and Development: Global Challenge and International Response* (London: Belhaven Press, 1990).

20 See below, chap. by S. Bell.

21 A. Cockburn, 'A Short, Meat-Oriented History of the World. From Eden to Matthole', *New Left Review*, 1996, pp. 16–42, esp. p. 30.

22 Ibid., p. 31.

23 C. Koonz, *Mothers in the Fatherland: Women, the Family and Nazi Politics* (London: Methuen, 1987).

24 This heuristic division remains bounded by the old terms of nature and culture simply as an organizing device.

25 J. Campbell, *The Masks of God*, 2 vols. (London: Souvenir Press, 1973), II, p. 237.

26 F. Mernissi, *Beyond the Veil: Male Female Dynamics in a Modern Muslim Society* (New York: John Wiley, 1975); L. Abu-Lughod, *Veiled Sentiments: Honor and Poetry in a Bedouin Society* (Berkeley, Calif.: University of California Press, 1986).

27 M. Douglas, *Risk and Blame: Essays in Cultural Theory* (London: Routledge, 1992), pp. 271–94.

28 *The Times Higher Education Supplement*, 26 April 1996.

29 K. Browne, *Divided Labours: An Evolutionary View of Women at Work* (London: Weidenfeld and Nicolson, 1998).

30 Bell (this vol.) concludes that there is no concept of women having a special relationship with nature in Theravada Buddhism; they may be seen as more ensnared in *samsara* but *samsara* involves both nature and culture. The Buddhist virtue of compassion for all life does not equate to an environmentalist concern for the conservation of threatened species since, in Buddhist thought,

nothing in nature has meaning or purpose and nor should we struggle for permanence.

31 J. Biehl, 'Ecofeminism and Deep Ecology: Unresolvable Conflict?', *Our Generation*, 19 (2) 1988, pp. 18–32.
32 A. Baring and J. Cashford, *The Myth of the Goddess: Evolution of an Image* (London: Penguin Books, 1993), pp. 672–73.
33 C. Jackson, 'Gender Analysis and Environmentalisms' in *Social Theory and the Global Environment*, eds T. Benton and M. Redclift (London: Routledge, 1994), pp. 113–49; M. Nanda, 'Is Modern Science a Western, Patriarchal Myth? A Critique of the Populist Orthodoxy', *South Asia Bulletin*, XI (1 & 2), 1991, pp. 32–61; M. Molyneaux and D. Steinberg, 'Mies and Shiva's Ecofeminism: A New Testament?', *Feminist Review*, 49, 1995, pp. 86–107.
34 H. Pietila, 'The Daughters of the Earth: Women's Culture as a Basis for Sustainable Development', in *Ethics of Environment*, eds Engel and Engel, pp. 235–44, esp. 236.
35 For example, see *New Catalyst Quarterly*, 1987/8.
36 D. Fuss, *Essentially Speaking* (London: Routledge, 1989), p. 4.
37 T. Benton, *Natural Relations: Ecology, Animal Rights and Social Justice* (London and New York: Verso, 1993), p. 32.
38 Ibid., p. 31.
39 B. Eastlea, *Science and Sexual Oppression: Patriarchy's Confrontation with Women and Nature* (London: Weidenfield and Nicholson, 1981), p. 43.
40 P. Dickens, *Society and Nature: Towards a Green Social Theory* (Brighton: Harvester Wheatsheaf, 1992).
41 P. Boyer, 'What Makes Anthropomorphism Natural: Intuitive Ontology and Cultural Representations', *Journal of the Royal Anthropological Institute*, ns, 2, 1996, pp. 83–97.
42 Ibid., p. 95.
43 N. Bird-David, 'Tribal Metaphorisation of Human-Nature Relatedness: A Comparative Analysis', in *Environmentalism: The View from Anthropology*, ed. K. Milton (London: Routledge, 1993), pp. 112–25.
44 Tim Ingold argues, however, that when the hunter-gatherer addresses the forest as a parent, this is not a metaphor to the people themselves, and that it is the anthropologist who represents it thus. The hunter-gatherers do not separate society and nature. See T. Ingold, 'Hunting and Gathering as Ways of Perceiving the Environment', in *Redefining Nature: Ecology, Culture and Domestication*, eds R. Ellen and K. Fukui (Oxford: Berg, 1996), p. 129. Animals have personhood, and humans and animals are distinguished only as varieties of organism-person such that 'anthropomorphism' and 'naturalism' become meaningless. However, Boyer's work on infant ontologies suggests otherwise.
    Although Ingold charges Bird-David with making her own interpretation of hunter -gatherer views of human-nature relatedness, Ingold, by claiming fidelity to hunter- gatherers own models denies his own subjectivity – both are methodologically problematic.
45 P. Murphy, 'Sex Typing the Planet: Gaia Imagery and the Problem of Subverting Patriarchy', *Environmental Ethics*, 10 (2), 1988, pp. 155–68.
46 Bookchin, *Ecology of Freedom*.
47 D. Haraway, *Primate Visions: Gender, Race and Nature in the World of Modern Science* (New York: Routledge, 1989).
48 M. Douglas, *Implicit Meanings* (London: Routledge, 1975).

49 M. Kheell, 'From Healing Herbs to Deathly Drugs: Western Medicine's War against the Natural World', *Living with Contradictions: Controversies in Feminist Social Ethics*, ed. A. Jaggar (Boulder, Colorado: Westview Press, 1994), p. 650.
50 Baring and Cashford, *Myth of the Goddess*.
51 Ibid., p. 332.
52 Biehl, *Finding Our Way*.
53 Baring and Cashford, *Myth of the Goddess*, p. 156.
54 Campbell, *Masks of God*, p. 160.
55 Baring and Cashford, *Myth of the Goddess*, p. 163.
56 M. Eliade, *Patterns in Comparative Religion* (London: Sheed and Ward, 1958); F. Padel, *The Sacrifice of Human Being* (New Delhi: Sage, 1995).
57 Mahapatra, 'Invocation. Rites of Propitiation', pp. 63–74, esp. p. 66.
58 A more useful understanding of meriah comes from the comparative work of Elisabeth Leigh-Stutchbury (1982) who, through socially contextualising the sacrificial institutions of both *sati* and *meriah*, is able to reveal connections between religious practices and social relations. Where *sati* is associated with caste society, a masculine deity, fire, purity, the sky and the transcendental, *meriah* is linked in Khond history to a chaotic and destructive female deity, to blood, the pragmatic and the earth, see E. Leigh-Stutchbury, 'Blood, Fire and Mediation: Human Sacrifice and Widow Burning in Nineteenth-Century India', in *Women in India and Nepal*, eds M. Allen and S. Mukherjee (Canberra: Australian National University Press, 1982), pp. 21–75.
59 Campbell writes of the women buried alive in Middle Kingdom Egypt, as wives and concubines, saying that in spite of the evidence of pain and suffering in the postures of the female bodies, 'these sacrifices were not properly, in fact, sacrifices at all; that is to say they were not particular beings. . . They were parts only of a larger whole; and it was only by virtue of their absolute submission to that in its unalterable categorical imperative that they were anything at all', see Campbell, *Masks of God*, pp. 63–65.
60 Baviskar, *Belly of the River*, p. 213.
61 Ibid., p. 240.
62 B. Morris, 'Woodland and Village: Reflections on the "animal state" in Rural Malawi', *Journal of the Royal Anthropological Institute*, 1 (2), 1995, pp. 301–15.
63 Ibid., p. 302.
64 M. Vannuci, 'Tradition and change', in *Indigenous Vision*, ed. Sen, pp. 25–34.
65 M. Gadgil and R. Guha, *This Fissured Land: An Ecological History of India* (Delhi: Oxford University Press, 1992).
66 W. Pereira, 'The Sustainable Lifestyle of the Warlis', in *Indigenous Vision*, ed. Sen, pp. 189–204.
67 Singh, 'The Munda Epic: An Interpretation', in ibid., pp. 75–90.
68 V. Xaxa, 'Oraons: Religion, Customs and Environment', in ibid., pp. 101–12, esp. p.107.
69 K. Vatsyayan, 'Ecology and Indian Myth', in ibid., pp. 157–82, esp. p.171.
70 Baviskar, *Belly of the River*, p. 161.
71 Ibid., p 162.
72 Ibid., p 168.
73 Ibid., p. 148. Baviskar gives an honest and reflexive account of her expectations at the start of her study, and her growing awareness of her own assumptions about adivasi culture and attitudes to nature and development.

74 For example, W. van Beek and P. Banga, 'The Dogon and their Trees', in *Bush Base: Forest Farm Culture, Environment and Development*, eds E. Croll and D. Parkin (London: Routledge, 1992), pp. 57–75; and see below, chap. by Nagarajan.

75 Pedersen, 'Nature, Religion and Cultural Identity', pp. 258–76, esp. p. 266.

76 R. Ellen, 'What Black Elk Left Unsaid: On the Illusory Images of Green Primitivism', *Current Anthropology*, 6 (2), 1986, pp. 8–13, esp. p. 10.

77 M. Palmer, 'The Encounter of Religion and Conservation', in *Ethics of Environment*, eds Engel and Engel, pp. 50–62, esp. p. 51.

78 G. Clarke, 1995 'Thinking Through Nature in Highland Nepal', in *Asian Perceptions of Nature*, eds Bruun and Kalland, pp. 88–102, esp. p. 99.

79 S. Sparkes, 1995 'Taming Nature – Controlling Fertility: Concepts of Nature and Gender among the Isan of Northeast Thailand', in *Asian Perceptions*, eds Bruun and Kalland.

80 Palmer, 'The Encounter of Religion and Conservation', in *Ethics of Environment*, eds Engel and Engel, p. 53.

81 Ibid., p. 55.

82 See below, chap. by Nagarajan.

83 D. Maxwell, 'A Social and Conceptual History of North-East Zimbabwe, 1890–1990' (Ph.D. thesis, University of Oxford, 1994).

84 J. Boddy, *Wombs and Alien Spirits: Women, Men and the Zar Cult in Northern Sudan* (Madison: Wisconsin University Press, 1989).

85 Maxwell, 'A Social and Conceptual History'.

86 Boddy, *Wombs and Alien Spirits*.

87 K. Kapadia, 'Impure Women, Virtuous Men: Religion, Resistance and Gender', *South Asia Research*, 14 (2), 1994, pp. 184–95.

Part II

The Sacred

3

Sacred Landscapes: Religion and the Natural Environment in the Classical World

Elena Kingdon

The Greeks had no sacred books. Information about religion is gleaned from the works of poets in hymns, epics and tragedy. Homer defined the Olympiç gods through the vicissitudes of the Trojan war and Odysseus's wanderings. Hesiod was a farmer-poet from Boeotia who, as he tells us, was impelled by the Muses to sing about the family of gods before time began. The narrative that follows is therefore interspersed with quotations to illustrate how the Greeks viewed their gods, goddesses and the natural environments.

Greek women, with few exceptions, as portrayed in the literature, were silent and belonged to the elite, being the wives, mothers and daughters of Athenian citizens. What is known about their lives, feelings and work was written by men, whose thoughts about women were dictated by socio-political mores and private prejudice. Nonetheless, women were essential to the performance of key rituals that ensured human and land fertility. In both Greek and Roman religion there were women priestesses. Women's link with the Earth was acknowledged by Athenian society, but fell short of any concept of 'custodianship'. What is more relevant, from a contemporary viewpoint, is that, among the attitudes towards the Earth and its resources in both the Athenian and Roman high culture, one can detect the beginnings of that pride in man's technological achievements which has animated so many endeavours in Western technological civilization.

This chapter is in two sections. The first illustrates some Greek and Roman attitudes towards the natural scenery, the second looks at the relation between women and the sacred.

Hesiod, inspired by Near Eastern cosmologies, systematized local mythical traditions into a *Theogony* or genealogy of the gods. In this composition the Earth is at first a spontaneous generative principle; she is the bearer of seas, mountains and sky, the abodes of the gods. In a second stage, under the influence of Eros and in sexual congress with Ouranos, the sky, she creates the second generation of divine beings. For Hesiod the onset of agricultural labour and the beginning of 'culture' bring about the separation between gods and men.

What the Earth meant to the Greeks, however, is better expressed in the first lines of a fifth-century Homeric Hymn,[1] which hails the Earth as mother of all and oldest of all:

> whose beauty nurtures all creatures that walk upon the land
> and all that move in the deep or fly in the air,
> O mighty one you are the source of fair children and goodly fruit,
> and on you it depends to give life to, or take it away from mortal men.
> (vv. 1–7)

Not as completely personified as other Greek deities, Gaia, the Earth, is nonetheless presented as female by the word 'mother' which reflects the life of women. It is easy for us to interpret the 'Mother Earth' of the Homeric Hymn in terms of our 'mother nature' allegory, but this does not convey the meaning it had for the Greeks, who felt the world of nature to be inseparably associated with the world of the gods; from mountains to the sea, down to caves, groves and springs, the Greek landscape was pervaded with divine powers embodied as gods or nymphs.

Can one therefore imagine how the Greeks perceived their immediate physical environment? First they saw a contrast between man-made landscapes and wilderness. The sight of cultivation and the promise of good harvests was dear to both Greeks and Romans. Rows of carefully tended vines, olive groves and fields of golden wheat reflected the order the gods had brought to the world. The olive was Athena's gift, wine Dionysus's, whereas cereal cultivation was identified with Demeter and Kore. These deities were not allegories. They represented the realities of cultivation interpreted as a reciprocal relationship with the gods, which involved agricultural labour punctuated by holy days and festivals. Non-cultivated land, the realm of nymphs and river gods, was scattered with shrines and sacred precincts where passers-by stopped to offer prayers, flowers and fruit.

The beauty of a country scene and its sacredness were closely associated in Greek consciousness. Indeed, Socrates' awareness that the spot he and Phaedrus have chosen is dedicated to some river god or nymph is right at the centre of his description of the scenery.[2] The tallness of the trees, the fragrance of the summer air, the coolness of the water, the green slope that forms a soft cushion for the head are all highlighted in turn; but the scenery Socrates evokes with such sensuous enjoyment is designed to provide order and comfort. It is the environment outside city walls, which is unlike the wild mountain ranges of shepherds and goats or the fastness of hunters and their prey.

The pastoral landscape was primarily associated with Pan. Pan, the god of shepherds and their flocks, can also be seen as the symbol of Mediterranean transhumance. In the *Homeric Hymn* 'he wanders through thick brushwood or careers through chalk-white lofty mountains, now protecting the flocks, now chasing a wild beast off mountain crests'.[3] Aeschylus writes of the 'Dancer who treads the briny shore'.[4] Pan is the sight of the shimmering sea at the end of the long tramp from mountain to plain. The sound of Pan's syrinx calms the restless goats and fills their udders with milk or leads them to the buck. It is music that both tempts and eludes and, like Echo the nymph pursued by Pan, resounds from rock to rock expressing the melancholy of unfulfilled longing. Pan merges into divine form the shepherd and the goat within the solitary pastoral landscape.

True wilderness belongs to Artemis, who was worshipped as Callisto in Arcadia, Pan's country of origin. Both Artemis and Callisto were aspects of the same divinity, of the Mediterranean *Potnia Theron*, the Mistress of Animals whom the Greeks transformed into chaste huntress, thereby maintaining her original dominion over animal life.

Artemis was also a child-rearing goddess, who presided over girls' transition rites. In the Brauron sanctuary of Attica, pre-pubertal girls danced for Artemis as 'little bears' supervised by bear-masked men and women.[5] Indeed Artemis protected all young life, human and animal. In the *Agamemnon* by Aeschylus,[6] Calchas, the seer, invokes Artemis 'so kind to the . . . young of beasts that stalk the wild'. Yet Artemis can also merge with the Gorgon; and it is with gorgonian fury that Clytemnestra will slay Agamemnon who sacrificed their daughter Iphigenia.[7]

As goddess of the chase Artemis is the patroness of hunters, who does not tolerate boasting or overkill, as the myth of Orion exemplifies. Xenophon recommends that leverets be left to the goddess and that hunters sacrifice a share of the chase to Artemis and Apollo.[8] We get a glimpse of Artemis's landscape in Pheadra's words:

> I am going
> Out to the hills and the woods, the pine forests
> Where hounds pace after blood
> And press close on the spotted deer!
> O gods! Were I there, shouting to the pack,
> Lifting the lance to my hair bright in the wind,
> Hurling the barbed blade.[9]

Artemis and Pan sanctuaries, situated far from cultivated land, acted as wildlife reserves, for hunters could not pursue prey within their precincts. Passers-by could rest in the shade of sacred groves provided they were ritually clean, without weapons or iron tools, and free from bloodshed. For the same reason, women could not enter sanctuaries for some weeks after childbirth nor at the time of the menses.[10] Shepherds were not allowed to graze their animals in sacred groves or cut branches for fodder. Infractions to these rules must have occurred, however, in spite of fines and spiritual penalties. In Aristophanes's *Birds* for instance, sacred precincts are said to offer birds little relief from traps and snares.[11] And, in Roman times, at the Parilia festival each year, the goddess Pales was asked to forgive shepherds for polluting springs and cutting foliage in sacred groves.[12]

Sanctuaries were often situated near springs or streams, because water was needed for rituals. In a passage of the *Critias* Plato mentions the presence of shrines as evidence that some mountains which, in his day, only supported bees, were not so long ago rich in woodlands 'and there were lots of tall cultivated trees which bore unlimited fodder for beasts . . . and the soil benefited from an annual rainfall that did not run to waste off the earth as it does today . . . and the shrines which still survive at these former springs are proof of our present account of the country'.[13] Plato's description of a landscape of 'not so long ago' is incidental to his account of a fictitious 'prehistoric' Athens hit by floods and deluges. Plato's reference to it shows, however, that his sequence of cause and effect ran from floods loosening soil, to uprooted trees and bare landscape. If he was silent over the human agencies responsible for causing the environmental degradation, this was because floods, not cut trees, were the perceived cause.[14]

The fifth century in which Plato lived had seen many important political, economic and social changes. Natural philosophy, Socratic dialectics and sophistic education had fostered new ideas and values. The democratic government of Athens offered its citizens opportunities for greater wealth and new careers. Philosophical speculation about the cosmos's first principles had affected religious belief among some intellectuals; but the Homeric gods were not deposed, nor was piety lessened or cults transformed. The new spirituality, however, denied anthropomorphism and explained the gods as allegories. Consequently, man's attitude towards the natural world was bound to change. Formerly, any attempt to control nature was seen as an act of defiance against the gods. This is evidenced in *The Persians*, for instance, where Xerxes's technical feat of yoking the Hellespont with a bridge of boats is considered an act of arrogance against the gods which justifies the rout of the Persians by the Greeks.

By contrast, only thirty years later, the chorus of the *Antigone* is not chary of singing the praise of man's technical achievements:[15]

Wonders are many, yet of all
things man is the most wonderful.
He can sail on the stormy sea
though the tempest rage, and the loud
waves roar around, as he makes his
path amidst the towering surge.
Earth inexhaustible, ageless, he wearies, as
backwards and forwards, from season to season, his
ox-team drives along the ploughshare.

. . . And speech he has learnt, and thought
so swift, and the temper of mind to dwell within cities

. . . Full of resources against all that comes to him
is Man. Against death alone he is left with no defence.
But painful illness he can cure
by his own skill. (*Antigone*, vv. 331–364)[16]

A word of warning still lingers, 'for the device and cunning of man brings him now to evil, now to good', but it is the law he must now observe. It is this definition of man in terms of city laws and institutions that will eventually bring about a separation (more evident still in Roman times) between the city and the world of nature.[17]

Greater changes were to follow in the wake of Alexander's

conquests and with the establishment of the Macedonian kingdoms after his death. By the time Rome had conquered Greece and was in turn captured by Greek culture, the countryside was idealized and viewed as a refuge from the cares of hectic city life. The Roman poet Virgil rejoices in his Italian homeland; for him the rural landscape with the small farms of his father's day represents the last bulwark of old Roman virtues. Virgil's *In Praise of Italy* can be contrasted to Antigone's chorus.[18] Here, the feats of human engineering Virgil mentions are described in a language that implies the intrusion they impose upon the natural environment. They are condemnations of technology evoked, perhaps, by 'the golden age' character of his praise of Italy; its temperate climate, luxuriant crops and fertile herds.[19] For Virgil the natural world is responsive to human emotion. This may reflect his own attunement to the natural objects in the environment; his concern for plants and animals, for the birds that have to abandon their nests when a tree is felled (*Georgics* II, vv. 208–12) for the aged horse which, when its strength fails, should be put out to grass. (*Georgics* III v. 99) Also Lucretius takes into consideration the feelings of animals, as is shown in his moving account of a cow's distress at the removal of her calf: 'Time and time again she returns to the byre, sore at heart with yearning for her calf . . . succulent osiers and herbage fresh . . . are powerless to console her . . . so obvious it is she misses something distinct and recognized.'[20]

The concern for animal life these two poets express is directly opposite to the callous disregard for animal suffering exhibited in the circus performances of late Republican and Imperial Rome, during which countless wild animals from all Roman dominions were slaughtered to glorify military victories and provide entertainment for the crowd. Roman intellectuals were not amused by the circus. Cicero and Seneca, both Stoic philosophers, expressed their contempt for it.

The Romans practical turn of mind inclined them towards Stoic and Epicurean philosophy, which emphasized reason and ethical systems which sought freedom from fear and equanimity in adversity. Roman writers versed in these traditions argued against superstition and for the naturalness of phenomena such as lightning, earthquakes and volcanic eruptions. In the course of their explanations, as French[21] has pointed out, the concept of nature shifted from the Aristotelian 'nature of a thing'; to the Roman 'Natura' which, supplanting the gods, governed the natural world with her laws. At the practical level of everyday life, this ordered, rational Stoic world found its most accomplished expression in the country villas of the Roman elite. Built on scenic spots by the sea or along rivers and lakes, the Roman villa combined the beauty of the landscape with man's art. The villa's interior, resplendent with marble and mosaic, its walls adorned with murals and paintings, looked out upon the surrounding garden from the colonnade of its portico. In the garden intricate plays of water gave out the shimmering reflections that so delighted Pliny the Younger. Further surprise for an onlooker came from the tonal contrasts of statuary and foliage. There, aesthetics and utility created not a sacred landscape but an essentially civilized environment representative of Rome's art of gracious living.

The Stoics saw the earth's plants and animals as having been providentially designed for mankind. According to Aristotle, reason was man's prerogative, for he came first in the great chain of being. The Stoics adhered to his viewpoint; fields and herds of cattle were esteemed for the profits that could be derived from them. As for the earth's metals, who but man could extract and use them?

In the attitudes of late Republican and Imperial Rome towards the natural environment one can detect the germs of the contemporary and irresponsible Western environmental exploitation. The consequences of deforestation were known to the Romans and some tree-planting was carried out by the state and encouraged on private properties. Over-grazing too, especially in regard to sheep and goats, was condemned, in theory if not in practice. Rich Romans who owned large estates favoured stock-breeding and neglected agriculture. Timber extraction was rife and the mining of marble and metals left visible scars in parts of Italy. Yet, nature could, to the great majority at least, still appear inexhaustible, especially as there were always more forests to fell further away in well-wooded Roman provinces. The damage to the environment, however, was neither consistent nor cumulative.[22] In fact, at the dissolution of the Roman empire, as the early Middle Ages emerged from the ravages of Barbarian invasions, large parts of Italy were once again taken over by forests and swamps, while agriculture dwindled to the self-sufficiency of small communities within the ambit of the Christian Church.[23]

Women and the Sacred

This section returns to the *Theogony*, to Hesiod's story of Pandora, how and why women originated. Pandora, Zeus's answer to

Prometheus's trickery, is herself a beautiful artifice. Her first action is to release from her jar (symbol of the womb) all the evils that beset mankind. Created separately from a race of men, who knew neither toil nor ills, Pandora inclines towards the animal world. The diadem about her head, which represents all the formidable creatures fostered by land and sea, is her emblem and animal similies describe her nature: 'As idle drones pile in their bellies the toil of worker bees, so are women a bane to hard-working men.'[24] The drone, as Roscalla has pointed out, was considered by the Greeks to be a subspecies of worker bees and is therefore a doubly appropriate analogy for Pandora.[25]

Hesiod's myth originated an ideology of separateness later 'confirmed' by philosophical discourse: women are a race apart from men not only intellectually (endowed with less efficient reason) but also physically. The latter difference is most forcefully expressed in Aeschylus's *Eumenides*:

> The woman you call mother of the child
> is not the parent, just a nurse to the seed,
> the new-sown seed that grows and swells inside her.
> The man is the source of life – the one who mounts.
> She, like a stranger for a stranger, keeps
> the shoot alive unless god hurts the roots.
> I give you proof that all I say is true.
> The father can father forth without a mother.
> Here stands our living witness. Look
> (exhibiting Athena) Child sprung full-blown from Olympian Zeus,
> never bred in the darkness of the womb
> but such a stock no goddess could conceive! [26]

In his eagerness to absolve Orestes from matricide, Apollo attempts to deny the fact that a child is born of woman. Aristotle does not fully rescue women from this absurd position; for they are but passive reproductive matter, the male alone being endowed with life-giving power.[27] Plato, often quoted for his enlightened attitude towards women (in his ideal state he allows them to be educated and share with men the duties of guardians) also disparages birth from women's bodies: women's offspring are mere mortals but immortal philosophical discourse is born of the love engendered by men in men's souls.[28]

So much for dominant male discourse but what about reality? Being multifaceted, reality is, as ever, elusive. All the more so when information about women has to be extracted from a literary heritage written by men. Nonetheless, some balance may be restored by examining the role played by women in ritual.

Women had a unique and central role in certain religious rituals and an important place in others. Indeed, as Winkler has affirmed, much was involved in women's connection with the sacred for 'through their activities concerning birth, nurture and the cult of the dead they controlled the fundamental course of life'.[29] In fact, far from ignoring women as generally assumed, the state acknowledged them to be men's partners in maintaining the essential relations between the world of the gods and the cultivated land on which the life of all Greek communities depended.

The *Thesmophoria* was an important women-only festival in honour of Demeter, goddess of agriculture. The cult's ritual, organized by citizen's wives, was secret and lasted three or more days depending on locality. On the first day women brought up from underground chambers the composted remains of piglets which they mixed with cereal seeds; on the second day they sat on the ground and fasted in memory of Demeter's sorrow at the loss of her daughter Kore; and on the third day there were sacrifices and feasting with much rejoicing and invocations to Kalligeneia, bringer of fine children. The *Thesmophoria* acknowledged the link between the fertility of women and that of the Earth, but there were other 'women's mysteries' also related to cultivation, the *Haloa*, held in honour of Demeter and Dionysus, and the *Skira*, previously assumed to be a harvest festival. Recent studies of the Athenian state calendar have shown that not only did these festivals feature on the calendar, but also that their timing correlated with the most critical periods of men's agricultural work. The *Thesmophoria*, falling at the end of October-beginning of November, preceded cereal sowing, vine trenching and pruning, tree-planting, and the picking and pressing of olives, whereas the *Haloa* marked the end of this hectic period of men's work. During the *Haloa* women held all-night bonfire parties accompanied by much scurrilous jesting. Priestesses were supposed to murmur lascivious counsels in the women's ears. Tables were laden with food and wine, and displayed dough representations of male and female genitalia. The *Skira* festival, named after the gypsum needed to plaster threshing-floors, occurred in mid-June after the sheaves had been stacked. The women, who carried the gypsum as a sacred object in procession, were responsible for performing the ritual (if not also the practical) replastering of the floor before the men began threshing. By including these women's festivals in the official calendar alongside those held by men, the city recognized their importance. Women alone could render men's agricultural work effective, because they mediated the relationship with the goddess of agriculture.[30]

The Demeter-Kore cult was also a celebration of the mother-daughter relationship. This festival, attended by women from all over Attica, offered mothers, daughters and sisters separated by patrilocal marriage, the opportunity of spending a few days together. In addition, medical research concerning the plants used both in the *Thesmophoria* and in the *Eleusinian Mysteries* has shown that, pomegranate, pine cones and the herb pennyroyal, contain plant oestrogens that may affect the reproductive cycle.[31] Pomegranate seeds were in fact one of the ingredients of ancient contraceptive pessaries. It is likely that, secure in the secrecy that surrounded these rituals, older women instructed younger ones on how to control their fertility.[32]

Greek women also attended the state sacrifice. A maiden in her late teens carried the basket in which the sacrificial knife was hidden under barley grains and all the women present uttered the shrill cry which marked the felling of the ox and culmination of the sacrifice. Although expressly excluded from some sacrifices, women were able to play a more active role in others; for instance, the animals sacrificed to Semele and Dionysus had to be consumed by women.[33] In the Pan festival, described by Menander in the *Dyscolos*, it is the matron with her retinue of women celebrants who first taste the victim's viscera, the exclusive privilege of participants having an official role in the ritual.[34]

The cult of Pan originated in Arcadia and became widespread in Attica after the battle of Salamis (480 BCE). (At Salamis the Greeks are supposed to have invoked Pan's help against the Persians.) In Attica, Pan's rituals and sacrifices took place in caves, often situated in mountainous pastoral areas of the country, well beyond cities and cultivated fields. Therefore Pan's cult disclosed to the general public aspects of the landscape previously frequented only by shepherds and their flocks.[35]

Mountains were also the favoured landscape of an old god in new guise, Dionysus, who, as the divine leader of Bacchic celebrants, can be said to escape the controls of cultivation and irrupt into the mountains with his women devotees. Dionysus is the god who opposes rationality with feminine enthusiasm. The women who follow him abandon their spinning and weaving and leap for joy 'like foals at pasture'.[36] With its interplay between myth and ritual, Euripides' *Bacchae* convey something of the ecstatic character of a cult of which very little is known. Accordingly, the Mysteries' secrets are not disclosed but Euripides sings of the rapture of freedom, of the pulse of dancing feet in the wake of the god. The Earth itself partakes in the Maenads' elemental joy and, true to primeval lore, streams with wine, milk and honey. This is a landscape of immense freedom in which women, like 'the fawn who has leapt free from the woven snare' draw breath and find peace in nature, in 'the blessed, lonely forest unmarked by human track' (*Bacchae*, vv. 865–79). Yet freedom taken to extremes ends in savagery, the very savagery of Pentheus's death at the hands of his mother. In real life, however, societies of Maenads were well regulated. As shown on ritual calendars, women raved at given times; at the annual *Lenaia* and at other festivals celebrated on alternate years.[37] The cult of Dionysus, in any case, allowed women to get away occasionally from the over-familiar, everyday landscape of home and fields.

In Rome, Dionysian frenzy gained subversive connotations. On the instigations of a priestess from Campania, Roman matrons started initiating their sons to wild Bacchic revels which took place at night. This religious innovation alerted the Senate to the dangers of women usurping the power exercised by the father in relation to their sons; and of the youths forsaking martial arts for female rituals. The Roman consuls reacted promptly to this scandal by suppressing the revels. With the senatorial decree *de Bacchanalibus* of 186 BCE, all Bacchic associations were disbanded throughout Italy.[38]

Rome had adopted or tolerated foreign cults before the Bacchanalia incident and would do so again later. It was women especially who, given their subordinate position in official worship, supported alien rites which promised greater freedom of practice.[39] The *Bona Dea* festival (also known as *Damia*) was restricted to women and celebrated in May when wheat was still growing in the fields. Pausanias recorded that Damia was one of Demeter's names on the island of Aegina. The Bona Dea priestess was Damiatrix; she cultivated medicinal herbs in the temple grounds and probably instructed women in their use. Little is known about this ritual but Roman matrons were supposed to drink wine (called milk) out of honey containers and to honour the goddess with games.[40]

The non-metaphysical disposition of the Romans manifested itself in the historicization of their mythology. Politics and religion were intertwined. When not mediated by their fathers or husbands, women's participation in official rituals was aimed at increasing human fertility or was largely commemorative of legendary themes from Rome's early history. The *Matronalia*, for instance, celebrated the marriage of Sabine women to their Roman abductors and their wifely role in reconciling two hostile populations. As the name implies, it was matrons only who attended this festival on the first day of March. On this day the matrons worshipped the birth goddess Juno Lucina at her temple on the Esquiline hill and entreated her to grant them fine children and easy labours.[41]

Unlike their Greek counterparts, Roman women did not mediate the success of men's agricultural work at the cosmological level. It was the Virgins that belonged to the Vestal priesthood, the custodians of the goddess Vesta's sacred fire, who represented female participation at essential agrarian ceremonies. The tasks of reaping, storing and grinding Far were entrusted to the Vestals.[42] Far was an early wheat reserved for sacrificial practice. With it the Vestals prepared the salted flour which was sprinkled on all sacrificial victims. The presence of the Virgins was therefore essential to the performance of all Roman sacrifices.

Most of the Vestals' duties had equivalents in the domestic sphere. During the *Vestalia* festival in honour of the goddess Vesta, her priestesses ritually cleaned the innermost part of Vesta's temple, which was called *penus* as was the store of every house. Also domestic rituals centred upon the hearth and its fire; and the store of each house contained, besides food, objects of cult, the *Penates*, images of mythical lineage ancestors. There were many speculations about what the temple *penus* concealed besides its store of sacrificial grain. In the archaic period it had probably sheltered the *Penates Populi Romani*, later perhaps emblems of Rome's power, but nobody really knew what the innermost part of the temple concealed. The correlation between temple and house and between the Vestals' duties and domestic rituals lay in the importance of the hearth fire, which represented the goddess Vesta and had, in its earliest form, been the open fire of the Latin shepherd's hut. The hearth, fixed to the ground in the central part of the dwelling, transcended domestic space and linked the house to the centre of the Earth, source of all creation.

The ambiguity surrounding the central part of Vesta's temple was also a feature of its priesthood. Vestal virginity was the cult's essential requirement, yet the Vestal Virgins wore matronly garb, a bridal head-dress, and enjoyed some exclusively male privileges. In addition, at an early age before menarche, the little girls of noble families selected to serve as Vestals were taken from their fathers' custody by the *Pontifex Maximus* in a ritual manner reminiscent of marriage by capture.[43]

These ambiguities have elicited various scholarly interpretations. Francesco Guizzi has attributed the Vestals' legal privileges (being preceded by a lictor, giving evidence in court and the right to bequeath property) to Etruscan influence.[44] As Rome developed from a cluster of villages to city-state, the Etruscans reorganized some of her priestly colleges and the Vestals were granted privileges which reflected the more independent position of Etruscan women. Other scholars have focused upon the ambiguity of the Vestals' position as brides-daughters, virgins-matrons. It was in the role of Brides of Rome that the Vestals enjoyed matronly status but their virginity was indispensable to guarantee the continued 'Romanness' of their adopted family, the Roman People's household.[45] As was postulated by Vernant for the Greek goddess Hestia, the hearth also represented 'fertility dissociated from sexual relations', in other words, the continuation of the paternal line through the daughter.[46] The permanence of Rome was therefore similarly enshrined in the virginity of the Vestal priesthood.

Furthermore, the paradoxical status of the Vestal has been shown to parallel the ritual condition of Greek wives during the *Thesmophoria* festival. In this ritual, Greek matrons recovered the state of *numphai*, virgins about to be tamed by marriage, therefore, like the Vestals, poised on the brink between virginal and matronly status.[47] Whereas Greek wives reactivated through ritual the potentiality inherent in wild femininity prior to the consummation of marriage on behalf of human and agricultural fertility,[48] the Vestal Virgins, symbolically on the verge of matronhood, equally promoted land fertility as well as representing a more lasting source of power on behalf of Rome and her citizens.

To recapitulate: Athenian women were directly involved in mediating divine sanction for the success of men's agricultural tasks. By including 'women's mysteries' (celebrating Demeter) on its calendar, the state acknowledged an aspect of gender equality which was vital to the city's farming communities. This partnership between women's rituals and men's work (with the added symbolism that grain signified civilization) incorporated women into the state cosmologically, socially and politically in contradistinction to the misogynous ideology of Greek poets and philosophers.

In Rome, on the other hand, it was the Vestal Virgins who carried out necessary ritual tasks on behalf of the farming community.

The ritual participation of Roman matrons was of historical importance, because it involved commemorating legendary female figures
or entreating the birth goddess to grant them fine children and
easy labours. In Rome the trials of parturition were seen as the
counterpart of those endured by warriors in battle. The permanence of Rome and its laws, symbolized by the ever-burning flame
of Vesta, was in character with a religion that had translated the
birth of Rome onto the cosmological plane.

Both in Greece and Rome, therefore, agriculture needed the symbolic intervention of the 'essential feminine' whose link with the
Earth was a given of women's actual or potential role in procreation. The modern concept of 'custodians of the earth' derives
from the same premise.

Notes

1 *The Homeric Hymns (To Earth Mother of All; to Pan; to Demeter)*, trans. A. N.
Athanassakis (London; Baltimore: Johns Hopkins University Press, 1976).
2 Plato, *Phaedrus*, trans. W. Hamilton (London: Penguin Classics, 1973), p. 230.
3 *Homeric Hymns*, trans. Athanassakis, vv. 1–15.
4 Aeschylus, *The Persians*, trans. P. Vellacott (London: Penguin Classics, 1961), v.
499.
5 The long seclusion of the female bear with her young was a symbol of successful child-rearing for Neolithic cultivators. Clay figurines of mother and child,
both wearing bear masks, have been found in settlements from the Aegean and
Central Balkans dated 5000 BCE. M. Gimbutas, *The Gods and Goddesses of Old
Europe* (London: Thames and Hudson, 1982), pp. 194–5. See also L. Bruit-Zaid-
man, 'Les Filles de Pandora. Femmes et Rituels dans les Cités', in *Histoires des
Femmes en Occident*, vol. I, eds G. Duby and M. Perrot (Paris: Plon, 1991), p.
368.
6 Aeschylus, *The Oresteia (Agamemnon and the Eumenides)*, trans. R. Fagles
(London: Penguin Classics, 1979), vv. 140–43.
7 Ibid., v. 156.
8 Xenophon, *Scripta Minora, On Hunting*, trans. E. Marchant (Leiden: Loeb Classical Library, 1971), v. 14 & vi. 13.
9 Euripides, *Hippolytus*, trans. P. Vellacott (London: Penguin Classics, 1953), p.
34.
10 J. D. Hughes, *Pan's Travail: Environmental Problems of the Ancient Greeks and
Romans* (Baltimore; London: Johns Hopkins University Press, 1994), p. 172.
11 Aristophanes, *The Birds*, trans. D. Barrett (London: Penguin Classics, 1978), v.
530.
12 D. Sabbatucci, *La Religione di Roma Antica: dal Calendario festivo all'Ordine
cosmico* (Milan: Arnaldo Mondadori Editore, 1988), p. 129.
13 Plato, *Timaeus and Critias*, trans. D. Lee (London: Penguin Classics, 1977), III,
p. 134.
14 O. Rackham, 'Ecology and Pseudo-Ecology: The Example of Ancient Greece', in

Human Landscapes in Classical Antiquity, eds G. Shipley and J. Salmon (London, New York: Routledge, 1996), p. 34.

15 Similarly, in the Mesopotamian epic of Gilgamesh, the hero-king, having failed to secure immortality, accepts the human condition and takes pride in his real achievement, the great walls that comprise the city of Uruk.

16 Sophocles, *Antigone*, trans. H. D. F. Kitto (Oxford: World's Classics, Oxford University Press, 1994), vv. 331–64.

17 C. P. Segal, 'Nature and the World of Man in Greek Literature', *Arion*, III, 1, Spring 1963, pp. 19–53, esp. p. 49; J. P. Vernant, *Myth and Thought Among the Greeks* (London, Boston: Routledge and Kegan Paul, 1983), p. 357.

18 Virgil, *The Eclogues and Georgics*, trans. C. Day Lewis (Oxford: The World's Classics, Oxford University Press, 1983.), 'In Praise of Italy' (*Georgics*, II).

19 R. F. Thomas, 'Lands and Peoples in Roman Poetry. The Ethnographical Tradition', *Cambridge Philological Society*, Suppl. 7 (Cambridge, 1982), p. 39.

20 Lucretius, *On the Nature of the Universe*, trans. R. E. Latham (London: Penguin Classics, 1951), vv. 331–98.

21 R. French, *Ancient Natural History: Histories of Nature* (London, New York: Routledge, 1994), pp. 152–3.

22 Hughes, *Pan's Travail*, p. 112.

23 Often overlooked by environmentalists: R. Hutton personal communication.

24 Hesiod, *Theogony and Works and Days*, trans. M. L. West (Oxford: The World's Classics, Oxford University Press, 1988), vv. 594–600.

25 F. Roscalla, 'La Descrizione di Se e dell'Altro: Api e Alveari da Esiodo a Simonide', *Quaderni Urbinati di Cultura Classica*, 29 (2), 1988, pp. 2–4.

26 Aeschylus, *The Oresteia (Agamemnon and the Eumenides)*, trans. R. Fagles (London: Penguin Classics, 1979), vv. 665–77.

27 G. Sissa, 'Philosophie du Genre. Platon Aristote et la Différence des sexes', in *Histoire*, eds Duby and Perrot, eds p. 83.

28 A. Cavarero, *In Spite of Plato. A Feminist Re-writing of Ancient Philosophy* (Oxford: Polity Press, 1995), p. 106.

29 J. J. Winkler, *The Constraints of Desire. The Anthropology of Sex and Gender in Ancient Greece* (London, New York: Routledge, 1990), p. 208.

30 L. Foxhall, 'Women's Ritual and Men's Work', *Women in Antiquity*, eds R. Hawley and B. Levick (London, New York: Routledge, 1995), pp. 97–108.

31 In the *Homeric Hymn to Demeter* the goddess asks to be brought a drink of barley meal and water with tender pennyroyal (v. 209).

32 L. Nixon, 'The Cults of Demeter and Kore', in *Women in Antiquity*, eds R. Hawley and B. Levick (London, New York: Routledge, 1995), p. 73.

33 R. Osborne, 'Women and Sacrifice in Classical Greece', *Classical Quarterly*, 43 (11), 1983, p. 399.

34 P. Bourgeaud, *The Cult of Pan in Ancient Greece*, trans. K. Atlass and J. Redfield (Chicago: University of Chicago Press, 1988), p. 167.

35 R. Osborne, *Classical Landscape with Figures: The Ancient City and its Countryside* (London: George Philip, 1982), p. 192.

36 Euripides, *The Bacchae*, trans. P. Vellacott (London: Penguin Classics, 1973), vv. 164–7.

37 W. Burkert, *Greek Religion*, trans. J. Raffan (Oxford: Blackwell, 1985), p. 290.

38 J. Scheid, 'D'Indispensables Etrangères', in *Histoire*, eds Duby and Perrot, p. 426.

39 For this reason the women and the rites were often considered subversive.

40 D. Sabbatucci, *Religione di Roma*, pp. 161–2.

41 Ibid., pp. 91ff.

42 An ancient prohibition forbade Roman women to grind wheat, prepare meat and drink undiluted wine. They were therefore excluded from all sacrifices. J. Scheid, 'D'Indispensables Etrangeres', in *Histoire*, eds Duby and Perrot, p. 435; O. de Cazanove, 'Exesto. L'incapacité sacrificielle des Femmes Romaines', *Phoenix*, 41 (2), 1987, pp. 159–73.

43 M. Beard, 'The Sexual Status of the Vestal Virgins', *Journal of Roman Studies*, LXX, 1980, pp. 15–17.

44 F. Guizzi, *Aspetti Giuridici del Sacerdozio Romano. Il Sacerdozio di Vesta* (Naples: casa Editrice Eugenio Jovene, 1968), p. 2.

45 Sabbatucci, *Religione di Roma*, p. 204.

46 Vernant, *Myth and Thought among the Greeks*, pp. 133–4.

47 H. S. Versnel, 'Transition and Reversal in Myth and Ritual', in *Inconsistencies in Greek and Roman Religion*, II, ed. Versnel (Leiden: E. J. Brill, 1993), pp. 284–6.

48 The Madurai temple in S. India is dedicated to the divine couple Minaksi and Sundarèsvara (forms of Sakti-Devi and Siva). A complex of daily rituals and special festivals insists on alternating Minaksi's status from independent goddess (apart from her consort) to subordinate wife united with him in sexual intercourse. One aspect of this ritual complex is related to agricultural fertility which is bound up with that of the goddess. When Minaksi is independent she possesses specific feminine powers that are vitally important for rice cultivation. Were she to remain independent for too long, however (heat generated through chastity), her power would become excessive and Minaksi would lose her pacific character. Rituals and festivals that alternately separate and reunite Minaksi and Sundarèsvara therefore keep the divine couple's relationship in constantly oscillating balance. C. J. Fuller, 'The Divine Couple's Relationship in a South Indian Temple: Minaksi and Sundarèsvara at Madurai', in Fuller, *History of Religions* (Summer 1961), pt 1, pp. 321–478.

4

Aboriginal Women and Sacred Landscapes in Northern Australia

Veronica Strang

In Australian Aboriginal society women have an exemplary role as 'sacred custodians' of the earth. The environmental values which characterize Aboriginal relations with land are deeply affective, and land is central to all aspects of Aboriginal life. There is little separation of the spiritual, the social and the material in Aboriginal culture and the sanctification and care of the landscape, and the reproduction of a particular kind of environmental relationship is represented in many everyday activities. In this interaction with the environment, with a belief that the connections between people and their 'country' are permanent and inalienable, women share with men a responsibility for caring for the land 'for all time'. Historically, women's interaction with white Australians has, to some extent, advanced their role as teachers of environmental and spiritual values, and today they retain key roles as communicators with the wider Australian society.

This chapter examines the lives of Aboriginal women as 'custodians of the earth', and considers how this role has been affected by the colonial experience. It draws mainly on fieldwork conducted in the Aboriginal community of Kowanyama, which is on the western coast of the Cape York Peninsula in Far North Queensland.

Culture and Cosmology in an Aboriginal Community

The community in Kowanyama consists of about 1,200 people and is composed of three major language groups: the Yir Yoront,

63

Kunjen and Kokobera people. Prior to colonial settlement at the beginning of this century, these groups occupied a much larger territory, their land extending well into the cattle properties which now surround the reserve area.

The Yir Yoront are well known in the anthropological literature, having featured in Lauriston Sharp's famous article 'Steel Axes for Stone Age Australians'.[1] Following his fieldwork in the 1930s, Sharp predicted that, because the missionaries had usurped male authority by giving steel axes to the women (when stone axes, he said, were a key symbol of patriarchal authority), the community would be completely undermined and moral collapse and bio-logical extinction would follow. Fortunately, this did not happen, and today the Yir Yoront number several hundred people – a popu-lation possibly larger than in the pre-colonial era. Their survival may be a testimony to the resilience of the community, but it is also worth asking whether Sharp's assumptions about political structures and male leadership were correct.[2] Like many Europeans investigating other cultures earlier this century, he assumed that in Aboriginal society women were subordinate to men. He empha-sized the supremacy of Yir Yoront systems of patrilineal descent, which define individual identity and rights to land, and he appeared to assume that property rights and responsibilities were a largely male domain.[3] This emphasis has by no means disap-peared: in battles over land tenure the complexities of multiple types of land rights, including rights to 'mother's country', are often still subsumed within a simpler model of patrilineal inheri-tance.

However, 'women's business' has proven difficult to ignore. Though patrilineal descent is a primary form of inheritance in the Far North of Queensland, as in most of the better watered and more densely populated regions of Australia, Aboriginal people also have significant rights to their 'mother's country' and lesser rights to that of more distant relatives. Modern ethnographic research into Aboriginal land tenure depicts much more fluid and less patriarchal systems of inheritance in which matrilineal rights and responsibilities play an important part. Similarly, closer atten-tion to the role of women in maintaining Aboriginal values and relations with land suggests that although women may take care of particular spheres of activity, and these may be less public than those of men, their status as elders is not necessarily a secondary position in a fundamentally gerontocratic society.

Gender roles in Aboriginal culture are highly circumscribed, and give men and women differing but often equal responsibilities. In Kowanyama, female and male elders share the leadership of the community, and as the following ethnography illustrates, this leadership does not reflect a Western model in which political power is equated with traditionally 'male' values. Instead, as in Aboriginal groups throughout Australia, leadership is characterized by values in which authority is linked with nurture – a responsibility to care both for the community and its land. It might even be said that Aboriginal women and men share equally the kind of affective concern for their community and their environment which, in Western industrialized societies, is often seen largely as the province of women. This raises a wider and important question as to whether a sense of community and a close and benign relationship with the natural environment can be achieved by any society unless it is held by all members – that is both genders – of that society.

Just as patriarchy, with Durkheimian predictability, is enshrined in the creation myths of Christianity, the creation myths which describe Aboriginal spiritual life reflect considerable gender equality. The creative era of Aboriginal cosmology is commonly known as the Dreamtime or in north Queensland as the Story Time.[4] According to Aboriginal belief, the world was created by many female and male ancestral beings who took myriad forms, appearing as birds, animals, insects, fish, clouds, thunder, water and material culture objects such as spears and dilly (string) bags. The ancestral beings emerged from flat and featureless ground, travelled across the land, and through their actions made all the features of the landscape and all the things upon it. Having completed this task and, in many instances, undergone transformations between human and animal, bird or even plant forms, the ancestral beings re-entered the land. There they remained, 'for all time' as a source of spiritual power, located in particular places, linked by story or 'song' lines, and maintained through the human re-enactment of their lives, through ritual activities and through a daily existence mirroring the way of life depicted in ancestral myth.

In re-entering and remaining in the land, the ancestral beings are said to have created a sentient landscape, animated by their persona. Each place is unique, formed by the actions of particular beings, and holding their particular story, characteristics and, of course, gender. The landscape is therefore not only humanized but also totemically gendered, providing the 'mothers' and 'fathers' of the ancestors' human descendants. Even today, people speak quite casually of the country as being their 'mother' or 'father', and having 'grown them up'.[5] The inherent equality of a cosmology in which ancestral beings are both female and male is thus translated into a vision of the earth as containing both genders in equal measure. This opens up a very useful question about the kinds of environmental relations which are enabled by such beliefs, as opposed to those in which there is a separation between female 'nature' and male 'culture', or in which a feminine earth is seen as the product of a male God.

One of the logical outcomes of the non-separation of nature and culture in Aboriginal life is that spiritual existence and the social and material aspects of existence are not compartmentalized. On the contrary, spiritual beliefs provide organizational principles for social and economic practices. Located in sacred sites, the ancestral beings provide both totemic and geographic foci for a network of traditionally organized clan groups. Rights to land are conferred by clan membership, which is the basis of personal identity. Thus people are placed within the landscape spiritually, socially, spatially and economically.

It is difficult to encapsulate briefly the immense richness and complexity of the cosmology expressed in Aboriginal stories. Every aspect of life is depicted in the ancestral myths, either literally or allegorically: marriage customs, maps of the land and its owners, moral order and ritual activity. The stories are also intensely practical, describing economic activities right down to the finest details of hunting, gathering, cooking and storing food, the making of tools and the maintenance of resources. The songs and stories about the ancestors not only provide a template of 'traditional' Aboriginal life, but also clearly delineate gender roles and social relations, laying down Ancestral Law about divisions of labour, kin obligations, cross-cousin marriage, avoidance relationships and sexual behaviour. In the ancestrally defined gender roles, women are primarily gatherers and men are given the responsibility for hunting. Isaacs presents a classic explanation for this:

> Sex roles are well defined in traditional Aboriginal communities. Women generally gather food; men hunt it. While men hunt large land and sea animals and catch fish, women collect vegetables, shellfish, small animals and eggs. Women, or course, as bearers and rearers of children, must carry out all their food-gathering activities with children present. However, they gather food extremely successfully and can provide up to 80 percent of the food in the community. I would suggest, therefore that the greatest repository of centuries of botanical

knowledge and experience lies with Aboriginal women, rather than men.[6]

This deep knowledge and the ethic of 'custodianship' emerge in the harvesting of resources, which is clearly directed towards long-term sustainability. For example, women teach the schoolchildren today is the 'custom way' of harvesting wild yams, which, as one elder explained, involves digging up the yams, but only taking the new growths and carefully reburying the main root:

> Same yam, when you put them old yam back again, he still grow . . . Next time when he's ready to dig out again, still there, same one, only take new one. (Interview, Doris Gilbert, 1992)

Another set of knowledge often provided by women is the bush lore relating to medicinal plants, which are still regularly used alongside the health care systems imported by the regimes of Church and State. Women also harvest many materials for the production of local crafts, and it is worth noting that just as 'nature' is seen to contain both genders, material culture is also composed of both female and male objects. These are quite clearly defined as one or the other, and seen to embody the qualities of each gender. Women typically produce soft, woven objects such as dilly (string) bags made of cabbage palm string, which are used for carrying gathered food such as eggs. The conceptual association between such objects and the uterus is underlined by linguistic overlaps such as the term *idn afum* for womb, which translates in Aboriginal English as 'breeding bag'. The term *afum*, also means 'breast' and is used as a kin term for mother or child. The fact that country may also be described as 'mother' serves to underline further the linkages between women's reproductive role and the role of the land in reproducing humans through the provision of resources and the spiritual essence which animates human beings.

Human spiritual life is seen to emerge from the sentient pool of ancestral force held in the land, thus shifting from the invisible 'Dreaming' plane outwards into material existence. At the end of life this spiritual essence has to be returned to where it came from, to be reincorporated into the land. Thus the human cycle of existence mirrors that of the ancestral beings in emerging, acting upon the land, and then re-entering the Dreaming. Women are inevitably central to the spiritual cycle of birth and death. 'Spirit children' are held within the landscape, most often at water sources or particular ancestral sites, and are said to 'jump up' into the body of a woman. The presence of this spiritual animation within her womb is revealed, often to the father or to a close relative (female or male), through a sign given by the landscape: an unusual event such as the discovery of an animal in an unexpected place, an extraordinarily large fish, or some odd behaviour by a bird or animal. The location of this event designates the spiritual and actual 'home' of the child, its *errk elampungk*,[7] which, within the context of clan membership, forms the basis of her or his personal identity, rights to particular tracts of land, and responsibilities for that land.

On death, a part of the human spirit – which in post-missionary terms may be called the soul – is said to 'go west' to another place called 'the sky country' or 'the land of the dead'. However it is to the 'spiritual home' from which they came that the Dreaming part of a person will be guided by the elders of the group, so that, like the ancestral beings, it can rejoin the well of spiritual power within the land. It must be returned to that specific place, and no other will do:

> My home errk elampungk. Go back to same place . . . home bla we again. Where him born you know – erk elampungk. (Interview, Lefty Yam 1992)

> We come back la our own country again . . . when I die they gonna send my spirit back here, that's my home see, my land. I gotta come back here . . . We bin come from here, we gotta come back here. Same place. (Interview, Winston Gilbert, 1992)

The Dreaming part of the person links them firmly to a particular totemic being. On death, through returning 'home', they are reunited with this being:

> After when we die, that spirit go back to errk elampungk . . . go back to what he[8] really came from. Like Brolga, from the beginning – because he was Catfish or a Goanna, like that – Wallaby – so he form back to those animals. (Interview, Alma Wason, 1992)

Because kin groups are geographically defined by totemic ancestors whose stories are located in particular tracks and places, people find themselves situated in a spatially organized network of kin relations. Kinship is no casual matter in Kowanyama: according to Ancestral Law, kin relations define marriage partners, exchange relationships, avoidance relationships, joking relationships and a host of other rules and responsibilities about social and economic interaction. Kinship is a central tenet in Aboriginal culture, and because it is mediated by the land responsibilities to care for the community and the land are not separable. In caring for the community women are also seen to be caring for the land, and vice versa. In their everyday lives, women spend a lot of time taking care of kin in both practical and abstract terms. As well as carrying most of the responsibility for bringing up the children, they also help to maintain social relations through ensuring that the complex kinship system is regularly reiterated and repeated, like a rosary of connections. Thus they perform an important teaching role in upholding the basic tenets of social organization and a stable and predictable sense of community.

The systemic nature of Aboriginal kin relations, and the still relevant (though increasingly disregarded) marriage laws and exchange obligations are, like pre-colonial systems of land care, clearly directed towards long-term sustainability and the careful management of people and resources. Before the demographic disruption of the European invasion, the spatially defined network of clans ensured that the population was balanced with resources, and inbuilt flexibilities in the system allowed for adaptations to environmental change.[9] However, although the outcome of this organization may have been intensely practical, ensuring a highly sustainable way of life, it was – and remains – founded upon spiritual beliefs, defined not by explicitly measured balances of people and resources, but by sentient and powerful totemic beings.

As well as being expressed by the creation of spirit children, the sentience of the Aboriginal landscape is revealed by the presence of ghosts of 'the old people', various kinds of devils, and by particular features – trees or rocks – which are said to embody specific ancestral beings. People in Kowanyama say that the land will provide or withhold resources according to who is trying to fish, hunt or find them, favouring those who own or have rights to the land, and denying sustenance to outsiders. The land is also believed to respond with grief when someone important within its particular clan dies. For example, Emu Lagoon, a permanent waterhole in Kunjen country, is said to dry up only when the primary owner of that country dies.

In Aboriginal terms then, both human reproduction and the reproduction of resources are generated and controlled by the ancestral forces within the land. Numerous different rituals enable Aboriginal people to interact with these sentient forces, and the ancestral stories provide the basis for gender specific ritual activities. These fall into two categories: those providing rites of passage for every stage of human life, including birth and death; and those which, through increase ceremonies and other rituals are designed to maintain resources and 'take care of' the land and the human community which inhabits it. For example, one of the rituals in which women have responsibility takes place at the birth of a child. They ensure that the afterbirth is buried with due ceremony at the child's 'home', ritually reaffirming her or his links with that particular place.

There are many such rituals in which elders intercede between the ancestral forces and 'newcomers' whether the latter are newly arrived babies or strangers from elsewhere. Because the country 'recognizes' its own people and looks after them, children and strangers, unless ritually introduced to the ancestral beings, are in danger and may be harmed or snatched away. As the Kunjen elders explain, at a place called White Water there are 'people you can't see' who have mirrors which can take your picture 'like a photo' and keep it, making you feel constantly sick and tired. To prevent this, they say, you must go there with the owners of the land who 'know' that country, and undergo a ritual which involves painting your face with the mud from that place. This, according to the elders, will keep you safe and ensure that the next time you go there 'they [the people you can't see] – will know you'. (Interviews, Judy Brumby and Alma Wason, 1992)

With the growing numbers of European Australians working with the inhabitants of Kowanyama there is an increasing need for rituals which introduce strangers to the ancestral inhabitants of the sacred landscape. Women frequently take on the responsibility for these rituals of 'baptism'. Though a Christian word is used to describe the ceremony, and they often do involve pouring the water of a sacred site over people's heads, it remains a ritual of introduction to the ancestral beings within the land, so that the stranger will be recognized by them, will be protected from the land's more malevolent aspects, and provided with resources.[10] The fact that in modern times this responsibility is often given to women may point to a fairly recent divergence between male and female roles as custodians of the land.

Aboriginal Women as Mediators and Teachers

To some degree, Aboriginal women have had quite a long-term role as mediators between Aboriginal people and European

Australian society. There are powerful historical reasons for this. The colonial era was characterized by an aggressive invasion by settlers who, in many instances, forced Aboriginal women into concubinage and killed Aboriginal men.[11] Later, when an uneasy peace was achieved, Aboriginal men often found that they could only remain on their traditional land by working for the newly established cattle station owners and permitting some continuance of sexual relations between the colonizers and Aboriginal women.[12] With few European women in the remote areas this arrangement continued for some time, and even today sexual relationships between the pastoralists and Aboriginal women, while often covert, are not uncommon. In the early days of settlement, as well as sometimes being involved in sexual relationships with the settlers, Aboriginal women were increasingly employed as domestic labourers as European women began to come and live on the cattle stations, and this also brought them into closer social contact with the European population.

At the same time that the stations were being established, other elements within British and white Australian society disapproved deeply of the settlers' violence towards Aboriginal people and the sexual exploitation of the women. To try to prevent both they set up mission stations, such as that in Kowanyama, where the mission (then called Trubanamen) was formed in 1905. The objective was to protect the Aboriginal people and to 'educate' them into 'civilization'. In reality, this largely meant that older and less tractable people were excluded, and the major recipients of 'education' – Christian beliefs and literacy – were young women and children.

Thus both in life on the cattle properties and on the mission stations, Aboriginal women found themselves placed, without much choice, in a closer relationship with the newcomers than the Europeans formed with the obviously more threatening Aboriginal men. They learned English, Christian beliefs, and Western ideas, and became mediators between the two groups of men. In a sense, this role also enabled them to intercede and protect their own community. Part of what they were protecting was the 'double life' led by Aboriginal people. Beyond their enforced lives, which involved working for and accommodating the missionaries and settlers, Aboriginal communities continued hidden, 'traditional' lives in which their own beliefs and customs were quietly maintained.

Unfortunately women became, to some extent, victims of their own mediatory skills. In Queensland in the 1930s and 1940s, as

71

relations between the indigenous people and the settlers improved, and the men on each side began to negotiate with each other rather than relying upon violence to resolve disputes, the patriarchal dominance which characterized European Australian society was communicated to Aboriginal men. Women were increasingly excluded from discourses between the two groups. For several decades, when Aboriginal people gained sufficient political power to begin demanding that their land should be returned to them, the negotiations about land ownership, control and management largely involved European Australian men talking to Aboriginal men. This problem has by no means disappeared: all too often, interactions between communities like Kowanyama and government organizations, industries and other outsiders still tend to mean 'high ranking' men coming in and expecting to talk to other 'high ranking' men. In taking over from the Church, the State has also imposed forms of government which tend to be patriarchal rather than gerontocratic: thus government officials have supported the election of middle-aged men to a European style local 'council' intended to lead the community.

These impositions have been resisted, however. With growing self-determination, Kowanyama has re-established its customary form of gerontocratic leadership by creating a female and male 'Counsel of Elders' [sic] which has an 'advisory' role to the local Community Council. The community thus retains a 'double life': one in which imposed norms are performed in interactions with outsiders, and another in which 'custom ways' are maintained. In the last few years, greater political freedom has meant that these 'custom ways' have been moving steadily to the fore.

Further afield, since the 1970s, persistent feminist questioning of gender and power relations within mainstream Australia has served to draw attention to the exclusion of Aboriginal women in governance and in the land rights debates. Today Aboriginal women have therefore regained some leadership in negotiating environmental and land issues, and in incorporating new ideas into Aboriginal culture. This reasserts their previous role in 'taking care' of the community in both practical and spiritual terms.

Throughout this century Aboriginal women have been particularly successful in dealing with the colonizing activities of the Church and managing the absorption of Christian ideas into indigenous beliefs. Just as the white men who took over the land were, by necessity, afforded a dominant role outside 'real' Aboriginal life, the male Christian God was cast expediently as a larger, –

more abstract and supreme kind of ancestral being, positioned 'outside' or arching over traditional beliefs. In this way, Aboriginal spiritual life and ritual activity remained relatively undisturbed. As Taylor found in the Edward River community, just north of Kowanyama: 'Despite their participation in the rites and ceremonies of the Christian faith . . . people remained firmly committed to their own worldview. Their Christianity was a thin veneer laid over a very traditional set of beliefs and values . . .'[13]

God was framed as a vague kind of ancestral overseer, or as two women in Kowanyama explained it:

> the Creator one, the one that created all thing . . . M'atat we call him . . . he walking and digging.[14] (Interviews, Alma Wason, Jessie Burrie, 1992)

Today the major churchgoers in Kowanyama are almost exclusively older women, and their activities through the church have become a stabilizing influence in a community still struggling to deal with massive social and cultural changes. Astutely, they have used the authority of the church and other imposed welfare institutions to confront the problems of violence and alcoholism which reflect the trauma of these changes. In Kowanyama, as in many such communities, the older women are often responsible for the care of several generations. They care for their elderly relatives, who in many instances maintain a wholly traditional view, often speaking little or no English; they try to help their sons and daughters as they struggle with the complexities of rebuilding the community; and they often assume primary responsibility for their grandchildren.

Aboriginal Women as Leaders

In common with Aboriginal communities throughout Australia, the people in Kowanyama have two major concerns: to ensure that their cultural beliefs and values – their 'custom ways' – and their vast lexicon of bush knowledge are maintained and passed on to the younger people; and to see their community regain its self-determination and economic self-sufficiency. Obviously the land is central to both of these concerns: all traditional life is rooted in it, and control over it offers the community its only major economic resource.

Aboriginal women take a leading role in attempting to meet

both of these aspirations. They have multiple roles as teachers: for example, in recent years, 'traditional knowledge' has (after considerable political lobbying) been made a part of the school curriculum. Thus, along with conventional lessons, the children are regularly visited by the elders of the community, who teach them about the maintenance of resources: how to take sugar bag (honey) without destroying the bees' nest; how to cut spear rods so that the tree will grow new ones. These lessons are also given in practice: as often as they can, the older people take the children 'out bush' and pass on to them, both formally and informally, their encyclopaedic bush lore, as well as their accounts of the ancestral myths. Thus they are carrying out an entirely traditional role as elders, providing both authority and nurturance to the young, and ensuring the inter-generational transmission of knowledge:

> It still important for us to keep it on and on . . . the old people, they are the ones that keep the custom. (Interview, Maureen Zingle, 1992)

Meanwhile a number of the younger women in the community are doing teacher training courses, so that Aboriginal teaching can be better incorporated into the standard curriculum. As a result, spelling lessons now focus on local names for flora and fauna, essays cover local resources and events, and many of the ancestral myths are being written down on word processors and used to teach both literacy and, of course, traditional cosmological beliefs.

As well as preserving the 'custom ways' of the community, Aboriginal women are very active in Kowanyama's efforts to reconstruct a self-sufficient local economy. In the Australian media, for obvious political reasons, Aboriginal relations with land are frequently romanticized as being largely spiritual, and bush lore framed as a kind of 'communion with Nature'. However, As Rose points out, this is an expedient mystification:

> Intimacy with the natural world is not 'natural', it is based on keen observation and understanding, and is a cultural construction of the environment.[15]

In fact, Aboriginal interactions with land are, and always have been, as firmly economic as they are spiritual, and the elders in Kowanyama are anxious to re-establish the economic aspects of their use of the land. Some pre-colonial economic activities continue in the community: although a Western diet prevails, people supplement this by hunting and fishing, and gathering bush foods.

A number of the older women have been heavily involved in creating an outstation at a place called Orinors, which is in Kunjen country. This is intended to be a 'dry' (i.e. 'no grog') centre where 'traditional' economic activities will predominate.

One such activity is the production of local material culture which is currently being revitalized, although for new purposes. Today craft items are made mainly to be sold to tourists, and it is the tourist industry that many people now see as being the key to economic self-sufficiency. The cattle business on Kowanyama produces very little income, and cannot possibly support 1200 people. Tourism, on the other hand, offers the prospect of a viable balance between traditional and modern life.

Several older women have proposed the creation of a small 'outstation' at a major site beside a river within their traditional country. Here they want to build a few houses, grow (as well as gather and hunt) their own food, and run a 'bush tour' type of tourist operation which will allow their family to maintain its own knowledge whilst also educating outsiders about Aboriginal culture:

> There's a nice sand ridge there, it got high bank, and it's good for us to stay there . . . settle down and make some garden – banana plantation, pawpaw and some vegetables, like potatoes, sweet potatoes, cabbage and lettuce, tomatoes, all them sort of vegetables. (Interviews, Alma Wason, Judy Brumby, 1992)

Part of the reason for this is to return to their own country:

> I got a good feeling for that place – make me feel good. We can settle down and live here, and bring our family up right on this ground, because this ground is my grandfather and grandmother, and mother and great grandparents, and all our ancestor used to live here, and that's what we feel, to be here on this ground, on their footprint. (Interview, Alma Wason, 1992)

The other half of this affective and spiritual concern for the land though, is to initiate economic activities and use of the resources which will complement, rather than conflict with, a traditional way of life:

> We could have something there, and cook for them. Tourist house, so they can stay in a proper house instead of down at the sand . . . proper building, have toilet and shower, and build up real nicely. Yeah, and plant some lawn and some garden there for them to see . . . If we have horses we can let the people go for a ride. Elders might take them out,

show them places, wildlife, show them what we have there, in that country . . . People like to see something you know, tourists . . . (Ibid.)

The venture would provide employment for both young and old, as guides and guardians of the land in both practical and spiritual terms:

We need Rangers to go around and visit our area, check up on the countryside, take some tourists, take them out and show them places around, and probably a few elders might go out too . . . to show the place where the sacred area, to show them where there's no-one to touch anything see . . . (Ibid.)

Thus Aboriginal women express a clear vision of the future, in which both land and people are taken care of, and in which relations with the wider Australian community are placed on a more equal footing. The viability of this vision is, of course, heavily dependent upon the resolution of some of the conflicts over land that have dogged Aboriginal and European Australian relations for two hundred years.

Conclusion

Today, in the political arena, Aboriginal women's experience as mediators assists them in a vital role. Increasingly, as well as being equal participants within the Counsel of Elders, they are now becoming more involved in the 'Western style' Community Council. In both levels of organization they are vocal, active and effective protectors of the community, its particular values, and its land.

This pattern recurs in many Aboriginal communities in Australia.[16] For example, Carolyn Merchant cites the leading role of Nganyinytja, who is the principal owner of land at Angatja, south of Alice Springs in the central Australian desert:

Women, she [Nganyinytja] says, have respect and power in the traditional tribal way of life. Her concern is to save her lands from degradation and mining. She says 'Let your heart and mind be as open as the land. The earth belongs to everyone, black and white. We all need to care for our environment with this kind of love and respect if we are to survive.'[17]

Nganyinytja has been active in the 'Back to the Homelands' movement and as a founder of the 'College in the Desert' in the

Musgrave Ranges and has, as Merchant says, become 'an ambassador for her people on behalf of traditional land rights in the federal capital in Canberra and the state capitals'.[18]

Thus, within their own communities, and as 'ambassadors' to white Australia, Aboriginal women are fighting to strengthen their ownership and care of the land. As representatives of Aboriginal culture they offer to the Australian and indeed to the international community a way of considering the environment that is both spiritual and pragmatic, and above all long-term. Their aspirations point towards a sustainable custodianship of the earth, not by returning to traditional hunting and gathering, or by enacting a romantic but impractical economic mode, but by carrying into modern ways of life a set of beliefs and values which balance human and environmental needs.

There are two major obstacles to a fuller understanding of the role of Aboriginal women as 'custodians'. One is a persistent tendency for Western societies to see indigenous cultures as intrinsically more 'feminine'. This is a common perception – that other cultural groups, particularly small scale indigenous societies, are more focused on feelings: 'in touch' with their emotions and with Nature. Indeed, they are often conflated with Nature, which in Western terms is cast as female, to be acted upon by 'male' culture. In their affective concern for the land, indigenous cultures are often presented as offering a feminine anima to the Western animus. The result of this projection is that the process of colonization and the imposition of Western technology is portrayed as a rape of Nature and, by extension, of indigenous cultures. Both are therefore cast as the passive victims of Western male aggression and exploitation. The ethnographic evidence, however, does not support the projection of femininity onto indigenous peoples, whose cultures contain wholly distinctive concepts of male and female, and whose activities are far more complex than is suggested by such rosy simplifications.

The other major barrier to appreciating the importance of the role of Aboriginal women is created by an equally persistent notion that Aboriginal cultures (and indigenous cultures in general) invariably subjugate women. It is perhaps much more useful to reject the assumption that traditionally prescribed gender roles, though different, are necessarily widely unequal. This enables us to consider instead the critical effects of gender equalities within other cultures – equalities which often continue tenaciously beneath imposed colonial models of patriarchal dominance. Aboriginal culture offers a useful example. It is a highly conservative culture in which gender roles are firmly prescribed. Yet through the gerontocratic bestowal of authority, and through the inheritance of rights to land and resources, women actually have considerable parity in political and economic terms – far more parity, in many respects, than is possessed by the vast majority of women in industrialized societies. Significantly, the ethnography suggests that this equality is, recursively, both reflected and enabled by cosmological beliefs in which deities are both female and male.

The effects of female parity at a social and cosmological level are, it seems, to create a relationship between human beings and nature which is similarly characterized by mutual interdependence, rather than by the dominance of one over the other. In communities such as Kowanyama, land and people are seen as equally important, and their fortunes inextricably bound together. In their role as 'custodians of the earth' Aboriginal women therefore demonstrate how particular environmental values can construct a more protective and sustainable interaction between human communities and their land. Their experiences also suggest some answers to the questions posed at the beginning of this paper: is it possible for human societies to achieve both a sense of community and a close and benign relationship with the natural environment unless these values are shared by all members – that is both genders – of that society? Can human societies maintain a sustainable relationship with Nature if it is cast as feminine and separated, unequally, from 'male' culture? The example offered by an exploration of the lives of Aboriginal women suggests that the answer to both questions is 'no', and thus that gender equality, at a material and at a cosmological level, is an essential part of creating greater 'equality' in the relationship between human beings and Nature.

If Western societies are seeking to learn from other cultures what kinds of values and organization enable better 'custodianship of the earth', this ethnographic example provides some quite radical lessons. It suggests that if we are to improve our environmental relations, we must first establish gender equality in all material and spiritual aspects of our own cultures. This implies significant political and economic changes and an unequivocal rejection of patriarchal cosmological beliefs and values. Such a radical revision may appear unpalatable to those committed to maintaining the status quo, but as the evidence accumulates that the status quo is unsustainable, the example provided by women in Australian Aboriginal communities may offer some potential ways forward.

Notes

1 L. Sharp, 'Steel Axes for Stone Age Australians', in *Man in Adaptation: The Cultural Present*, ed. Y. A. Cohen (Chicago: Aldine, 1974 [1952]).
2 L. Sharp 'The Social Anthropology of a Totemic System of North Queensland' (Ph.D. diss., Harvard University, 1937).
3 L. Sharp 'Tribes and Totemism in North-East Australia', *Oceania*, 9, 3 (1939), pp. 254–75.
4 Ibid.; U. McConnel, *Myths of the Munkan* (London: New York: Melbourne University Press, 1935); J. von Sturmer, 'The Wik Region: Economy, Territoriality and Totemism in Western Cape York Peninsula, North Queensland' (Ph.D. thesis, University of Queensland, 1973); V. Strang, *Uncommon Ground: Cultural Landscapes and Environmental Values* (Oxford, New York: Berg, 1997).
5 R. Layton 'Anthropology of Landscape', unpublished seminar paper, Oxford University, 1990, notes similar conversations in the central desert region, where his informants described 'this rock here is my father'; 'this tree is my mother'.
6 J. Isaacs, *Bush Food: Aboriginal Food and Herbal Medicine* (Willoughby, NSW: Ure Smith Press, 1987), p. 16.
7 This Kunjen phrase translates as 'the home' (*am pungk*) 'place' (*errk*) of your 'image' (el).
8 Aboriginal English uses the pronoun 'he' to describe both female and male persons as well as gender neutral objects.
9 See H. Morphy, 'Cultural Adaptation', in *Human Adaptation*, ed. G. Harrison (Oxford: Clarendon Press, 1993).
10 In other parts of Australia this 'baptism' may consist of being passed through the smoke of a fire.
11 R. L. Jack, *Northmost Australia* (London: Simpkin, Marshall, Hamilton, Kent and Co., 1921); H. Holthouse, *Australian Geographic Book of Cape York* (NSW: Australian Geographic, 1973), H. Reynolds, *The Law of the Land* (Victoria, London, New York: Penguin, 1987).
12 See F. Stevens, *Aborigines in the Northern Cattle Industry* (Canberra: Australian National University Press, 1974), F. Merlan, '"Making People Quiet" in the Pastoral North: Reminiscences of Elsey Station', *Aboriginal History*, 2 (1978), pp. 70–106; E. Kolig, *The Noonkanbah Story* (Dunedin, NZ: University of Otago Press, 1987). A. McGrath, *Born in the Cattle: Aborigines in Cattle Country* (Sydney: Allen and Unwin, 1987).
13 J. Taylor, 'Of Acts and Axes: An Ethnography of Socio-Cultural Change in an Aboriginal Community, Cape York Peninsula' (Ph.D. thesis, James Cook University, 1984), p. 465.
14 There are various examples of conflation between Aboriginal myths and biblical stories: for example, myths concerning floods quite often incorporate Noah as an ancestral being.
15 D. B. Rose, 'An Aboriginal Land Ethic' (unpublished seminar paper, Australian Institute of Aboriginal and Torres Island Straits Studies, 1986), p. 17.
16 See F. Gale, ed., *Women's Role in Aboriginal Society* (Canberra: Australian Institute of Aboriginal Studies, 1970); D. Bell, *Daughters of the Dreaming* (Sydney: McPhee Gribble/George Allen and Unwin, 1983); M. Carter, 'Nganyinytja: Teaching the Circle of Life', *ITA*, trans. D. James, June 1991, pp. 72–77.
17 C. Merchant, *Earthcare: Women and the Environment* (New York: Routledge, 1995), p. 192.
18 Ibid.

5

The Separation of the Sexes Among Siberian Reindeer Herders

Piers Vitebsky and Sally Wolfe

People and Land in the Far North-East

Where better to be a 'sacred custodian of the earth' than in north-eastern Siberia? Rushing stony rivers, lined with groves of vanilla-perfumed poplars, drain out of immense swamps. Wispy larch forests rise to ridge upon jagged ridge of bare, lichen-speckled rock. While spiritually powerful bears and eagles patrol around them, the tiny groups of humans who pick their way laboriously across this landscape leave offerings at the graves of shamans and make peace with the spirit owners of each site where they pitch their tent and light their fire.

Why then is this landscape occupied almost entirely by men? To suggest that women are 'sacred custodians of the earth' implies that there is some sort of universal essence of womanhood which sets women off from men in a particular way. This privileged female relationship to earth and landscape, however, should be seen as no more than an ideological construct until it has been tested against a wide range of evidence and forced to confront historical and social circumstances. This custodianship should be examined, not as a presupposition, but as a hypothesis. It may apply in some societies, economies and periods but not in others.

This chapter examines the situation of a community of semi-nomadic native reindeer herders in Siberia, belonging to the Tungus-speaking Evén people.[1] Virtually without exception, women are increasingly looking for their frame of reference to the village, and beyond that to the city, rather than to the vast landscape. They are becoming ever-less involved with the 'sacredness' of the earth because their own sub-sector of the economy is no longer based on direct contact with the earth. They have been led or driven off the land by several generations of a Soviet policy which denied the sacredness of the land, at the same time as radically overhauling gender relations.

The entire economy of the community depends, however, on reindeer herding for the production of meat, skins and other commodities.[2] This herding is done by some of the men who have stayed on the land, although they suffer great hardship. They stay there partly because someone still has to, partly because some of them like the sense of freedom, and partly because they do not have anywhere else to go. For these male herders, however, their vestigial remaining sense of the sacredness of the earth has become a symbol of a life they wish, forlornly, they could still live satisfactorily. If there are any remaining custodians of the earth, they are men, but not all men.

There is a complex system of status, one could even say of class, in which those men who stay on the land are at the bottom of the scale. Because of the nature of the landscape and of the recent history of settlement, institutions and power, women occupy many positions near the top of the scale. But the people at the very top of the status system are men.

The Sakha Republic, previously known as Yakutia, is part of the Russian Federation. It lies in northeastern Siberia and occupies an area roughly the size of India. The population of just over one million belongs to a mosaic of ethnic groups, both indigenous and European. Each people is traditionally associated with a different ecological niche and sector of the region's economy. Thus, the Sakha/Yakut are horse and cattle herders, while Russian, Ukrainian and other white immigrants are associated with trade and mining. The Evén (Russian plural Evény) are one of nearly thirty minority indigenous peoples of Siberia. They number some 17,000 and are scattered in small communities across the *taigá* (Siberian forest) living mainly by hunting and reindeer herding.

The Republic's capital of Yakutsk is six hours flying time northeast of Moscow and with its population of some 300,000 has the air of a booming frontier town. Several days of negotiation may enable one to charter or hitch on a little biplane or helicopter which takes two hours to reach the village of Sebyan-Kyuyel' in the heart of the Verkhoyansk Mountains to the north. The population of this village, which is still organized as a state farm (*sovkhoz*), are mainly Evén and graze their reindeer across a territory almost the size of Wales.

The Collectivization of Reindeer and the Changed Nature of Being a Woman

In pre-Soviet times, herds were not large since domestic deer were used mainly for riding and pulling sledges in order to hunt wild reindeer and other animals for food (herders continue to hunt wild animals to avoid eating too many domestic reindeer). Clans had traditional hunting routes and people lived a nomadic life, largely in nuclear families. Without idealizing what was a very harsh life, one can say that men, women and children lived and worked together, so that the kinship unit and the productive unit overlapped or were identical. Gender relations were complex, with a great deal of etiquette concerned with modesty and the maintenance of personal distance while living at close quarters.

Across the Russian North, the new Soviet regime 'collectivized' domestic reindeer in the 1930s by confiscating them and placing them in state-owned herds, employing the previous owners as herders. This process intensified in the 1960s. The previous system was labelled 'nomadism as a way of life' (*bytovoye kochevaniye*) and was downgraded by contrast with the new system called 'industrial nomadism' (*proizvodstvennoye kochevaniye*). In the latter system, the only people allowed on the landscape were 'the able-bodied population directly concerned with reindeer herding for whom nomadism is essential'.[3] Yet the reindeer still needed to stay in the vast landscape beyond, moving around an extensive annual cycle, attended by herders living in tents. These herders were men and their employment was modelled on that of the Russian miner or oil worker prospecting on a remote frontier.

The aims of collectivization were various: to introduce a system of meat production based on economic rationality; to 'civilize' the nomadic natives by settling them in central villages built specially for the purpose, with schools and clinics;[4] and to attack the patrilineal clan as the basis of a 'backward' social organization. In this last aim, women were singled out for special attention:

> By 1930 it became clear the 'the real and most authentic proletarians' of the north were women. At the end of the nineteenth century the

missionaries had decided that the combination of oppression with a special role as keepers of the hearth and protectors of children made women the ideal candidates for early conversions and successful proselytizing. Independently but for the same basic reasons, the new missionaries of Communism also arrived at the conclusion.

Women were 'the mainspring through which the old way of life could be changed', the key to a healthier domestic and social life for the natives. Teach them new skills, and the children and men will have no choice but to follow.[5]

Special efforts were therefore made to remove women to the villages, and this was also justified by economic rationality. Since women were 'not directly involved in reindeer herding', they were considered to be 'unutilized labour resources' and new, village-based occupations were introduced for them. These were, and still are, typical Soviet female occupations such as cleaner, cook, administrator, bookkeeper and teacher. Since about the 1970s, virtually all women have been living full-time in the village, as do their children, and about three-quarters of the men. If they are closely related to a man working as a herder, they may join him in his nomadic camp for the summer holidays. Very occasionally, an unusually spirited young girl may enjoy working as a herder before marriage.

The lives of women were radically altered in their relationship both to men and to the land. Previously, women were integral to family camps. The area around the hearth in each separate tent was the domain of a woman as wife and mother, and babies were born there. The tent represented a domestic clearing in the wilderness, a space of largely female activity set in a wider landscape of largely male activity.

To a considerable extent this sense of concentric gendered space around the tent still holds – except that there are hardly any women at the centre to do the women's job. The tent as centre of its own world has itself become peripheral to a new kind of centre. Women's concept of home has shifted from the isolated tent in the mountains to the log cabin in the village. If their man is a herder he is absent from his home almost all the time.

Consequently, the far-flung tent now exists in a gender vacuum. Babies are born in the village hospital or even in town. Except during the summer holidays, the hearth of just one tent in the camp is the domain of one woman who is employed by the farm as dinner-lady and housekeeper combined (*chumrabotnitsa*). The other tents clustered around are like small bachelor dormitories, while the tent with a woman in it becomes like a canteen.

Collectivization and the imposition of a productive rationality took control of the significant roles of both men and woman in the hunting and herding camp. In this process a tightly woven nexus of obligation, authority and indigenous expertise was unravelled. While some men were kept on the land as their roles as hunters and herders were transformed into regulated employment, for all women, except the *chumrabotnitsa*, the changes wiped out any commitment to a way of life on the landscape. Some of the old roles were then given back to women, but in an institutionalized form. Rather than being basic elements of a full, kin-based social identity, they were reconstituted as paid activities answerable to the State Farm (*sovkhoz*) or Collective Farm (*kolkhoz*) adminis-tration. Apart from the job of *chumrabotnitsa*, these jobs were car-ried out entirely in the centralized village.

The impact of the political and economic changes can be observed in three areas or clusters of women's roles. The first con-cerns motherhood. With children removed to the boarding school (except for the possibility of stays during the summer holidays), it became virtually impossible for a woman to live in the *taigá* and practise motherhood except with very small infants. By contrast, some of the women who left the *taigá* became kindergarten and boarding school teachers, nurses and so on to other people's chil-dren. As with other activities much of the community's motherly activity was collectivized and placed in the hands of paid employ-ees. Virtually everybody who grew up between the 1960s and the late 1980s is a product of the boarding school, with its Russian, urban-focused curriculum. With the liberalization of *perestroika*, these schools came under a barrage of criticism from their former inmates who revealed (among some good and dedicated teachers) a horrifying catalogue of neglect, misery and victimization. Some children even died in the wilderness trying to flee back to their camps, while others later wrote that while they remembered their teachers well they could hardly recognize their own parents. They also lost much of their native language in favour of Sakha or Russ-ian. A growing sense of the need to protect their children from these schools added to the flow of women off the land and into the village. In the 1990s many boarding schools closed and school-children now reside with their mothers or other relatives in village households.

The traditional role of wife as housekeeper or 'tentkeeper' was transformed. The housekeeper or 'tentkeeper' became a *chum-rabotnitsa* – a paid job within the employment structure of a state agricultural and economic enterprise, instead of a gender role within a family structure. Consequently, it involves very few women. In Sebyan-Kyuyel', with a total population of around 800, there are roughly ninety herders in fourteen brigades who are looked after by just fourteen or so women working as *chumrabot-nitsa*. The job is so unattractive to most women that some of the brigades have to spend long periods without a woman, and one of the men has to take on the job of cook and housekeeper, leaving the herders one man short: 'When there isn't a *chumrabotnitsa*, what can you do? . . . Someone has to stay at home and light the stove, one of you stays behind to prepare the food and the fire-wood.'

In terms of marital relations, most herders live the greater part of their lives in a state of enforced celibacy. Those who are married see their wives quite rarely, mostly when on leave in the village. On such occasions they tend to get drunk and behave in a way which the younger village women find uncouth. In addition to a school education which makes them unfit for the traditional work, one of the main reasons why young men are reluctant to live in the camps is the social isolation: 'There just isn't anyone out in the forest. You don't meet girls sitting on the back of a reindeer! So no-one wants to work here. Young lads go and get any job they can in the village for a month or a year, as a boiler-house attendant, go to dances. But out here there's nothing.' This frustration certainly seems implicated in the very high levels of alcohol abuse and deaths from accidents, violent fights and suicide. It may also be related to the depressed birth-rate. While the male herders are trapped in the situation, women have found a way round it which has important implications for demography and for inter-ethnic relations and status.

The erosion of the old *partnership* between men and women in decision-making and running the camp and herd is a third major break with tradition. There is still considerable continuity between the former role of a senior man as manager of a family herd and the role of the Brigadier (a significant Soviet militaristic title) as head of a herding 'brigade'. There is a comparable continuity in the roles of the junior herders, the constantly changing groups of bach-elors and other younger men who cluster around the Brigadier and make up the full population, often up to six men at a time, of the herding camp.

This system never found a place for more than one woman in each camp. Observing the life of a modern *chumrabotnitsa*, it seems that the scope of a woman's life in the *taigá* has narrowed in two senses. In the first place, it has become diminished in terms of authority and mental sweep. The few remaining old women who continue to live on the land radiate an air of authority which comes not just from seniority, but also from a lifetime's habit of making significant decisions on their own or jointly with their husbands.

In the second place, it has become diminished in terms of actual movement across the landscape. Except when the whole group migrates from one camp site to another, a *chumrabotnitsa* hardly ever moves more than a few hundred metres away from the camp, summer or winter. The same applies to the additional women who come out with their children for the school summer holidays. They pick herbs, berries and mushrooms, collect fresh larch branches and lay them down for flooring, tend the deer when the men periodically bring them near to the camp, and do endless small jobs around the camp such as fetching water.

Crudeness and Sensitivity on the Land

The work of the women, and children, is vital to the survival of male herders. They go out for twelve to fifteen hours at a time, ranging up to fifty kilometres or more, generally without food (they eat only in camp), guiding and reassembling the deer who keep dispersing and are constantly vulnerable to injuries, diseases such as foot-rot, inappropriate diet and attack by wolves. The men may come back at any time from different directions, frozen and exhausted. The 'tentkeeper' immediately drops whatever else she is doing and serves hot tea and meat. As one *chumrabotnitsa* put it: 'I milk the does, catch the foals and tie them up, boil the kettle, make the bread, cook the meals, feed everybody five or seven times a day. I rest only when I go to sleep.'

However, the same woman also said, 'I like the camp life, I prefer to stay here rather than in the village. The air's fresh, everything's fresh. I like fresh reindeer milk best of all. Even if the work's hard, it's good all the same.' On another occasion she said about the village, 'Who wants to get crushed underfoot by all those crowds?'

Whether the village is really a crush, is a matter of perspective.

When one first reaches it from the town in a little twelve-seater biplane, bumping along the tiny airstrip on a heap of sacks containing basic supplies (and some unlikely luxuries like elegant ladies' clothing), one imagines this is the remotest place possible for humans to live. Returning after several months in a nomadic tent, 100–200 kilometres still further into the mountains, it does indeed seem like a metropolis, an arena of ceaseless activity and talk. Even in the near-dark of a midwinter day, one can see heavily-padded female figures trudging through the snow carrying supplies or going on a visit to gossip around the stove with slices of meat or fish brought in from the *taigá* and hung up to store in the freezing atmosphere.

The village is the magnet and centre of the women's world, the place which becomes the centre of the world for even the most enthusiastic herding girl when she marries and becomes a full adult. From the school holiday treks one can observe the extreme difficulty of collecting supplies and organizing horses or reindeer to ride back out to the camps. As one *chumrabotnitsa* put it, 'You have to bring your own reindeer skins [to sleep on] – they don't have enough in the camp [to put everyone up]. The only people who have this stuff are the people who go out there all the time anyway: ropes, saddles, bags, all the things one needs, drinking mugs. You can't just make up your mind and set off. It needs a lot of planning.'

One could add to her list knives, guns and the sheer skill to make anything work. The distances, dangers and logistic demands of moving and surviving on the landscape create two separate worlds of preparedness (a widespread phenomenon in the Arctic, captured in the title of Barker's book on the Eskimo of Alaska, *Always getting ready*).[6] To be mobile on the land requires a state of mind which is easy to lose and hard to regain. Young women, when asked why they did not want to live on the land, gave answers couched in various terms.

The simplest answer is that it is too cold in the camps. This remark alone suggests a significant shift of lifestyle in a setting where it is normal to work out-of-doors for hours at a time in a temperature of minus fifty degrees or lower. Many younger women could be said to be 'addicted' to the comforts of the village, with their well-insulated log cabins and their electricity, television and videos (whenever there is fuel for the village generator).

There is, however, more to it that this. Many women will add that life in the camps is not civilized (*tsivilizóvanoe*) or cultured (*kul'túrnoe*). In the camps, it is impossible to wear elegant leather boots and clothes flown in from the city. The well-groomed younger village women see the reindeer herders as coarse and uncouth as they enter the village in their muddy clothes on their occasional home leave and hit the bottle.[7]

Women also perceive the *taigá* to be synonymous with swearing and bad language.[8] One Evén friend and informant insists that, like vodka, his people did not have swear words in their language before the Russians introduced them. Swearing is perhaps a common phenomenon of men living alone. The loss of gender complementarity is self-reinforcing: as the frontier model of the male industrial worker takes over, life in the *taigá* becomes ever-more masculinized and unattractive to women who are aware from literature, magazines and television of a whole range of alternative lifestyles.

Behind this idea of 'culture' (*kul'túra*) lies a a question of shifting kinds of sensitivity, articulacy and communication. Village girls say that they cannot imagine marrying a reindeer herder because they have no conversation, that herders communicate as if by telepathy. This non-verbal communication is a skill or disposition which is highly valued out on the land and is associated with a nexus of taboos, silence and awe of the landscape,[9] but which is drowned out by the noise of life in the village. Many of the young lads in the camps today are impatient, too quick, and cannot work well with animals.

Out on the landscape, one must be in a state of constant awareness. This is a sensitivity to other people and to the environment, a kind of discretion. So one must not sing, whistle or make a loud noise, because this might offend the spirits who own the forest. It is important not to do the wrong thing, not to touch the grave of a shaman, not to offend the Keeper of the Animals. Rather, one must show respect for the moods of animals and maintain a low, modest profile in all one's movements. Only then will one catch animals, avoid accidents and stay alive.

The hunter is in a state of intense communion with the land, and any person from the human world who gets in the way of that could interrupt that flow of sensitivity that they need in order to be good hunters. It feels as if the whole of that forest is a space in which, though animals and birds roam free, there are no sudden human noises, no human interruption. The silence is unbroken.

Relations with other persons require a similar kind of non-verbal sensitivity. People develop a sensitivity to each other's moods which could go unnoticed in a more fully verbalized environment. It is clear that people always know exactly what is going on, everywhere in the camp, even when nothing is said. They are intensely aware of slight changes of mood and of how it is very important for the group in the camp to work well together, whatever the tensions and rivalries.

This brings us back to the concept of 'custodianship' of the earth. These men live on the land, sometimes for six months at a time without visiting the 'crowded and busy' village, never seeing more than four or five human companions, and often fewer – but having a great deal of communion with animals, rivers and mountains. On this land, they pass ancient graves of ordinary people or shamans and make offerings; they have erotic dreams of sexual intercourse with female spirits who vouchsafe them a successful hunt the following day; they notice changes in the mood, animals and vegetation of every place; they remember the names and stories of these places, sometimes adding new names and stories.

Land, Gender and Values

Within the range of relationships between women, men and the land, several scales or contrasts running in parallel are observable. These concern the overall political and social life of the community, but also have very specific implications for concepts of gender and the earth.

There is a scale from wild, or uncouth, to civilized. This scale applies to virtually all aspects of conduct, dress, and physical and domestic comfort. Earlier Evén culture had elaborate codes of modesty and etiquette and gender relations, but these pre-existed the village and were based on a shared nomadic life in the *taigá*. The current terms *kul'túra* and *tsivilizátsiya* are Russian words which carry heavy Soviet ethical baggage.[10]

This scale is mapped out across the face of the earth, along a continuum from wilderness, through the village, to various provincial towns and the city of Yakutsk. On this scale, the wilderness is downgraded. While Sakha intellectuals and artists in the city talk of reviving the spiritual values associated with the earth,[11] here there is no scope for this kind of validation of Earth and Nature – perhaps because people in the village are still too close to it.

The scale from wild to civilized, from wilderness to village, is also paralleled by a scale of articulacy, in which verbalization is increasingly valued over non-verbalized kinds of sensitivity. The indigenous languages are extremely expressive – for old-fashioned kinds of communication, in which a veiled, allusive style of expression was fundamental. But village television and videos are largely in Russian, a modern European language. This is also the language of colonialism, of passionate novels, high drama, popular magazines, cinema, and pornography. Even the discussion of Nature in Russian magazines is cast largely in the alienated global idiom of the 'environment'.

All of these scales run in parallel and reinforce a growing contrast of gender. The uncouth or wild is assigned to the wilderness which is populated and worked almost exclusively by men. It is not clear whether one should say that the landscape has been masculinized, or defeminized rather, perhaps, that it has ceased to be an arena for the playing out of any kind of gender complementarity.

If there is a loss of contact with the land for women, does their commitment to advancement in education at least give them command in the village? The answer is: not entirely. This kind of question, however, with its feminist overtones, is not what counts in local perceptions of power and social survival.

The village, of course, is not entirely, or even predominantly, female. It is an arena of complex gender relations which may be seen either as a complementarity or as a further imbalance. If there are ninety male herders out of a population of 800, then allowing for various demographic adjustments, more than three-quarters of the male population also live in the village. Most men in the village are employed in the management, control, processing or servicing of the herders' primary productive activity of growing reindeer. A wider view of gender and power in the village shows that though many administrative posts in the *sovkhoz* are held by women, especially in what we have called the professionalized or collectivized caring roles, such as senior posts in the school and clinic, nonetheless the key posts involving political or fiscal control are held largely, and in this village, entirely by men.

Of course, these are not the same men as the ones who herd reindeer. In this economy of networks and favours, in which everything is scarce, local people are not interested in whether this or that is controlled by women or men, but to which faction they belong.

The small number of men actively employed at the sharp end of herding is largely excluded from the political processes of the village. As reforms gathered pace from the late 1980s, public meetings, debates and votes about issues directly affecting the herders were often held at short notice and with an almost complete absence of the herders themselves. In many cases it was only the presence of a forceful wife or other close female relative that the interests of the herders were represented at all.

During this period the multi-ethnic policy of the Soviet regime brought in immigrants of all nationalities into the village, such as Sakha (Yakut) veterinarians and Russian and Ukrainian radio operators, tractor mechanics and boilermen. For the Evén, this region is their homeland. For the newcomers, by contrast, it is a remote frontier. They generally come as single men and easily form temporary or permanent relationships with Evén women. Sometimes they stay on, sometimes they take their Evén partner back to the city. Women are interested in such men for several reasons. Village technicians are better paid than the herders. Women make an association between the professions and material comforts of the immigrant men and the possibilities for greater educational advancement for their own children. Finally, the withdrawal of air links between villages (flights go now only to the city) has ended a pattern of intermarriage between a chain of villages over hundreds of miles. The inter-village marriage had met the shortage of potential partners within the village who were not too closely related. Few young people now know how to travel overland between villages and survive.

All these scales meet in one process of demographic change which focuses on Evén women and their changing values. These women are advancing themselves and the prospects of their children. Whether as the wife of an absentee herder, or as one of the village's many single mothers, or by marrying up and out, village women frequently push their children into further education and still further away from the occupation of herding.

The grandeur of the crags, the fresh air and reindeer milk, the life-or-death self-sufficiency hold little or no attraction for most women. For the appreciation of a role of 'sacred custodianship of the Earth' one may have to wait at least a generation of living away from the Earth.

It would hardly be an exaggeration to say that there is a kind of class system, with gender implications. From being the heroic hunter in a shamanic cosmology, the capable Evén man on the land was transformed by socialism into a kind of wilderness proletarian. While the going was good, he could also be a socialist hero of productivity, and certainly in the late 1980s, herders were still very well paid – although already at the heavy price of an unsustainable pattern of family life. Under the new pseudo-capitalism, herders have sunk to an abandoned, unsupported proletariat. The same herders who ten years ago, even when living away from their wives, used to say, 'Any other kind of life would be completely uninteresting', are now suffering depression and inertia. This is not because they are men, but because they are at the face of production, and because they live on the land. As in many other parts of the world, those closest to the 'earth', even if glamorized by outsiders, have the lowest status. There are different kinds of roles available and the role of productive herder, as opposed to administrator of the herder's production, falls only to men. As a result, there are no longer enough women out on the land to sustain a sub-culture of their own based on a complementarity with men.

The following conversation illustrates this. The first speaker is a young woman who lives in the village, a cultural activist and composer of songs about her love of the land, where she has not lived since she was a girl. The other speaker is a very old woman who has struggled alongside her husband to stay on the land and run their own herd for twenty years against many social and political odds. The singer is visiting the old lady's camp, one of the remotest tents in the entire mountain range:

Singer: (enthusiastically, to anthropologist) [In the old days] when men were around, a woman was not supposed to bare herself at all. She couldn't get on with female activities like bathing. But my grandmother told me that in autumn when the animals are fat, the men would leave the camp and go off on a [long] hunt leaving the women on their own. Then the women would get on with whatever they wanted. They would [bathe and] sing improvised songs to thank Bayanay [the spirit of the forest] for sending animals to the hunters, to drive evil spirits away from the camp, or to make an offering to the fire to heal sick reindeer.

   Then turning to the old woman she asked 'What do you do now when the men are away?' The reply came: 'It's all the same whether they're here or not – we don't do anything special.'

Reflecting on the above one may perhaps detect a certain romanticism on the part of the young woman, but also note the differentiation in the roles of the younger women in the villages, where they may hold jobs in the modern sector, and the feeling of loss on the part of some of the older generation.

Notes

This research is based on fieldwork since 1988 (PV) and 1995 (SW). We are grateful for funding from the British Academy Small Grants Award Scheme and from the Economic and Social Research Council's programme on Global Environmental Change.

1 Though there are many variations of language, culture and environment among the hunting and reindeer-herding peoples of the Russian North and Far East, a uniform Soviet policy has led to certain similar consequences all the way from the Norwegian frontier on the Kola Peninsula to Chukotka, facing Alaska across the Bering Strait, and Kamchatka and Sakhalin, across the water from Japan.

2 This was true until around the mid-1990s. It is now unclear whether any activity at all could genuinely be economically viable in these communities. See P. Vitebsky, 'The Northern Minorities', in *The Nationalities Question in the Post-Soviet States*, ed. G. Smith (London and New York: Longman, 1996), pp. 94–112. At any rate, reindeer herding provides survival rations in a largely cashless situation.

3 B. Lashov, *Nekotoryye voprosy razvitiya natsional'nyk rayonov kraynego severa* [Some questions regarding the development of the ethnic regions of the Far North] (Yakutsk, Siberia, 1973), p. 94.

4 P. Vitebsky, 'Landscape and Self-determination among the Evény: The Political Environment of Siberian Reindeer Herders Today', in *Bush Base, Forest Farm: Culture, Environment and Development*, eds E. Croll and D. Parkin (London: Routledge, 1992), pp. 223–46.

5 Y. Slezkine, *Arctic Mirrors: Russia and the Small Peoples of the North* (Ithaca and London: Cornell University Press, 1994), p. 231.

6 J. H. Barker, *Always Getting Ready – Upterrlainarluta: Yup'ik Eskimo Subsistence in Southwest Alaska* (Seattle and London: University of Washington Press, 1994).

7 H. Kwon, 'Maps and Actions: Nomadic and Sedentary Space on a Siberian Reindeer Farm' (Ph.D. thesis, University of Cambridge, 1993).

8 We are grateful to Rane Willerslev for reminding us of this.

9 S. Wolfe, 'Healing, Landscape and Experience in Siberia', *Race and Cultural Education in Counselling*, 13, 1997, pp. 13–16, esp. p. 15.

10 P. Vitebsky, 'Landscape and Self-Determination among the Evény', pp. 223–46.

11 P. Vitebsky, 'From Cosmology to Environmentalism: Shamanism as Local Knowledge in a Global Setting', in *Counterwork: Managing Diverse Knowledges*, ed. R. Fardon (London: Routledge, 1995), pp. 182–203; M. M. Balzer, 'Perilous States', in *Perilous States: Conversations on Culture, Politics, and Nation*, ed. G. E. Marcus (Chicago and London: University of Chicago Press, 1993), pp. 131–64; Balzer, 'Changing Images of the Shaman: Folklore and Politics in the Sakha Republic (Yakutia)', *Shaman*, 4 (1), 1996, pp. 5–16.

6

Priestesses and Environment in Zimbabwe

Terence Ranger

In late pre-colonial Zimbabwe – as in the Communal Areas to the present day – women had few rights to land. In the patrilineal system of Shona and Ndebele society, wives moved into their husband's home area. They were regarded as intrinsically strangers to that environment. The right of the community to land was vested in the spirits of male patrilineal ancestors; the ancestors of wives, whether male or female, did not exercise any influence. Yet women carried out most agricultural tasks. As the Zimbabwean novelist, Chenjerai Hove, expressed it in *Bones*, 'most women are just "one big scar" which has blighted the earth which has systematically denied them their rights for ages'.[1]

This sounds like a classic context for the secret nurturing by women of the beliefs and rites of 'witchcraft', maintaining underground an old female fertility religion which had been displaced by the incursions of new peoples and the rise of patriarchy.[2] In fact in Zimbabwe witchcraft belief and practice did not work in this way. There were plenty of other positive rites of fertility; both men and women regarded witchcraft as the evil opposite of social religion; the witch damaged the environment by blighting crops or withholding rain. Female participation in positive rituals of the environment did not work in hidden opposition to patriarchy. Instead women occupied public religious roles either within the lineage patriarchal cult system, or in the cult of the High God or Creator God which operated independently of, or 'above', patriarchy. These roles profoundly modified the idea of women as 'a scar' upon the land.

Women's Environmental Roles within Patriarchal Religion

Ecological religion[3] typically operated in Zimbabwean patriarchal society in the form of a hierarchy of male ancestor spirits. The founders of a chieftainship and their immediate successors were known as *mhondoro* (lion) spirits. Such spirits possessed human mediums. Through these mediums the *mhondoro* spirits legitimated chiefs of the same ancestral line, cleansed the land from the stain of incest, made rain, and gave out ritually treated seed. The graves of dead senior ancestors were surrounded by sacred groves which were never to be cut. Such graves were usually on mountains, and these spiritually powerful high places marked out the territory of the chief. Environmental catastrophes such as drought were explained as the result of one or other infractions of the spiritual order – witchcraft, incest, disrespect to the ancestors, disobedience of the *mhondoro*. In some chiefdoms every medium of a *mhondoro* spirit was male; so too were the acolytes, messengers, drummers and *mbira* (thumb-piano) players who attended them. [4]

This archetypal structure allowed for many exceptions, however. There were many powerful female mediums and important female rainmakers. In some exceptional chiefdoms every *mhondoro* medium was female, no matter whether the possessing spirit was thought of as a man or as a woman. In 1974 the Rhodesian Front administration of Ian Smith commissioned a total Index of Spirits, which listed and described every significant medium throughout the country. The result is very much an official overview rather than an anthropologically sensitive study. But some large contrasts emerge. In Mount Darwin district, for instance, Chief Makuni and Chief Rusambo had only female mediums, even for male spirits; neighbouring chieftaincies had only male mediums, even for female spirits.[5]

There were similar contrasts in the operation of chieftainship. In most chieftaincies a single male office-holder reigned. But in Mtoko district, Chief Mtoko was obliged to nominate a female chieftainess, Charewa, who ruled over half the territory of the chieftainship. Moreover, Charewa cared in her village for the female medium of Nehoreka, the chieftaincy's apical ancestor:

> Nehoreka, son-in-law of Dzivaguru, is the founding ancestor. He settled the area between the Nyadiri and Chitora rivers, which now forms the chieftaincy of Charewa . . . He set himself up as the tribal High Priest

and convinced the elders that, after death, he would possess a woman and she was to be immediately installed as his svikiro [medium]. Thereafter he would speak through this woman. Nehoreka further strengthened his position . . . by introducing various reciprocal obligations of a religious nature, including . . . Chief Mtoko's obligation to nominate a woman to fill the post of Chieftainess Charewa . . . The svikiro lives in Charewa's Dzimbahewe [sacred area] where she is cared for by Wa-Dziva – a woman who can be characterized as the Chieftainess's handmaiden . . . Rainmaking ceremonies are also held under the auspices of the Chieftainess and Nehoreka.

The District Chief, Mtoko, emphasized that the Nehoreka spirit had 'built up a reputation as a rain-god of no mean ability'. But the rain was made by women.[6]

These exceptions and many others seem to have arisen in three main ways. The first is that early rain and environmental shrines in Zimbabwe had taken the form of sacred pools tended by the 'spirit wives' of the High God[7] and were, what have been classified as, territorial shrines. This pattern was disrupted by newcomers with a different social structure based on patrilineality and the the rise of patriarchal chieftainship but it could not be entirely obliterated. Secondly, in the conquest of earlier polities the patriarchal chieftainships often turned defeated – and murdered – predecessors, both male and female, into powerful spirits of the land. Thirdly, in some chiefdoms the male ruler drew upon female relatives in order to balance male rivals; characteristically such 'chieftainesses' and 'princesses' had a special responsibility for the environment. In all these ways an important female sub-text was constructed to the main text of patriarchal religion.

Early Female-Operated Environmental Shrines

A number of Africanists have written on the importance of women in religious cults among African matrilineal and uxorilocal peoples, such as the Chewa, in what are now Malawi, Zambia and Zimbabwe.[8] More recently the Malawian feminist theologian, Isabel Phiri, has written on the religious experience of Chewa women in Malawi in general and in particular on 'African Traditional Women and Ecofeminism'.[9] She demonstrates that in early Chewa religion between 900 and 1600 CE 'the religious roles of women were very clear and accepted at the territorial rain shrines. Women, known as spirit wives, *Mbona*, were the controllers of these shrines. The women received messages from God to the community when in a state of ecstacy.' Some of these female religious leaders exercised ritual political control as well, as in the case of the *Mwali* priestess who ruled over the Banda clan. One of the rain-shrine priestesses bore the title Chauta, which was a name for the High God among the Chewa. Phiri maintains that the 'Chewa recognized the feminine nature of God', stressing the woman as mother of all people and as nurturer of the environment.[10] This tradition of priestesses or priests' wives with a role in worship continued in some areas into the nineteenth century.[11]

At a later date, Phiri argues, 'the role of spirit medium passed over from women to men due to changes in traditional religion brought about by external factors such as conquest and the predominance of a new cult ideology'. In one striking case, the *Mbona* spirit wife was replaced by *Mbona*, a male martyr.[12] Vail, writing in the 1970s, found that among the Chikulamayembes of Malawi, although change to patrilineality was accompanied by the office of priest going from father to son, the office-holder was still called the 'wife' of the God.[13]

It seems likely that similar patterns and processes operated in Zimbabwe. Before the sixteenth century the main rain shrine in north-eastern Zimbabwe took the form of a sacred pool set among white trees. Here a manifestation of the High God, Dzivaguru or Great Pool, was venerated. The shrine was tended by the *Chikara* (High God) priestess who guarded spirit wives of God. Requests came in from a wide area for rain and for divinely treated seeds. The shrine monitored the environment drawing on symbols of female fecundity.[14]

Further to the south the main rain shrine in this early period was established and operated by a brother and sister who belonged to the Dziva (Pool) people. The Dziva culture was strongly feminized; its totem was the pool; its ritual experts were recognized as great rainmakers. The central figure of what later came to be called the Musikavanhu cult was in these early days the priestess Chapo, possessor of the rain charms.[15]

Conquest and the Ritual Power of the Conquered

Just as in Malawi, therefore, the central shrines of original Zimbabwean ecology-religion were controlled by women. Similarly the shrines were conquered by incoming rulers, who legitimated their power by reference to male ancestor spirits. The result was a 'masculinization' of ecology-religion. So far as the Dzivaguru cult was concerned, this process was commemorated in a myth first recorded by the Portuguese, Pacheco, in 1862. Matope, the conquering founder of the Munhumutapa Empire, found himself cut off by the powerful princess Chikara with a large army. He learnt the secret of her magic power, protected his men against it, and she vanished into the Nyamakate pool at the Dzivaguru shrine.[16]

Thereafter, in the Mutapa Empire, state religion (with a focus on ancestral spirits) balanced the influence of the *mhondoro* mediums of the founding kings – and particularly of Matope – with the ritual power of the officials of the Dzivaguru cult. Two male representatives of the cult, the Netondo and Bushu priests, attended on the Mutapa at all times and officiated at his coronation and burial. Chikara, now usually thought of as male, was said by Portuguese observers to be the chief priest of the Empire; royal messengers went every season to the Dzivaguru shrine and pool, which Chikara controlled, to ask for rain and good crops. But even if Chikara was now a male priest, there were still virgin wives at the pool, controlled by the Mushongavudzi, a woman past child-bearing age who after assuming office was recognized as a chief.[17]

These historical processes account for some of the exceptional female rainmaking and environmental powers recorded in the 1974 survey. The Charewa chieftainess, guarding the female spirit medium of Nehoreka, and balancing the political power of Chief Mtoko, is obviously a legacy of this sort of history. The chieftainess and the medium are probably survivors of an old Dzivaguru shrine which was partially brought into the patriarchal system by the device of making the ancestor, Nehoreka, a son-in-law of Dzivaguru.

We may suppose that the chieftaincies where every medium was female, or where the dominant spirit was female, also looked back to similar transitions from female shrines to *mhondoro* spirits. The 1974–75 survey gives another example from Mtoko district. In Chief Chimoyo's area there are male mediums of *mhondoro* ancestors. But by far the 'most important spirit of all in the Chimoyo area' is incarnated by a woman medium who is *not* related to the chief at all. She represents the original rainmakers who owned the area before Chimoyo moved into it. She 'holds major rainmaking rituals [and] plays an important part in testing other mediums in Chimoyo's area'.[18] Of all the autochthonous cults which predate the arrival of the Korekore people the one of especial fame is the Dzivaguru.[19]

In addition to cases in which the conquered indigenes became spiritually powerful, thus preserving some elements of the older female eco-religion, there were cases where the incoming conquerors tried to co-opt important female spirits by inserting them into their genealogies. Thus under the Mutapas the female mediums of the Nehanda spirit were crucial in 'ensuring the fertility of the nation and the crops'. Official Mutapa ideology insisted that Nehanda was the sister and wife of Matope. But it is much more likely that the Nehanda spirit long predates the Mutapa Empire, operating as the major rainmaker in the areas to the west of the Dzivaguru and Musikavanhu cults. The Nehanda spirit's medium has always been a woman; it has two distinct manifestations – 'the Head' and 'the Foot', in the north and south respectively; it has always been superior to chiefly *mhondoros*; it owns sacred pools which are death to whites who see them. David Lan's structuralist reading of the Mutapa myths of origin sees Nehanda as standing for the procreative power of the vagina, a 'wet and fertile mother', from whom flowed the rivers.[20]

Female Power Deployed by Male Chiefs

There are some manifestations of female ecological authority within the patriarchal system which are not the result of survivals from earlier times. In some chiefdoms, particularly among the Manyika-speakers of eastern Zimbabwe, ruling chiefs made use of female relatives to control sensitive areas and to perform eco-rituals. At the end of the nineteenth century, the then Chief Mutasa recognized several 'princesses' to whom he gave chiefdoms. One of these was Muredzwa, so famous as a rainmaker that it was said that rain fell into her footsteps as she passed. In the 1980s a later Mutasa revived the system of women chiefs.[21]

More recently, the current Chief Makoni, who lacks the support of the *mhondoro* mediums of the chieftaincy, has revived the ancient institution of the princesses. These are women drawn from each of the Makoni chiefly houses. They report to the Chief on events in their area; they sit with him to hear domestic cases; and they enforce traditional ecological laws. Since 1998 they have prohibited the sale of caterpillars and locusts – which God sent for food not as a marketable commodity; they have rebuked men for fencing in pools which ought to be public resources; they have tried to stop the cutting down of sacred groves. These princesses are certainly not 'a scar on the land'.[22]

Above Patriarchy: The Oracular Cult of the High God

In the south-west of Zimbabwe there still operates a system of eco-religion which is autonomous of any African king or chief and is not part of the patriarchal system; it draws pilgrims from hundreds of miles and from many different language zones, and seeks ritually to control the environment and its use. This is the cult of Mwali, the High God, whose Voice can be heard in the cave shrines of the Matopos. These shrines control the environment, determining which areas can be cultivated and which not, where trees can be cut and where not, and where streams and pools can be used and where not. They also control the agricultural year, providing seeds soaked in the water of the caves and decreeing when planting can start, when fire can be used for clearing the land, what the rest days shall be, and when harvesting can commence. Here one might expect to find female eco-religion operating as it has not done anywhere else in Zimbabwe since the sixteenth century.[23]

Indeed, female spiritual and environmental principles are much more apparent in the Mwali cult than in the *mhondoro* system, though here too there is conflict between male and female; not now between male conquerors and female priestesses, but between men and women for the control of the main Mwali shrines.[24]

For its adepts, the Mwali cult is not about lineage and succession, even though the shrines endorse candidates for the chieftainships. The cult is about creation, fertility, rain, and the environment. Hence there is no barrier to full emphasis being placed on both the male and the female attributes of God.[25] Indeed, I have speculated that the cult was originally more exclusively female. The word *Mwali* is a widely dispersed Bantu term connected with female puberty, female initiation, and female ecological power.

At the shrines priests present praises to each of the triple manifestations of Mwali – *Shologulu*, the father; *Banyachaba*, the mother; and *Lunji*, the needle or shooting star, who runs errands between the father and the mother. At Njelele, the senior shrine of the cult, priests praise *Shologulu* for the might of the thunder and *Lunji* for the penetration of the lightning; they praise *Banyachaba*, the female manifestation of God, as the protector of helpless animals, and as 'the pool that supplies the whole world with water'.[26] A myth which describes Mwali's return to earth, after a period of

101

withdrawal and punishment, combines all three manifestations: 'the sky became pregnant by the clouds and God's Voice came like a needle which sewed up the earth, and a stone began to speak'.[27]

The shrines are called 'the rocks of the pool'; each oracular cave contains within itself a perennial pool, which myth compares to the amniotic fluid.[28] Chenjerai Hove's marvellous book, *Guardians of the Soil*, quotes an old woman from eastern Zimbabwe:

Ambuya Manditsera is the memory of the landscape, of the people of the living and the dead. She talks about the womb of a woman as a shrine, like those caves in the hills.[29]

In the Matopos it is the other way around – the shrine caves and their pools are compared to the womb of a woman. In these pools there live female water spirits, *Njuzu*; Mwali adepts are said to go down into the pools for years on end, there to be taught by the *Njuzu*, learning among other things how the environment should be managed and protected. All the rivers and streams of Zimbabwe are said to be peopled with *Njuzu*, who originate from the shrines of the Matopos. They constitute an 'underwater' – rather than an underground – female ecological army.

Among the shrines themselves, some are thought of as male and some as female. In the eastern Matopos the Dula shrine is 'male' (and connected with war) and the Dzilo shrine is 'female' (and connected with fertility); the male manifestation of God travels between them to be with the female. Dzilo is supposed to be controlled by a succession of matrilineally inheriting priestesses, though in the twentieth century this sequence has been blurred by the claims of husbands and brothers.[30]

This long-standing duality has been complicated in more recent times by frustrated priestesses breaking away and founding new shrines. One of these shrines is Bembe. Minye Ncube lived at Dzilo, that female shrine all too often controlled by men. In 1961 she was herself possessed by a rain spirit:

Minye had to set up her own kraal. The site of this had been indicated to her in a dream when she was a child. In the dream she saw a boulder falling down the side of a hill and she knew that when this happened the time would have come for her to take up her duties. In 1963 a huge rock rolled down the side of Bembe Hill and Minye set up home at the base of a shrine where the boulder fell down.[31]

The Voice of God was heard from the overhang; the fall of the rock seemed to portend a major symbolic and cosmological upheaval;

Bembe became a place of mass pilgrimage and especially renowned for rainmaking. When the District Commissioner came to test her powers Minye made so much rain that he had to beg her to stop![32]

At other shrines, where men have long been in charge, it has been suggested that the Voice of Mwali is articulated by a series of women, inheriting matrilineally.[33] But in any case there are gender-neutral shrines which may be controlled by either men or women, whichever reveals the greatest ecological power. One of these is the Ntunjambili shrine, seventy kilometres north-east of Njelele. It was once controlled by a male priest, Daba, who figures largely in early colonial records. But when he died it was his daughter, Nhlangiso Mmeke Ncube, who became priestess, because her mother was the only one of Daba's wives who could germinate sorghum in her clenched fist. Her half-brothers were furious and bewitched her.[34] In her extreme old age she remains the priestess today.

Indeed in the 1990s the record of female priesthood in the Matopos is an impressive one. Minye controls Bembe; Nhlangiso controls Ntunjambili; even at the senior shrine, Njelele, a woman priestess, Ngcathu Ncube, has recently been installed. In the face of allegations by rival male claimants that no woman could be in charge of Njelele, Ngcathu told me that she had received a message from Queen Elizabeth II to say that women should rule! More seriously she told Jocelyn Alexander and JoAnn McGregor in 1996, that 'Njelele's power covers the whole world. All these mountains – Dzilo – power comes from Njelele. Zimbabwe is very good in farming. You can go to Botswana, but we refer to Zimbabwe as Canaan, the land of milk and honey and that's because of Njelele.' And she insisted that 'it is traditional in our [Kalanga] culture that women were in charge'.[35] Ngcathu became the accepted interpreter of the recent ecological woes of southern Matabeleland, where there was a terrible drought, and was cited even in the *Financial Gazette*!

Finally, the Matopos shrines, and especially the female shrine of Dzilo, have long been associated with prophetic ecological movements, led by women adepts.[36] The latest of these swept across southern Zimbabwe in the 1990s. It was led by the prophetess, *Mbuya* Juliana, whose professed aim is to restore the balance between humanity and nature. Juliana claims to have been empowered by the *Njuzu* in the pool at the Dzilo shrine, where she lived underwater for four years. 'The Njuzu said: "Go and teach the people, so they will live again according to law and order, so the rains will come again."' Juliana blames drought on government development plans, imposed from above, and on dynamiting for dams. A holy silence needs to be restored in which the *njuzu* can again operate.

Juliana attracts a huge following. She holds meetings on the mountain tops sacred to the chiefs and displaces the *mhondoro* spirits of the patriarchal system. Her authority is at once female and a-sexual – she says that if any man looks at her with desire he will explode![37]

Despite the dominance of patriarchy in Zimbabwean land ownership, inheritance, politics and ritual, women mediums, priestesses and prophets still play a major role in eco-religion. The environmental role of men is important – and many chiefs, Mwali priests and male *mhondoro* mediums are passionate about the right relationship of humanity, animals and the environment.[38] My argument has not been that women represent Nature and men Politics. Creation myths celebrate male potency as well as female fecundity. I have been concerned to show here that, despite the constraints of patriarchy, men and women play complementary roles in Zimbabwe's eco-religion.

Notes

1 Hove is cited in A. Mutsakani, 'Mumbengegwi Fights for Women's Land Rights', *Financial Gazette*, 24 Sept. 1998, p. 6.

2 Across a broad stretch of central Africa people who were matrilineal and uxorilocal were settled before newcomers, including the Shona who were patrilineal and virilocal, arrived.

3 See J. M. Schoffeleers, ed., *Guardians of the Land: Essays in Central African Territorial Cults* (Gwelo, Zimbabwe: Mambo Press, 1979), p. 3. Scholeffeers quotes R. A. Rappaport to define the religion as 'a ritually directed eco-system'.

4 A classic account of the way this system operates is D. Lan, *Guns and Rain. Guerrillas and Spirit Mediums in Zimbabwe* (London: James Currey, 1985). Lan emphasizes that 'very few *mhondoro* mediums are women' and that if a woman claims to be possessed it is always 'possible to conclude that they are possessed by a low level ancestor', pp. 70, 88.

5 File S 3276/2, National Archives, Harare. Index of Spirits. Mount Darwin.

6 Ibid., Mtoko District, S 3276/2. During the month of Sept. 1998 Chief Mtoko faced a unanimous call from his headmen to resign because he had not given Chieftainess Charewa due respect. The current chief is a Christian and the Charewa office-holder stands for 'traditional' religion and environmental practices.

7 The High God's characteristics have been defined by W. van Binsbergen in 'Explorations in the History and Sociology of Territorial Cults in Zambia' in *Guardians*, ed. Schoffeleers, as being an invisible entity, who may be considered

the ultimate Creator and tends to be associated with the sky and meteorological phenomena p. 82 n.25.

8 See essays in *Guardians*, ed. Schoffeleers.

9 I. Phiri, 'African Traditional Women and Ecofeminism: The Role of Women at Chisumphi Cult in Preserving the Environment', *Religion in Malawi*, 5, 1995 and Phiri, *Women, Presbyterianism and Patriarchy: Religious Experience of Chewa Women in Central Malawi* (Blantyre: Claim, 1997).

10 Ibid., pp. 21–32.

11 See, for example, H. L. Vail, 'Religion, Language and the Tribal Myth: The Tumbuka and Chewa of Malawi' in *Guardians*, ed. Schoffeleers.

12 J. M. Schoffeleers, *River of Blood: The Genesis of Martyr Cult in Southern Malawi, c.AD 1600* (Madison: Wisc., University of Wisconsin, 1992.)

13 Vail, 'Religion, Language and the Tribal Myth', p. 222.

14 I have here extended the argument in S. I. G. Mudenge, *A Political History of Munhumutapa, 1400–1902* (Harare: Zimbabwe Publishing House, 1988) esp. pp. 42, 84, 87, 95, 121, 122, 127, 130, 131.

15 J. K. Rennie, 'From Zimbabwe to a Colonial Chieftaincy. Four Transformations of the Musikavanhu Territorial Cult in Rhodesia', in *Guardians*, ed. Schoffeleers.

16 Mudenge, *Political History*, p. 42.

17 Ibid.; M. F. C. Bourdillon, 'The Cults of Dzivaguru and Karuva amongst the North-Eastern Shona Peoples', in *Guardians*, ed. Schoffeleers.

18 Index of Spirits, Chimoyo area, Mtoko, S 2376/2.

19 *Guardians*, ed. Schoffeleers, p. 240.

20 Lan, *Guns and Rain*, ch. 5.

21 H. Schmidt, 'Muredzwa: Superwoman', unpublished paper, Oxford.

22 I owe this information to Mercy Wachtmeister, who is carrying out doctoral research in Makoni District on women and water.

23 I have discussed the Mwali cult extensively in T. O. Ranger, *Voices From the Rocks. Nature, Culture and History in the Matopos* (Oxford: James Currey, 1999). The environmental role of the cult is discussed on pp. 23–25.

24 Infighting over control of shrines has a long history. The importance of shrines to national politicians in recent times is discussed in my *Voices from the Rocks*.

25 I. Phiri reminds us that the Chewa initiation ceremony for girls is called *chinaMwali*; that the *Mwali* priestess presided over the Mankhamba rain shrine; and that the Banda clan assert that they were once ruled over by a female ritual leader called *Mwali*. I focus here on the current condition of the cult in which male and female power is complementary without either being dominant. It is worth noting, however, that among Tonga speakers in northern Zimbabwe the rainmaker is seen as a hermaphrodite figure, representing simultaneously male and female spiritual power.

26 L. Nthoi, 'Social Perspective of Religion: A Study of the Mwali Cult of Southern Africa' (Ph.D. thesis, University of Manchester, 1995).

27 H. Aschwanden, *Karanga Mythology* (Gweru: Mambo Press, 1990) p. 217.

28 Ibid., Aschwanden thoroughly explores the sexual symbolism of the shrines.

29 C. Hove and I. Trojanow, *Guardians of the Soil: Meeting Zimbabwe's Elders* (Harare: Baobab, 1996) p. 30.

30 The matrilineal succession at Dzilo, established by District Commissioner I. G. Cockcroft, is recorded in the 'Shamanism Book', a compilation on Zimbabwean religion drawn up in 1973 by the Internal Affairs 'expert', A. Latham.

31 'The Making of a Rain Goddess', *Sunday News Magazine*, 26 Oct./8 Nov. 1988.

32 Interview with M. Ncube, Bembe, 27 July 1989.
33 L. Nthoi, 'Social Perspective of Religion', p. 373.
34 Ibid., p. 384.
35 Interview between J. Alexander, J. McGregor and N. Ncube, Njelele, 2 Sept. 1996.
36 For an account of earlier movements see T. O. Ranger, 'Religious Studies and Political Economy: The Mwari Cult and the Peasant Experience in Southern Rhodesia', in *Theoretical Explorations in African Religion*, eds W. van Binsbergen and J. M. Schoffeleers (London: RKP, 1986).
37 G. Hansson interview with M. Juliana, Mudavanhu, 3 Nov. 1993; A. Mawere and K. Wilson, 'Socio-religious Movements, the State and Community Change: Some Reflections on the Ambuya Juliana Cult of Southern Zimbabwe', paper presented at Oxford, 23 April 1994.
38 Hove and Trojanow in *Guardians of the Soil* (interview of nine men and two women).

7

Rice, Women, Men and the Natural Environment among the Kelabit of Sarawak

Monica Janowski

In this chapter, I look at the way in which both male and female are fundamental to the construction of what one might describe as full and proper humanity for the Kelabit of Sarawak. I suggest that neither gender can be seen as being more 'sacred' than the other through a special, closer relationship with what might be termed 'nature'. Rather, both genders may be said to be sacred through their role in generating humanity via the relationship which the Kelabit have with their natural environment.

The 'Euro-American' dichotomy between 'nature' and 'culture' has been explored by Strathern.[1] I would suggest that it is not only in 'Euro-American' societies that there is a conception of a distinction between that which is not under the control of humans – which we may describe as 'the wild' – and that which is – which we might describe as 'culture' or 'civilization'. Among the Kelabit of Sarawak I found that, although there is no word which could be translated as 'culture' or 'civilization', there is a conception of something called *ulun,* which I shall gloss as 'human life'. *Ulun* implies a special human way of life based on rice-growing that is distinct from simply 'being alive' (*mulun*) which is applicable to wild living things. As is arguably the case in Euro-American societies, for the Kelabit too, to be truly human means to transcend a way of life which is entirely within the sphere of the wild, even though having *ulun* is, in fact, only possible because of a reliance on something I shall gloss as 'wild life force' (*lalud*).

Both for Euro-American societies and for a group like the Kelabit, gender is profoundly significant in the way in which people order the cosmos in terms of this type of dichotomy. However, male and female cannot be mapped in a simplistic way onto the tension or relationship between 'the wild' and 'the human', whether one describes these as 'nature' and 'culture' or not. This has been explored by contributors to the book edited by MacCormack and Strathern, *Nature, Culture and Gender*.[2] As MacCormack points out in her introduction, it seems more valid to propose that, in general terms, 'they [women] (and men) might better be seen as mediating between nature and culture' and that 'both men and women are nature and culture'.[3] This, indeed, is what I found to be the case among the Kelabit. Here I will explore the subtle way in which gender is related to notions of rice-growing and the forest, both of which are the essential elements in the Kelabit notion of the relationship between what is 'proper human life' (*ulun*) and what is not.

The Kelabit of Sarawak: Rice-Growers and Hunter-Gatherers

The Kelabit are a hill tribe living in the interior of the Fourth Division of Sarawak on the island of Borneo, on a highland plateau about 3,500 feet above sea level which is one of the sources of the Baram river. They probably now number about 7,500, about half of whom live in the highland area – half have migrated temporarily or permanently to the town of Miri, which is near the mouth of the Baram.[4] The Kelabit in the highland area live in small settlements consisting of one or two longhouses. The majority of Kelabit settlements in the highlands are now grouped in an area known as Bario, where the government has built a small airstrip, a clinic and a secondary school. In the period 1986–88, and again in 1992–93, I carried out fieldwork in a settlement known as Pa' Dalih in the southern part of the Kelabit Highlands, about twelve hours walk from Bario.

For the Kelabit, their physical relationship with the natural environment involves two major areas of interaction: rice-growing on the one hand and hunting and gathering in the forest (*polong*) on the other. They practice both wet and dry cultivation of rice, in which they are very successful, and they also plant tubers, mainly cassava, and maize, for snack foods, and a variety of other vegetables to be eaten with rice as side dishes at the rice meal. In the primary and secondary forest they hunt animals for meat, and gather vegetables as well as materials for crafts. All of the meat eaten on an everyday basis and a large proportion of the vegetables eaten with rice at the rice meal are derived from hunting and gathering, demonstrating the importance of these activities in terms of subsistence.

A profound distinction is made by the Kelabit between rice on the one hand and wild plants and animals on the other; the latter are said to 'grow on their own' (*mulun sebulang*), while rice is considered to need human help to grow. All cultivated plants except rice are treated as 'wild', and also as 'growing on their own'. They are given away freely as are wild plants and meat, in contrast to the way in which rice is very explicitly owned and is not given away without creating a debt.

These two areas of interaction with the natural environment – rice agriculture and the exploitation of plants and animals which 'grow on their own' – are, in Kelabit eyes, very different from a symbolic point of view. Rice cultivation, for the Kelabit, enables them to be fully human, distinguishing them from animals who are dependent solely on the forest and also from humans who depend purely on hunting and gathering, such as the Penan who share the forest with the Kelabit. Rice-growing is judged, probably rightly, to be a considerable achievement in the context of the surrounding rainforest. It requires planning, foresight and skill. Above all, rice-growing work is *lema'ud*, a category of activity which is close to the English notion of 'work'. Hunting and gathering, on the other hand, are described as *raut,* a word also used to describe the play of children – something enjoyable, which one engages in willingly.

Play, Work and Gender

As they grow up, marry and have children, both young men and young women have to make a transition from purely *raut* activities as children to becoming involved in *lema'ud* and rice-growing. This is always perceived as involving a certain effort of will.

There is a sense that humans will easily revert to *raut* activities in the wild unless a constant effort is made to engage in *lema'ud* activities. Unlike *raut* activities, those of *lema'ud* are not conceived of as pleasurable, although there is considerable satisfaction in being successful in them. I use the phrase 'revert to' because I had a strong sense that hunting and gathering are seen by the Kelabit as a way of life which comes naturally, easily. It is, in fact, to a large degree equivalent to what Euro-Americans conceive of nowadays as 'natural'. Rice-growing, on the other hand, is, for the Kelabit, something which humans have imposed upon the natural environment.

Men are particularly attracted to *raut* activities. While young women almost invariably make the transition to becoming rice-growers smoothly, well before they are married and have children, young men do not. They resist the necessity of giving up a life of daily hunting in the forest. Some young men fail to make the transition even after they have become fathers, which is seen as the time when it is essential to take up adulthood and rice-growing. Men, then, may be said to be, in some senses, more closely associated with the wild where *raut* activities take place, and to be less closely associated with *lema'ud*. Things are not, however, quite as straightforward as this.

Gender, the Couple, and the Generation of 'Human Life' from the Life Force of the Forest

What is the meaning of rice-growing? Why should the Kelabit want to impose rice upon the rainforest? I would suggest that this is because, for the Kelabit, growing rice means being able to generate *ulun* 'human life'. This is achieved through the rice meal. The rice meal is provided by the leading couples of households, described as 'big people' (*lun merar*), for their dependants and descendants (described as their *anak*, or 'children', although they are not always biological children).[5] Such households are described either as 'houses' (*ruma'*) or as 'hearths' (*tetal*). I describe them as 'hearth-groups' because of the focal role of the hearth, where the rice meal is cooked and next to which it is consumed.

Rice has the central position in the rice meal. The meal consists of both rice and wild foods (or cultivated vegetables, which are treated as 'wild') cooked as side dishes. The fact that it is described as 'eating rice' (*kuman nuba'*), however, highlights the central position of rice in the meal; side dishes are described as *nok penguman*, literally 'something to eat with [rice]'.

At the rice meal *ulun* is generated which is passed from the couple who provide the meal to their dependants and descendants. This process is dependent on the provision of *lalud* (wild force) through the wild foods eaten with rice. Without these wild foods a rice meal cannot take place; at the very least a meal must consist of rice and salt, which is a wild food processed from brine springs in the forest. Although there is a public insistence on the importance of rice, wild

110

foods, and particularly meat, are as essential as rice to the meal. This is made clear at *irau* feasts, where domestic animals are slaughtered and a great deal of emphasis is placed on the provision, by the hosts, of plenty of domestic meat which has a monetary value.

The Importance of both Unity and Division of Male and Female

Errington has suggested that in insular South-East Asia there is a broad distinction between what she terms 'centrist' and 'exchange' societies.[6] In 'centrist' societies, there is an emphasis on the generation of power or potency[7] within focal centres in society, whereas 'exchange' societies emphasize the generation of potency through exchange between entities (most importantly, houses).[8] The Kelabit belong to the geographical area which Errington categorizes as 'centrist'.

Errington stresses the 'unity' of the genders in 'centrist' societies. In South-East Asia, male and female tend to be complementary and together make up a whole,[9] and the union of male and female is very potent; deities are often male plus female.[10] The Kelabit data, however, underlines the fact that it is important not to overstate this unity. At least for the Kelabit the separation of the genders is important as well as their unity.

I would suggest that the Kelabit hearth-group, with the 'big people' couple, is a potency-dispensing centre. Among the Kelabit, the gender make-up of this centre is vital to the process of generating *ulun* out of *lalud*. The couple is not only represented as unitary, a seamless whole whose division into male and female is veiled, but also as being clearly separated into its component genders, male and female.[11] The first representation is projected through the everyday emphasis on the cultivation of rice by the couple, on the rice meal as a *rice* meal, and on the delineation of hearth-groups through rice, which is very clearly owned by the hearth-group, unlike wild foods. The other representation of the couple as made up of male and female becomes apparent at communal meals, particularly at *irau*, child-naming feasts.

The suggestion that in 'centrist' societies of South-East Asia men and women are fundamentally the same sort of being has been made by some writers. Atkinson, for example, states that the Wana of Sulawesi 'underscore the fundamental likeness of the sexes'.[12] In the case of the Kelabit this would be too simplistic an analysis.

Among the young it is definitely not true. For the 'big people' couple, it is both true and not true, since there is an emphasis *both* on the 'sameness' of the two members *and* on the difference between them, and both perspectives are vital.

The concept of power, life force or potency in South-East Asia has been discussed in unitary terms.[13] For the Kelabit, however, there is a distinction between the concept of *ulun*, or human life, dispensed by 'big people' through the rice meal, and that of *lalud* or wild force, which is accumulated by the 'big people' in order to be processed into *ulun*. The role of the 'big people' within the hearth-group at the rice meal is to achieve this processing. Kelabit men and women *must* be different in order to make the generation of *ulun* possible.

In South-East Asian 'centrist' societies, power and stillness are concentrated the closer one gets to the very centre of the society, while activity is associated with the periphery. The Kelabit associate the centre with the longhouse, the ricefields and the hearth, while the periphery is the forest and mountains where hunting takes place. The centre is associated with the female, the periphery with the male. The male association with the periphery does not imply a superior, or a more powerful, role any more than the female association with the power-dispensing centre does. Men, in their association with the forest, have a vital role in accumulating *lalud*, the wild force necessary for the generation of human life. Rosaldo and Atkinson have noted a similar association between men and forces from outside the settlement for the Ilongot and the Wana.[14] But *lalud* would be meaningless without being brought together with rice, associated with women, at the rice meal. In the same way the powerful, still centre associated with the female, and rice which is linked with it, could achieve nothing without the *lalud* contributed by men.

It cannot be said that either male or female, among the Kelabit, are more associated with power or potency. Men are associated with access to wild life force, *lalud*, but women are more closely associated with the centre which processes this into human life (*ulun*). There is also a sense in which both men and women are connected with that *ulun*-generating centre, through the symbolism of rice.

The Complex Association between Rice and Gender

Rice is associated with women. It is women who are specialists in rice-growing, although their husbands may become expert assistants and spend almost as much time in the ricefields as their wives. It would probably not be possible for a man to cultivate rice without a woman (I know of no cases where this occurs) while there are cases of women cultivating rice without a man. Certain key activities, in particular seed selection, are not done by men. It is women who, in the past, were said to have had special relationships with the deity associated with success in rice cultivation, Deraya, and who may still be said to have 'good *deraya*', using the word as a noun equivalent to 'luck' in English.

Rice stands symbolically for the entire rice meal. This is projected linguistically through the fact that the rice meal is described as '*kuman nuba*', literally 'eating rice'. Rice is cultivated together by the 'big people' couple and it stands for their achievement together, as a whole. From this perspective the couple is a seamless unity within which the distinction between male and female is minimally visible. Rice is associated with the 'big people' couple in opposition to the childless, who are described as *anak*, or 'children'. Young people rarely engage in rice-growing, although girls do so more than boys. It is once a young couple have children and have taken parental names that they begin to become seriously involved in rice-growing, and they spend more and more time together in the rice-growing enterprise as they grow older, reach grandparenthood, and take grandparental names. Rice, then, has the capacity to join the two genders together productively. It stands for their unity, which is achieved in relation to child-related status.

Rice is attributed an ambiguous position. Although closely associated with women it also represents the unity of the couple and 'stands for' the *ulun*-dispensing centre. Rice is counterpoised to the other vital element of the rice meal, wild foods, and particularly meat. A rice meal cannot take place without side dishes consisting of foods which are either actually wild or which are treated as such. This includes cultivated vegetables for side dishes, which have been simply planted and left, unlike rice which has to be protected and weeded.

Wild Life Force and the Forest

Meat is strongly associated with men. It derives, on an everyday basis, solely from the forest (*polong*). The forest is described as 'bigger' the less it is controlled by humans, and the more this is so the more it is associated with men. Although women gather vegetables in secondary growth, they do not enter big secondary growth and they almost never enter primary forest, being afraid, they say, of the spirits which dwell there. Men, on the other hand, say that they are not afraid of spirits, and indeed some have developed 'friendships' with forest spirits.

The natural environment beyond the longhouse and the rice-fields is quite explicitly a source of *lalud*. It is the abode of spirits carrying *lalud*, the most important of which is named Puntumid. Puntumid's *lalud* gives him the power over life and death. It is said that, before the Kelabit became Christian, Puntumid made friends among the young men and gave them substances carrying *lalud* – *tabat* (the same word as is used for modern medicines) which gave them the power to heal and kill, the power over life and death. Puntumid can also give success in hunting, and apparently before the Kelabit became converts men used to pray to Puntumid for hunting success; now they pray to God, who is believed to be an even more potent source of *lalud*. The environment beyond the settlement is also said to be the abode of other peoples, similar to the Kelabit but existing on a mythical plane, who have great *lalud* and with whom mythical Kelabit male heroes, also carrying great *lalud*, have done battle according to the stories.[15]

Men, then, through their hunting, bring back *lalud* to the settlement. In the past, until perhaps 1940, men were also involved in headhunting, although much less frequently than among some other tribes in Sarawak such as the Iban. Headhunting is a major source of life force in many tribal societies in South-East Asia.[16] Among the Kelabit it would seem that headhunting, practised by men, was a means of bringing back *lalud* although *lalud* from this source was not fed into the rice meal.

Although side dishes at the rice meal consist of both meat and vegetable foods, it is meat which is the most highly valued and significant. It is to hunt and obtain meat that men normally enter the forest. The centrality of meat as the most important complement of rice at the rice meal is made clear at *irau* naming feasts, where only meat is eaten together with rice. Here, the association between men and meat is made explicit and is given value in a way in which it is not on an everyday basis. *Irau* are held, nowadays, to mark the birth of a child, which is, of course, the basis of parental status for his or her parents and of grandparental status for the grandparents. Parental, and particularly grandparental, status is vital, together with diligence and success in rice-growing, in the development of 'big people' status for a young couple, and hence the considerable significance of *irau*. The co-resident grandparents of the child, who are the 'big people' of the hearth-group to which he or she belongs, are the hosts of the feast. On these occasions, side dishes consist of domestic meat from highly valued buffaloes and pigs which are accumulated with great effort by the host hearth-group. The amount of meat provided is noticed and commented on widely by the guests, and it is distributed with ceremony. The distribution is by men, and men engage in fat-eating competitions, underlining the association of men with meat.

The Veiled Significance of Wild Life Force

Only at *irau* and other communal feasts is the central importance of the wild and of *lalud* in the generation of *ulun* explicit. The Kelabit emphasize their identity as rice-growers; indeed, throughout the geographical area there is a tendency to play up rice-growing and to downplay the very widespread reliance on the wild.[17] This relates to the association of the young with hunting and gathering. Not only is the access to wild resources associated with men, it is also associated with the young and childless. Young men in settlements like Pa' Dalih spend a very large proportion of their time hunting in the forest, both primary and secondary, engaging in activities which are very strenuous and skilled but which are nevertheless categorized as 'play' (*raut*) by their rice-growing elders (who also like to indulge in them whenever they have time). For their part young women and girls spend a lot of time gathering vegetables in the secondary forest.

There is undoubtedly an emphasis placed on the need for youngsters to make the transition to rice-growing. The implication is that hunting and gathering must be left behind as a way of life, to be replaced by one based on rice-growing. Hunting and gathering is seen as the easy, straightforward choice, being what, in effect, comes 'naturally'; rice-growing is the difficult option. One is tempted to draw a parallel to the Euro-American evaluation of the taming of the natural environment as associated with civilization. Like Euro-American civilization, rice-growing creates a human site, distinct from the wild, pushing back nature.

Underlying this concept, however, is a recognition by the Kelabit, which is demonstrated at every rice meal, but particularly at *irau* feasts, that the contribution of the wild, and of *lalud* from the wild, is vital to the success of the generation of *ulun*, which cannot be derived solely from rice. The significance of the association of men with the wild is that men, unlike youngsters, are able to feed *lalud* into the centre because they are part of of it. They are able to harness this wild force, in the form of meat, with rice, in order to make the generation of *ulun* possible.

Nevertheless, although access to *lalud* is important, gaining access to *lalud* is not, in Kelabit eyes, the great human endeavour. The great human achievement is successful cultivation of rice. The transition to being a rice cultivator, which occurs at marriage and particularly after the birth of the first child of a couple (when they begin to be regarded as 'big people' to some degree), is represented as difficult and painful, particularly for men. Some men continue to spend a good deal of time hunting even when they are established parents and grandparents, but this is ridiculed and leads to their being referred to in disrespectful ways behind their backs, for example, through the use of their childhood name rather than their parental or grandparental name or title. This indicates that they have not made a successful transition from childhood to adulthood. The fact that this transition is more difficult for men underlines their greater closeness to the wild and to the hunting and gathering way of life.

Conclusion

I would suggest that among the Kelabit it is not only women, but both women and men, separately and together, who are 'sacred custodians of the earth'. The natural environment, if we equate this with 'the earth', is the source of what, the Kelabit believe, enables them to live truly as human beings, and we can perhaps equate this with what is, to the Kelabit, sacred. Both men and women relate in vital ways to this natural environment – women through their focal role in rice agriculture and their stronger association with rice, and men through their access to the *lalud* (wild life force) of the natural world 'growing on its own'. This distinction between men and women is important. The two vital components of the rice meal provide the means of generating *ulun* (human life). Men and women in the 'big people' couple, however, are also united in rice agriculture, which stands for the entire endeavour of creating something distinctly human. Together, they form a powerful male-plus-female whole which has the capability of processing *lalud* from the forest, brought in by the male mem-

ber of the couple, with rice, associated more strongly with the
female member of the couple. The result is *ulun* – human life.

Notes

1 See for example, M. Strathern, *Reproducing the Future. Anthropology, Kinship and the New Reproductive Technologies* (Manchester: Manchester University Press, 1992).
2 C. MacCormack and M. Strathern, eds, *Nature, Culture and Gender* (Cambridge: Cambridge University Press, 1980), pp. 9, 17.
3 In *ibid.*, pp. 9, 17.
4 There were estimated to be 5,057 Kelabit in 1987 and a growth rate of 4% from 1970 to 1980, so it is probable that the total is now about 7,500. T. H. J. Ko, 'Minor Indigenous Groups in Sarawak', *Sarawak Gazette*, CXIII, 1987, pp. 31–35.
5 M. Janowski, 'Rice, Work and Community among the Kelabit of Sarawak' (Ph.D. thesis, London School of Economics, University of London, 1991); M. Janowski, 'The Hearth-Group, the Conjugal Couple and the Symbolism of the Rice Meal among the Kelabit of Sarawak', in *About the House: Levi-Strauss and Beyond*, eds J. Carsten & S. Hugh-Jones (Cambridge: Cambridge University Press, 1995).
6 S. Errington, 'Recasting Sex, Gender and Power: A Theoretical and Regional Overview', in *Power and Difference. Gender in Island Southeast Asia*, eds J. M. Atkinson and S. Errington (Stanford: Stanford University Press, 1990).
7 B. Anderson, 'Power', in *Culture and Politics in Indonesia*, ed. C. Holt, *et al.* (Ithaca, NY: Cornell University Press, 1972).
8 Carsten & Hugh-Jones, eds, *About the House*; C. McDonald, *De la hutte au palais: sociétés 'à maison' en Asie du Sud-Est* (Paris: CNRS, 1987).
9 Atkinson and Errington, eds, *Power and Difference. Gender in Island Southeast Asia*, see esp. S. Errington, 'Recasting Sex, Gender and Power: A Theoretical and Regional Overview', in ibid.
10 J. Hoskins, 'Doubling Deities, Descent and Personhood: An Exploration of Kodi Gender Categories', in *Power and Difference*, eds Atkinson and Errington.
11 Janowski, 'Hearth Group'.
12 J. M. Atkinson, 'How Gender Makes a Difference in Wana Society' in *Power and Difference*, eds Atkinson and Errington.
13 B. Anderson, 'Power'; S. Errington, 'Recasting Sex, Gender and Power' in Atkinson and Errington, *Power and Difference*; C. Geertz, *Negara. The Theatre State of Nineteenth-Century Bali* (Princeton: Princeton University Press, 1980).
14 Atkinson, 'How Gender Makes a Difference'; M. Rosaldo, *Knowledge and Passion: Ilongot Notions of Self and Society* (New York: Cambridge University Press, 1980).
15 C. Rubenstein, 'Poems of Indigenous Peoples of Sarawak – Some of the Songs and Chants', pt II. *Sarawak Museum Journal*, XXI, 1973, pp. 723–1127.
16 J. D. Freeman, 'Severed Heads that Germinate', in *Fantasy and Symbol: Studies in Anthropological Interpretation*, eds R. H. Hook and G. Devereux (London: Academic Press, 1979); J. Hoskins, *Headhunting and the Social Imagination in South East Asia* (Stanford: Stanford University Press, 1996).
17 C. Helliwell, 'Autonomy as Natural Equality: Inequality in "Egalitarian" Societies', *Journal of the Royal Anthropological Institute*, 1, 1995, pp. 359–76. This describes what I call hearth-groups as 'rice-groups'.

Part III

The Great Religions

8

Ecology and Christian Hierarchy

Anne Primavesi

In classic Christian hierarchy the bridge between divine Being and those in the 'lower' states of being, that is, below the human, is taken to be the human person himself, the generic male. He, after the example of Christ, assumes a mediating role as steward, guardian/custodian or pastor/shepherd. Such male metaphors signal particular features in hierarchical ordering which have not only excluded women, *a priori*, from a custodian's role in regard to the Earth, but also, as we shall see, sanctioned the oppression of both women and Earth.

As a theologian, being asked to consider 'custodianship' as a possible role for women in relationship to the Earth means bringing this hierarchical 'order of things' within Christianity into view, since, in common with such paradigmatic structures, it is so generally accepted as to be almost invisible. In his Preface to *The Order of Things*, Michel Foucault refers to these structures as the rules which, epistemologically and systematically, keep things in order, come into play to make discourse coherent, and which, at the time it is written and accepted, give the order its practical application. They constitute the grid of identities, similitudes and analogies through which we sort out many and different things. They result from precise operations and the application of preliminary criteria. Order, he says, is at one and the same time that which is given in things as their inner law, the hidden network that determines the way they confront one another, and also that which has no existence except in the grid created by a glance, an examination, a language; and it is only in the blank spaces of this grid that order manifests itself in depth as though already there, waiting in silence for the moment of its expression.[1]

What order, network, or grid of identities connects women with the Earth? Who has created this particular grid, and on what preliminary criteria? What happens if the 'blank spaces' are given expression? The answer to some if not all of these questions is, I will argue, found in a particular hierarchical ordering within Christianity. This order, and its practical application in matters such as custodianship, has indeed rested on a preliminary criterion, that of a particular order of being, and the fact that both practical and preliminary order never had existence except in the grid created by theological language has not weakened its hold on the Christian theological imagination. This chapter will attempt to give expression to this preliminary order, and by raising it into view, weaken its imaginary hegemony. Doing so, it will also put in question the very notion of women (or men) as 'custodians' of the Earth, since such a concept can only arise from a view of humankind as in some way fitted by Nature to have custody of the planet and its life-support systems in all their mysterious complexity. When viewed from this angle, the absurdity and arrogance of the concept becomes apparent. And yet, as I shall show, the refusal to grant women such a role does not rest on its absurdity, but on an arrogant and equally misconceived perception of male power.

In a Platonic schema, the question of 'who will have custody of the custodians themselves?' implies a prior order as criterion on which their custodianship is presumed to be based. It presupposes that their actions result from, or depend on, or are in some way determined by their relationship with this prior order, as well as by what they are in themselves. The implication is that they themselves need a custodian. And this would also seem to apply to the Earth which they (presumably) have in custody. This too has an order of being which must, in some way, depend on that of its putative custodians, and through them, ultimately, on that which has a prior order of being.

Such an ontology, such a conception of things being ordered on the basis of what they are, may leave unspecified the organizational principle on which the beings themselves are ranked in relation to each other. So scientific organizational principles, such as cellular formation or nutritional modes, take certain observable individual characteristics or marks or behavioural habits of organisms as criteria for deciding which beings will be included or studied in various taxonomies.[2] General conceptions of how reality is ordered, however, cannot be so specific or so easily decided. They derive from ancient and often obscure ontological presuppositions, all the more powerful for being unstated, or taken for granted. Foucault refers to this as 'the site, the mute ground upon which it is possible for entities to be juxtaposed'.[3]

Hierarchy as a Principle of Order

The foundational concept in question here, which, though largely muted in Western culture, is no less powerful for that, is hierarchy: an organizational principle governing, and ranking the order of being, which is itself ordered on a primary notion of Being (routinely capitalized). This concept has functioned within Western culture as the formulation of a general order of existence; as the way things are in sheer actuality; as the most comprehensive idea of order. It has served as a model of the relations between the world and the self.[4] With it, we move from an Aristotelian schema to a neo-Platonist one, in which this primary Being is identified with God as the ultimate reference point to which we are bound. It is still the primary Christian ordering of the universe. As such, this principle of ranking beings in relation to God, the supreme Being, has, to a large extent, determined Western cultural perceptions of human identity as distinct from the identity of Nature/Earth, as well as what it means to be female rather than male. Its characteristic feature is its implicit/explicit acknowledgement of the sacredness of central authority, and its acceptance of certain key male figures, characterized in certain ways, as symbolizing, embodying and exercising that authority.

This binding together of ontology and theology, of what we say we are and what we say God is, takes God's sacred being as 'the mute ground' of all being. 'In God we live, move and have our being'.[5] Such an ontotheological presupposition was given consummate coherence by the late fifth-century Christian mystic and neo-Platonist known as Denys (or Dionysius) the Areopagite. He is credited with first use of the term *hierarchia* (hierarchy), a coinage from two Greek words meaning 'sacred', and 'source or principle'. He expounded the principle while writing about 'the two hierarchies', the celestial and the ecclesiastical. The first 'consists of three ranks, each consisting of three types of angelic being'. The second hierarchy also consists of 'three ranks of three, of which the first rank consists not of beings but of rites – sacramental rites'. The second rank in this hierarchy is that of sacred ministry: bishops, priests and ministers. The third rank is that of the laity, and includes monks (in the Eastern Church, they traditionally refused ordination), the baptized, and those excluded from the celebration of the sacraments. The purpose of the hierarchies is assimilation to God and union with him [sic]. This is accomplished by each being fulfilling its proper role in the hierarchy.'[6] The often ignored or forgotten aspect of hierarchy which I want to highlight here is that it ranks or grades all beings, even the angelic ones. And as each rank is graded, so is its role (in this instance, that of custodian). And each rank, grade or role is assumed to be determined by divine decree. A popular hymn endorses such hierarchical ordering, addressing God in his [sic] heaven as one who has determined the relative high and low estate of the king and of the poor man lying at his gate.

This divine ordering, made explicit by Denys, is still implicit in mainstream Christian thinking. It assumes that the two hierarchies outlined above are in fact part of a triad of being, with the Thearchy, or Trinity, ranked above the other two. The concept of hierarchy is then actually a cosmic, theocratic pattern of government in which the Trinity presides above the angels, who are above the ecclesiastics who are above the laity. This ranking is more than order. It refers also to what this sacred ordering makes possible: the knowledge and activity of those so ordered (the order of action). Denys's overall understanding of hierarchy sees it as the overflowing emanation of God's love, of God's active search for humankind and gentle persuasion of fallen human beings. A very important principle for him is that we do not receive our *being* from other creatures ranked higher than us, for we are created immediately by God, and each of us has an immediate relation to God by virtue of God creating each of us. However, those ranked above us have a mediating role between us and God, conveying and ordering knowledge of God (revelation) and directing our activity in accordance with God's will for all members of the hierarchy. They are, for Denys, a community seeking to draw near to God and draw others near to God. They are a community being saved and mediating salvation, and their presence expresses the transcendent love of God made immanent.[7]

This magnificent vision of order and harmony throughout the world shaped Christian and Western consciousness for centuries, most obviously in its religious and political order. Its organizing principle of graded levels of being carried through, for Denys, into the material order, manifested for him most clearly in physical church structures, where the architecture gives primacy to the sanctuary. A computer-generated model of a traditional church seen from above without its roof, reveals a hierarchically ordered space, where the sanctuary and its ministers stand at the apex of the building and the congregation fan out below them. The hierarchical order of those who use the building follows from this, with the ministers in the sanctuary separated from the laity outside and below it, the latter dependent on the ministers for access to God through sacramental mediation. The physical and spiritual boundaries between the orders are thus established, impregnable because ratified by the highest authority, God.

The ordering was formalized internally and externally, and its systematic application became and remains normative in theological and ecclesiastical systems. The 1960s Second Vatican Council document on the Church, *Lumen Gentium*, contains a long chapter on 'The Hierarchical Structure of the Church'.[8] In a recent interesting and influential theological/scientific study, Nancy Murphy and George F. R. Ellis argue that the hierarchical ordering of the natural and human sciences is marked by top-down causation and 'emergent order', in which with each step 'upward' in the hierarchy of biological order (from cell to organism to community) novel properties emerge that were not present at the 'simpler' levels of organization. In the light of this they define 'top-down causation' as both *effects*, which determine the detailed evolution of the hierarchical system, and *action*, which occurs when human volition is involved. They propose a hierarchy of the natural sciences which for them is incomplete without a metaphysical, or preferably theological, 'top layer'. This unifies the hierarchies by providing a single theory of divine *purpose* which answers 'the ultimate questions arising from each branch of the hierarchy'. For the authors, the purpose is that humankind (or at least ethically aware self-conscious beings) 'might exist', and the ultimate questions, in particular those raised by violence, are answered by a theology which sees God as refusing to do violence to creation, whatever the cost to God. This view for them, as Christian pacifists, holds direct implications for human morality in that it implies a self-renunciatory, non-violent ethic, one modelled on 'God's own self-sacrificing love'.[9]

In secular monarchies, particularly where, as in the Holy Roman Empire and the British monarchy, the monarch's 'divine' right to rule was, and is, ratified by the established Church or religion, hierarchy endorsed the political and military authority of royal institutions. Clifford Geertz gives a fascinating historical account of the symbolics of spiritual power previously attached to monarchies as diverse as those of England, Morocco, and Java. These symbolics might seem, at first sight, irrelevant as well as redundant in today's secular society. However, he points out that though both the structure and the expressions of social life change, the inner necessities that animate it do not. Thrones, he says, may be out of fashion, but political authority still requires a cultural frame in which to define itself and advance its claims, and so does opposition to it. It is no accident that Stuarts get Cromwells and Medicis Savonarolas. It is, he says, only a certain view of 'the affinity between the sort of power that moves men and the sort that moves mountains' which died in the French Revolution (to the degree that it did). The sense that there is such an affinity did not die.[10]

This assumed affinity between sacred and secular order, internalized and no less powerful for its religious origins becoming increasingly remote, has, however, been contested this century by political and liberation theologians for its conjunction of deity and domination;[11] or monotheism and monarchy,[12] or monotheism and violence;[13] or capitalist hegemonies supported by right-wing churches.[14] It is contested also by those theologians who find hierarchical authority structures exercising undue and oppressive influence on the lives of women.[15] Standing back, as it were, from these hierarchical structures within which they are enmeshed, are those philosophers and theologians who see that in classical hierarchical organization, where women and children are assigned to the lowest grade or rank, even that is denied to what is called 'Nature/Earth'. The dividing line, the ontological space between human and animal is so absolute that non-human 'beings' in our environments are 'non-entities' below any grade: are totally 'de/graded'. They are considered, if at all, to be outside of that community seeking to draw near to God and to draw others near to God; outside that community whose presence expresses the transcendent love of God made immanent. The secular version of this has been evident in the struggle by animal rights activists within the European Union to have farm animals graded as 'sentient beings' and not as 'agricultural products'.

I am not saying that divine 'collusion' with grading, degrading and exclusion is routinely or publicly claimed, endorsed or enforced, or that Denys is required reading for constitutional historians. But as Geertz points out, political, religious and military power still requires a cultural framework, a coherent system in which to define itself and advance its claims, and while the ecclesiastical institutions remain the most visible hierarchical framework, 'inner necessities' for an order of action and of being also remain potent within social and political structures. It is at that subliminal level that hierarchy, with its assumption of affinity between divine and human power, remains potent. Civil religious ceremonies, such as a Presidential Inauguration, the State opening of Parliament or Armistice commemorations in Europe, are its most public expression today.

It is no accident then that some of the most contested contemporary issues in public life have been women's challenges to a political and ecclesiastical order of being which excludes and degrades them (challenges epitomized in their claim to the right to vote and to officiate in the sanctuary) and the challenging of political and economic order by environmental movements which see that, for practical purposes, 'Nature' and its role have been degraded in, or excluded from, the community of being. Both these movements challenge what Geertz calls 'the master fictions', that is, the hierarchies of being and the mimetic processes by which the prevailing social order condones certain acts of violence toward certain classes of being: in Nature's case, by making it a 'non-being'. For at the heart of hierarchical separation lies a claim to divine and human independence of, and power over, Nature and any being identified with Nature.

Modes of Hierarchical Ordering

Hierarchical ordering remains theologically, politically, economically and ecologically oppressive as long as we subscribe to a system in which the *value* of 'being' (whether ours or that of any other living entity) is ranked in relation to a supposed order of nearness to the highest Being, God. Hierarchy assumes that the 'highest' value of all is ascribed to God's Being, which, through a type of 'top-down causation', is taken as the source of all value. By implication, whatever is placed furthest away, in the 'lowest' states of being, is furthest from God, and so of 'lesser' value. God 'functions' as the definitive source of value and at the same time, sets limits to one level of value in relation to another. So even though Denys was at pains to insist on the principle of immediate causation, or creation of each being by God, there is at least an implicit claim in hierarchy that the value of each one's being is not the same. It derives from where one is ranked relative to others' ranking. Therefore, it denies the value of what one is in oneself and/or how essential that presence and activity might be for another's existence and well-being.

In scientific coevolutionary theories, such as Gaia theory, which presuppose the integral and interdependent structural coupling of all organisms and their environments, the valuing which counts is based on an individual's interactivity with and contribution to the sustaining of life. We must, on this criterion, attribute intrinsic value to bacteria as well as to ourselves, and cannot consider beings in isolation, or as divided off from one another in any meaningful way. From such a non-hierarchical perspective, each entity can be considered unique and, therefore, essentially ungradeable. At a practical level of course, one may count more than another. But in this biological 'order of things', the valuing of one life form does not imply, or need, the degrading of another. And accepting that we are sustained through relationships of interdependence too complex for us to grasp in their totality does not allow us to claim, or to exercise absolute power over, or in this instance to 'take custody' of, the Earth.

Those theologians who base the intrinsic value of each human being on the gratuity of God's love for each one, for the least one, for the most forgotten one, assert that that love too is essentially ungradeable. The loveworthiness of each is not derived from class, wealth, education, religion or race, nor is it based on relative moral worth. It is based on their uniqueness before God. For me, when liberation theologians such as Gustavo Gutierrez see each poor person, without rank or power in human eyes, as altogether fresh and vivid in the memory of God, this echoes Jesus' claim about God's direct interest in sparrows and in each lily in the field. This notion of intrinsic value extends far beyond that of human life. Yet usually, the most value given other creatures, and the most accepted defence of their right to a habitat, is their contributing to 'quality of life': *our* life, not theirs.

In Christian church documents based on hierarchical ordering, there are explicit limits set and boundaries to be kept between one rank of being and another. There is presumed to be a defining and predetermined hierarchic blank 'space' between God and the other states of being which can only be bridged by *the* mediator between God and man [sic]: Jesus Christ. He brought knowledge of God to men, who then preached this knowledge to other men, women and children. This ontological limit to knowledge of God is so accepted as to be largely unrecognized. No trickle-down effect is envisaged in orthodox theology, although popular understanding has St Francis preaching to the birds and to the wolf. Yet here too, the presumption is that *he* was telling *them* about God, since it was assumed that otherwise they would not have this knowledge. The idea that he might have heard something about God from them would have been dismissed as, at best, ridiculous.

However, an intimation of the reverse order of mediation is given in the saying attributed by some to St Francis and by others to Rabindranath Tagore:

I asked the tree,
Speak to me about God
And it blossomed.

In classic Christianity, however, the bridge between divine Being and those in the 'lower' states was the generic male. He, representing Christ, assumed a mediating role as steward, guardian or custodian, or as pastor or shepherd. Women were excluded *a priori* from an intermediary custodial role in regard to the Earth.

The Place of Nature and Women in Hierarchical Ordering

The devaluing process within hierarchy has been recognized by feminist theologians and philosophers as a significant factor in the ordering of women and Nature.[16] In a hierarchical pyramid which ranks God at its apex, and men (for practical purposes we can discount angels) immediately below God, then women, children, animals, plants, and the soil/dirt/earth form its base. Once this 'ranking' has been established, God-concepts function in relation to women, children, animals, and the Earth as validation of their subordination and consequent exploitation. God is presented as the ultimate arbiter who distinguishes women from men in order to degrade the former. When this distinction is publicly expressed in binary codes which rank 'male' characteristics above 'female' ones, the degrading is formalized. The binary codes in themselves can be taken as a linguistic device for implying a whole which cannot be adequately expressed. But Christian binary codes of heavenly/earthly; sacred/secular; human/animal; male/female; spiritual/material always reflect, implicitly at least, a prior hierarchical ordering derived from neo-Platonism or ontotheology.

It is a moot point here whether hierarchy precedes patriarchy or merely sanctifies it. What matters is that when binary codes routinely attribute opposed male/female characteristics to men and women (such as rational/emotional; objective/subjective; logical/illogical; strong/weak; active/passive), the attribution is not neutral. What matters is not the position of one word relative to another, but their connotations within a hierarchical ranking.[17] The effects of this are obvious in a culture where, for centuries, the relative status of men and women in society has reflected this ranking. It has affected the power relations between men and women, whether religious, political, economic or social. It has affected the relations between men and their environments. The effects of this last, and its allied effects on women, have been quantified in studies of the disproportionate impact of environmental degradation on women, children, indigenous peoples and the poor.[18]

Degradation of the biophysical environment itself reflects hierarchical attitudes which reduce it to instrumental or commodity value alone. The degradation has been validated, consciously or not, by the identification of male/female with culture/nature, with overtones of mastery by the male. This conceptual relational field has been one of the most contested areas of feminist discourse, with the contest centred, for the most part, on whether or not women are to be identified with Nature or with Culture. Much of the analysis has been the work of secular feminists, who are often blind to the fact, as Curthoys points out, that there is a prior devaluing inherent in the terms which the terms in themselves do not carry. The understanding of this 'prior devaluing' offered here is that it rests in large measure on prior Christian hierarchical descriptions of the order of being, where women and Nature are presumed to belong on the level of the 'fallen' and 'disordered', and their subjugation and the recovery of order is validated publicly as 'divine rule', or civilization.[19] And I do not find it convincing when theologians protest that this is not what Denys meant by hierarchy. This is what it has meant for women and Nature up to now, as secular scholars like Merchant and Curthoys make clear.

Effects of Hierarchical Ordering

My theological concern is that within this perspective God functions as hierarch, as an idol who presides over an order of being in
which the poor, women, indigenous peoples and the Earth are
devalued and their oppression validated. For throughout history, as
Hugo Assmann avers, the God of the rich and the God of the poor
are not the same God. Perspective really matters here. God, he
says, has been pulled from one side to the other. As hierarch, he
has been the last of the Roman emperors and the first and last of
the medieval kings. Now he is a captive of capitalism, playing the
role of the god of the mighty dollar: 'in God we trust'.

This, Assmann says, is 'true idolatry':

> Idols are
> the shining fetishes
> with divine names
> and broad smiles,
> with creeds
> with worship
> with prayers
> with laws
> with sacred and divine power
>   power to oppress
>   power to exploit
>   power to kill.
>
> The dominators,
> the idolatrous,
>   will never make the mistake
>   of declaring themselves atheists.[20]

On the contrary, as Assmann knows, the dominators often
parade their Christianity. Pinochet, when under house arrest in
Britain in 1998, had his personal chaplain flown over from Chile to
celebrate Mass in the house. He is described, and describes himself, as 'a devout Catholic'. Within this idolatrous hierarchy, 'God'
is assumed to sanction the effects of military, political, social and
economic oppression, visible in the violence inflicted through mil-
itarism; in inequality of power and the incapacity to achieve well-
being; in over-exploitation of the Earth by industry and in the
effects on it of overpopulation by humans. For, in regard to the latter point, if it is assumed that the divine purpose in creating the

Earth and all its inhabitants is the emergence of humankind, the only value attached to Earth becomes its value to us. Human multiplication then, our right to exist whatever the cost to the Earth, can be taken as part of that purpose. And 'custodianship', ultimately, is geared to making human existence as comfortable, and as prolonged, as possible. Whatever biotechnology is proposed, and whatever its impact on the environment, the overriding and apparently unassailable argument in its favour is *always* its benefit to human well-being.

Women and Nature

One of the strongest and most enduring patriarchal/hierarchical distinctions made by men (understandably based on a biological one) has been that between them and women. This has been paralleled by an identification of women with Nature, which in turn has led historically to a personification of 'Nature' as female, and to images of Earth as maternal, nurturing, fruitful, passive and virginal, images bolstered by metaphorical clusters around seed, womb, fertility and barrenness which imply an active partner, man.[21] The enduring relationship between man and woman, 'husbandry', was used to describe his closest working relationship with the Earth, with its connotations of 'penetrating' virgin forest or soil, sowing seed on the analogy of marital sowing, and ploughing for the procreation of children.[22] When made on the basis of a hierarchical order of being, it has led to femaleness, either in women or Nature, being defined, in every sense, solely from the dominant male perspective. Indeed within this order, the male form itself has been taken to define complete or perfect humanness, and the use of the male form, whether in body or in language, taken as generic. An *Atlas of Physiology and Anatomy of the Human Body*, first published in 1906 and reprinted in 1984, illustrates the male body alone.

This physical apartheid has been linked to another important element in women's struggle for identity, the dichotomy between Nature and Culture, in which men are identified with culture. One of its supporting pillars has been the distinction in Hellenic culture between the supremacy of order (cosmos) over meaningless desolation (*chaos*). The achieving of this supremacy formed part of the worldview of the Greeks and every European ruling class which followed them. Carolyn Merchant traces its influence throughout the American capitalist project, where the city epitomizes 'the transformation of female Nature into female Civilisation through the mutually reinforcing powers of male energy and interest-earning capital'. The city became the locus of power operating in the natural world, sweeping everything towards its centre: the bridge between civilized female form and the raw matter of the surrounding hinterlands, transforming natural resources into capitalist commodities.[23] Building cities became synonymous with building culture. Culture then became identified with the supremacy of male power over *chaos*; with imposing order on a very Earthy substantiality which included slaves, foreigners, pagans or country-dwellers, women and potentially unruly freedmen, and which, prior to its ordering through cultural categories and projects, remained in a state of flux.

Christianity, from this perspective, can be seen to have overcome its chaotic origins in Galilee and through the preaching of Paul in the cities around the Aegean, and then through its assimilation into the Roman Empire, become largely an urban religion.[24] Its ceremonies became confined within hierarchical church structures, the largest being built in, or even creating, cities, and those outside city boundaries under the jurisdiction of urban episcopal centres. Any other form of worship was, and is, anathematized as 'pagan'.

A defining moment in the Christian imaginary of the city was the metaphorical cluster in the New Testament book of *Revelations*, which opposed Jerusalem (which comes down from God out of heaven) and Babylon, the latter the dwelling place of demons, the haunt of foul spirits.[25] Augustine's magnum opus, *The City of God*, built on these metaphors, presented the spiritual history of the City of God invisibly intertwined with the secular history of the City of Man. The first represents the collectivity of the saved, the second the 'lump of perdition'. In the latter, 'the lust for domination lords it over its princes as over the nations it subjugates; in the other, both those put in authority and those subject to them serve one another in love, the rulers by their counsel, the subjects by obedience'. At the last Judgment, these cities will separate from each other finally and visibly. Then the City of God will appear as the New Jerusalem.

Catherine Keller, making this analysis, remarks that Augustine's allegorical dualism reinforces a foundational (if not uncritical) loyalty to the imperial and civil order. His secondary metaphors of the *civitas pellegrina*, the pilgrim city, passing through the degraded *civitas terrena,* the Earthly city, obeying its rules but not becoming attached enough to challenge the unjust ones, led, she says, to a sublime aloofness. 'The Augustinian reduction of all things creaturely to means to the timeless End secures the Western disconnection of spirit from the time rhythms of the Earth.' The 'timelessness' of eternity, Augustine argues, means that 'in eternity there is no change'. In other words, says Keller, 'changelessness is the very essence of the immovable God, whose omnipotence is steering us unwaveringly through time towards the final confrontation. Then life will be frozen eternally into one of the two possible conditions.' Once free of time (and of the Earth), the self will again reflect the image of God, in which it was created, or rather, Keller notes, in which men were created. For Augustine, women, while redeemable as such, only possess the image of God inasmuch as they are coupled with men, as body to head.[26]

Defining Nature/Earth

These historic processes have built on and built up a perception of Nature/Earth, women/body as material, irrational, passive, dependent and immanent, needing to be subordinated to, and dominated and civilized by, culture, man, reason and spirit which are rational, active, independent and transcendent. This perception has been publicly and religiously expressed in Christian teaching about women which describes them, after Eve, as temptresses, fallen, lacking a soul and incapable, by Nature, of redeeming themselves or mediating the knowledge of God to others. Hierarchical principles, such as male control of the household, of the city and of public order, were given the seal of sacred authority. God was to be envisaged for, and to be experienced by, women as father, husband, patriarch, king, lord, steward, custodian, pope and bishop.[27]

These hierarchical notions have applied, *a fortiori*, to Nature/Earth. And it seems to me that in the West, for men and for women, it is the concept of Nature, prior to its identification or personification with either sex, which must change and is changing. Some of the changes are charted in *Remaking Reality: Nature at the Millennium,* in which the editors point out that political-economic transformations, technological changes of astonishing power and unfathomable extent, and apocalyptic pronouncements of ecological catastrophe have put 'Nature' on the agenda as never before. They and the contributors argue for a concept of 'social Nature', that is, a Nature ordered up, manipulated and constructed, as well as animate, unpredictable and consequential. They do this while describing three different and co-existing concepts of Nature: 'first' Nature: a Marxist term for a bourgeois concept and representation of Nature as external to society (and implicitly, the city); 'second' Nature, described by Donna Haraway as 'not pre-existing its construction, but something made by us, materially and semiotically (and, implicitly, encompassing whatever is within as well as beyond the city boundary)'; and 'third' Nature, a term used for the simulated Natures of visual media, or the extraordinary optics of the geographical information system (GIS), all of which provide powerful means of manipulating Nature as 'information'. These approaches, the editors conclude, show that it is 'increasingly impossible to separate Nature off into its own ontological space. Thus, the remaking of Nature(s) has wider implications – it becomes, quite simply, a focal point for a nexus of political-economic relations, social identities, cultural orderings, and political aspirations of all kinds.'[28]

While I value the contribution made by this discussion, it is, however, clear that there are important connections between a hierarchical ordering of Nature and the Marxist perception of 'bourgeois' 'first' Nature, and between hierarchical power relations and their implications for the role and perception of women, Nature and Culture in the concept of 'second' Nature as a place and product of human construction. But against that, and more importantly for the evolution of the Western worldview, is the recognition that it is now impossible to consider Nature as outside political-economic affairs and social identities. Included in this latter are the complexity of human-environment relations and the preconceptions we bring to their description.[29]

R. G. Collingwood, in *The Idea of Nature*, finds no less than seven definitions given by Aristotle for the Greek term *physis*, usually translated as 'Nature', one of which, *the essence of things which have a source of movement in themselves*, Aristotle regarded as the true and fundamental meaning. This definition, is, according to Collingwood, to be understood as what things are when left to themselves, before 'culture' or society adapts them to our needs and desires, or, as he puts it, before they are interfered with by us.[30] (This corresponds to 'first' Nature.) But, as Donna Haraway and others point out, and as Gaia theory and its study of the interactions between life and its environment demonstrates, once we have arrived, as it were, on the scene, the things are no longer left to themselves. Once life, in the form of living organisms, emerged from Earth's environment, 'Nature' was no longer 'alone'. It was subsumed in a relationship between things as they are in themselves and what they are when they are interacting with other things: a relationship of identity-in-difference. It was subsumed in the order of being called organism-with-environment/environment-with-organism. The relationship between the two constitutes their structural coupling. What kind of anthropology, what ordering of our being emerges from this coevolutionary, relational premise of interdependence and interactivity?

Belonging to the Coevolutionary Order

The premise of a hierarchical paradigm is a Platonic, neo-Platonic, Christian anthropology, based on assumed ontological spaces between the human and the animal which precede and establish dichotomies between Culture and Nature, between reason and instinct, between morality and physicality. Tim Ingold enumerates and then vigorously challenges these 'stale dichotomies', as he calls them. His work brings together some of the important anthropological issues raised by a coevolutionary worldview. Specifically, his descriptions of what it means for us to belong to, and to dwell within, the order of organism-in-environment parallels a coevolutionary order, in which being and activity are so related as to assume fundamental similarities between humans and animals while exploring differences between them.

This paradoxical similarity/dissimilarity, according to Ingold, resides in the fact that 'the difference between (say) a goose and a man is not between an organism and a person, but between one kind of organism-person and another . . . [P]ersonhood is not the manifest form of humanity; rather the human is one of the many outward forms of personhood.'[31] Within this one world, he says, humans figure not as composites of body and mind but as undivided beings, 'organism-persons', relating as such both to other humans and to non-human agencies and entities in their environment. 'Between these spheres of involvement there is no absolute separation, they are but contextually delimited segments of a single field.' It is, therefore, as entire persons, not as disembodied minds, that humans engage with one another and, moreover, with non-human beings as well, and vice versa. 'They do so as beings in a world, not as minds which, excluded from a given reality, find themselves in the predicament of having to make sense of it.' He coins the term 'interagentivity' to describe the constitutive quality of their world.[32]

Ingold's descriptions of personhood as a relational event, a process, an activity, remind me of Gerard Manley Hopkins's lines:

> Each mortal thing does one thing and the same;
> Deals out that being indoors each one dwells;
> Selves – goes itself; *myself* it speaks and spells
> Crying *What I do is me: for that I came.*[33]

The relationship between being, activity and environment is such that, in regard to the assumed dichotomy between Nature and culture, Ingold concludes: 'The world can exist as "Nature" only for a being who does not belong there, and who can look upon it, in the manner of the detached scientist [sic], from such a safe distance that it is easy to connive in the illusion that it is unaffected by his presence.' This accords with the coevolutionary premise, and with Ingold's own, that there can be no organism without an environment, and no environment without an organism. For environments are forged through the activities of living beings, and as long as life goes on, both are continually under construction.[34] (This, for me, is another way of describing coevolutionary process.) Therefore he takes the human condition to be 'that of a being immersed from the start, like other creatures, in an active, practical and perceptual engagement with constituents of the dwelt-in world'. This ontology of dwelling, he contends, provides us with a better way of coming to grips with the Nature of human existence than the alternative Western ontology. Its point of departure is that of a mind detached from the world, one which has literally to formulate that world prior to any attempt at engagement. For Ingold, however, and for an organism structurally coupled with its environment: '[A]pprehending the world is not a matter of construction but of engagement, not of building but of dwelling, not of making a view *of* the world but of taking up a view *in* it.'[35]

How could we then, taking such a view of ourselves and of the Earth, and realizing that we have emerged out of it and depend totally on the infinite complexity of its life-support systems, see ourselves as its custodians? Or considering its age, how can we think our 'custody' essential to it, since it managed on its own not only since it was formed, but in the billions of years it evolved before we emerged? And considering what we have done to it, would naming ourselves its custodians not seem, in James

Lovelock's forceful phrase, rather like giving a goat custody of a garden, one it had already almost stripped bare? What does its present state tell us about its 'sacred' Nature, sacrificed to the 'sacredness' we claim for our own? And what will become of it, and of our children, if we continue to see it as the Augustinian *City of Man*, the Earthly, decaying city through which we make a pilgrimage to the heavenly, unchanging Jerusalem where God walks on sapphire pavements?[36] All of these questions permit more than one answer.

Notes

Some of the arguments covered here are treated at greater length in my book: *Sacred Gaia: Holistic Theology and Earth Systems Science* (London: Routledge, 2000).

1 M. Foucault, *The Order of Things: An Archaeology of the Human Sciences* (London: Routledge, 1970), p. i–xx.
2 Ibid., pp. 128–45.
3 Ibid., p. xvii.
4 C. Geertz, *The Interpretation of Cultures: Selected Essays* (London: Fontana, 1993), pp. 87–125.
5 Acts 17:27–28.
6 A. Louth, *The Origins of the Christian Mystical Tradition: From Plato to Denys* (Oxford: Clarendon Press, 1990), pp. 162–78.
7 A. Primavesi, *From Apocalypse to Genesis: Ecology, Feminism and Christianity* (Tunbridge Wells: Burns and Oates, 1991), pp. 89–99.
8 W. M. Abbott, ed., *Documents of Vatican II* (London: Geoffrey Chapman, 1966), pp. 37–56.
9 G. Ellis and N. Murphy, *On the Moral Nature of the Universe: Theology, Cosmology and Ethics* (Philadelphia: Fortress, 1996), pp. 19–37, 202f.
10 C. Geertz, *Local Knowledge: Further Essays in Interperative Anthropology* (London: Fontana, 1993), pp. 121–46.
11 D. Nicholls, *Deity and Domination: Image of God and the State in the Nineteenth and Twentieth Centuries* (London: Routledge, 1994).
12 J. Moltmann, *Trinity and the Kingdom of God: The Doctrine of God* (London: SCM, 1981).
13 R. M. Schwartz, *The Curse of Cain: The Violent Legacy of Monotheism* (Chicago: University of Chicago Press, 1997).
14 Articles by F. Hinkelammert and H. Assmann, in *The Idols of Death and the God of Life: A Theology*, eds P. Richard and B. E. Campbell (Maryknoll, New York: Orbis Books, 1983).
15 R. R. Ruether, *Sexism and God Talk: Toward a Feminist Theology* (Boston: Beacon Press, 1983); N. Morton, *The Journey is Home* (Boston: Beacon Press, 1985); J. Plaskow, *Standing Again at Sinai: Judaism from a Feminist Perspective* (New York: Harper Collins, 1990); Primavesi, *Apocalypse to Genesis*.
16 Primavesi, *Apocalypse to Genesis*, pp. 195–222; V. Plumwood, *Feminism and the Mastery of Nature* (London: Routledge, 1993), pp. 165–90.

17 J. Curthoys, *Feminist Amnesia: The Wake of Women's Liberation* (London: Rout-
    ledge, 1997), p. 70.
18 P. K. Brubaker, *Women Don't Count: The Challenge of Women's Poverty to Chris-
    tian Ethics* (Atlanta, Ga.: Scholars Press, 1994); C. S. Robb, *Equal Value* (Boston:
    Beacon Press, 1995).
19 Primavesi, *Apocalypse to Genesis*, pp. 85–110; C. Merchant, *Earthcare: Women
    and the Environment* (London: Routledge, 1995), pp. 27–47.
20 H. Assmann, in *Idols of Death and the God of Life*, (Mary Knoll, New York: Orbis
    Books, 1983) eds P. Richard and B. E. Campbell, p. 204f.
21 C. Merchant, *The Death of Nature: Women, Ecology and the Scientific Revolution*
    (New York: Harper and Row, 1980).
22 Primavesi, *Apocalypse to Genesis*, pp. 33–36; pp. 46–54; pp. 61–64.
23 Merchant, *Earthcare*, p. 47f.
24 W. Meeks, *The First Urban Christians: The Social World of the Apostle Paul* (New
    Haven: Yale University Press, 1983).
25 Rev. 3:12; 18:2–3.
26 C. Keller, *Apocalypse Now and Then* (Boston: Beacon Press: 1996), pp. 97–103.
27 Primavesi, *Apocalypse to Genesis*, pp. 46–48, pp. 198–202.
28 D. Harraway in *Remaking Reality: Nature at the Millennium*, eds B. Braun and
    N. Castree (London: Routledge, 1998), pp. 3–42.
29 K. Milton, 'Nature and the Environment in Indigenous and Traditional Cultures'
    in *Spirit of the Environment*, eds D. Cooper and J. Palmer (London: Routledge,
    1998), pp. 86–99.
30 R. G. Collingwood, *The Idea of Nature* (Oxford: Oxford University Press, 1960),
    p. 80f.
31 T. Ingold, 'Hunting and Gathering as Ways of Perceiving the Environment' in
    Redefining Nature: Ecology, Culture and Domestication, eds R. Ellen and K.
    Fukui (Oxford: Berg, 1996), p. 132ff.
32 Ibid., pp. 128–9.
33 G. M. Hopkins, *The Poems of Gerald Manley Hopkins*, ed. R. Bridges (Oxford:
    Oxford University Press, 1930), p. 53.
34 T. Ingold, in 'Culture, Nature, Environment: Steps to an Ecology of Life', in
    Mind, Brain and the Environment, ed. B. Cartledge (Oxford: Oxford University
    Press, 1998), pp 158–80 at p. 170.
35 Ingold, 'Hunting and Gathering', pp. 120ff.
36 Exodus, 24:10.

9

Text and Practice: Women and Nature in Islam

Tahera Aftab

And Allah has produced
You from the earth
Growing (gradually)
And in the End
He will return you
Into the (earth),
And raise you forth
(Again at the Resurrection)
And Allah has made
The earth for you
As a carpet (spread out)
That ye may go about
Therein, in spacious roads.

(S.71:17–20)

In the relationship between women, earth and environment in Muslim societies there are two dimensions to consider: ideological and ethical frameworks from the perspective of the *Quran* and the Hadith; and the ways in which institutions and persons in authority have acted antithetically to processes of justice (*adl*), and equity (*ihsan*), thereby de-linking women from their natural roles. An approach is proposed in which women's role as 'custodians of the earth' can be restructured, resulting in community development initiatives. Thus, the chapter seeks to provide a broad-based spectrum of human beings' relationship with earth, nature and the cosmos, a relationship which is not limited to one single group or a community but a relationship which moves far beyond all frontiers. The core argument is built around women's lives and emerges out of a conviction that a negation of women's central role as guardians and upholders of Earth's sanctity is a major act of violence against women, children and society and is an abrogation of women's human rights. Societal impingements and increasingly the usurpation of women's rights by men has created barriers between women and their access to the resources of nature. This restriction is often justified as a safety measure to protect the identity of the Muslim community, the Ummah. This usurpation is an act of violence with repercussions on the whole of society.

During the last few decades there has been much research and many publications on various aspects of Muslim women's lives. Of these publications, the majority are concerned with the ineffectiveness of Muslim women as active partners in life within their respective communities. A common concern is the presumed role of Islam as a retrogressive factor in curtailing women's equality. Although empirical evidence documenting the horrible episodes of the 'harem's in-side stories' and women's helplessness in Muslim societies grows, analytical bias-free studies are few and less accessible to the general reader. Scholars of Islam, both within and outside the community, have selected the themes of their research and writings that contest the issue of power for the sake of perpetuating and creating power hierarchies.

Equality of Women and Men:
The Quran's Perspective

As I understand it, with the revelation of the Quran began a movement committed to the elimination of gender bias and sexist oppression. Not only was woman absolved of being the original sinner and of enticing and seducing Adam into disobedience and the subsequent Fall (S.2:36), but the Quran by declaring that, 'O mankind! ('*Ya ayyu-han-nasu*' – the Arabic word '*nas*' means human beings and therefore it is worth noting that both men and women are addressed in this verse) reverence Your Guardian-Lord, Who created you from a single soul (*Nafsin vahedatin)*'(S.4:1; 7:189; 39:6) establishes beyond all doubt that men and women are created equal. In another revelation the Quran explaining the process of creation says, 'We created man (*Khalaq-nal insana)* from sounding clay, from mud moulded into shape' (S.15:26).

Woman as Khalifa on Earth

In any discussion on the theme of women, gender, and human relationships, it is essential to note that there are three distinct ways in which God chose to address human beings in the Quran. First, the Quran addresses all human beings, men and women, Muslims and non-Muslims, living on this earth or in some other worlds. Secondly, it addresses specific communities and groups. Thirdly, it addresses Muslim men and women, together or separately. The themes of the verses also differ according to the persons addressed. Issues and themes related to life in general, rules of ethics, worship, and conduct are addressed to all human beings. One must note that there is a difficulty arising out of the translations of the Arabic text of the Quran into other languages, particularly the English language. Thus, for instance, the Arabic word *insana*, which means 'human beings' is usually translated as *man*, creating a fallacy of gender discrimination. Taking this further when studying God's revelations in the Quran one notices that the word *Adam* and *insana* are used for human beings, men and women both. Thus when God says 'I will create a viceregent on earth' (S.2:30) it is equally applicable to both men and women.

A viceregent (*khalifa*), as all understand the term, is one who represents the appointing authority. Thus the human being created out of clay (S.33:7) with God's breath into him (her) (S.33:9) was sent down on this earth *not* as a punishment but to fulfill God's commands as his servant (*abd*).

What are these commands which the human beings agreed to perform? The Quran refers to these in terms of a Trust (*amanh*). The ethics of human relationship with Earth is deeply rooted in this verse. The Quran says:

> We did indeed offer
> The Trust to the Heavens
> And the Mountains:
> But they refused
> To undertake it,
> But man undertook it:
> He was indeed unjust
> And foolish. (S.33: 72)

There are certain prerequisites for a holder of the Trust, even when the deal is between two human beings. This Trust is between the Creator, who 'is the Cherisher and Sustainer of the Worlds' (S.1:2), and not of one exclusive, privileged community of one world and of one particular time. In *Sura Nisaa* (the women) the Trust holder is 'commanded to render back your trusts to those to whom they are due'. Trust is explained as doing justice and doing good work on this earth: 'but do thou good, as Allah has been good to thee, and seek not mischief on this earth. For Allah loves not those who do mischief' (S.28:77).

It is to these human beings, who entered into a covenant with Him that God bestowed all that is on earth, 'Seest thou not that Allah has made subject to you all that is on the earth, and the ships that sail through the sea by His command' (S.22:65). This bestowal increases further with an example of those who are wayward and dispute about God's Bounty in S.31:20, 'Do ye not see that Allah has subjected to your (use) all things in the heavens and on the earth, and has made His bounties flow to you in exceeding measure, [both] seen and unseen? Yet there are among men (*annas*) who dispute about Allah, without knowledge and without a Book to enlighten them.' It is important to note here that this subjection of all that is on earth (*ard*) and in the heavens (*samavat*) is not purposeless. The 'subjection of all things' is not meant to be the subjugation and appropriation of all things. The Quran, referring to this subjection, warns: 'behold, in that are the signs indeed for those who reflect'(S.45:13). Those who follow the path of righteousness and ponder over these signs, men or women, will be judged the best. Thus the Quran says: 'He it is Who created the heavens and the earth in six days and His Throne was over the Waters – That He might try you, which of you is best in conduct.' (S.11:7) In this verse, *Sura Hud,* a Meccan verse, 'stress is laid on the side which deals with justice and the punishment of sin when all Grace is resisted'.[1] The reference to the 'best conduct' in conjunction with the earth and heaven is worth noting in the context of the theme of this chapter.

Before analysing the relationship between women and earth let us attempt to understand the concept of 'best conduct' (*ahsanu amala*) as explained in the Quran. In several verses the Quran says that 'verily the most honoured of you in the sight of Allah is (the one who is) the most righteous (*a-taqaakum*) of you'. The 'best in conduct' is one who is 'the most righteous'. The word *taqwa,* often translated as piety and righteousness, is 'a unique balance of integrative moral action to protect oneself against the harmful or evil consequences of one's conduct'.[2] Arguing further, Rahman says that 'when a man or a society is fully conscious of this while

conducting himself or itself, he or it has true *taqwa*. An exact opposition of *taqwa* is the moral perversion and moral apathy[3] which
impels a person to commit one of the various forms of *'fasad-fil-ard*
(corruption on earth) (S.2:11, 27) thereby causing a loss of peace,
prosperity, and power. What is this corruption or *fasad*? The Quran
explains its meanings in various passages. One example will illustrate this wrongdoing:

> When he turns his back,
> His aim everywhere
> Is to spread mischief
> Through the earth and destroy
> Crops and cattle.
> But Allah loveth not mischief. (S.2:205)

Is *taqwa* enacted by men only? Amina Wadud says that the two
components of *taqwa*: 'faith and action or mental consciousness
and good practice remove *taqwa* from any possible disparity on the
basis of gender'.[4] One fundamental aspect of the Quran is the uni-
versality of its message for both men and women. Thus, *taqwa*
transcends gender difference. Indeed the Quranic vision of
women's activities and role is not confined by any boundaries.
Taqwa, therefore, is a virtue to be sought both by men and women,
as the actions of both can create a good life or cause corruption on
this earth. That women are, and should be, active agents in keeping God's Trust on earth is made clear in the Quran statement :

> And he that works a righteous deed –
> whether man or woman – and is a believer –
> Such will enter the garden of Bliss. (S.40:40)

In the Quran the word *earth* (*ard*) is used 460 times, the expression 'heaven and earth' (*samawat wal ard*) occurs well over 200
times.[5] Although a mere numeration of words used in the Quran,
without an understanding of the spirit of the Word itself, will not
instruct the reader as to the exact purpose of the revelation, it suggests the emphasis that Allah wishes to place on earth, heaven and
its inter-connectedness with human beings. Explaining the verbal
root of the word *ard* Murata says 'it means to thrive and produce;
to become fruitful; to be soft when trod upon and pleasant when
sat upon; to be lowly, submissive, naturally disposed to do good'.[6]
The earth, therefore, is assigned a series of roles, each sustaining
and drawing upon each other, with the sole purpose of protecting

and guarding Divine creation. This role of the earth is clearly charted in *Sura al-Hijr*, the central theme of which is to show the Divine Signs (*ayas*) 'that make things clear'. (These are the Ayats of Revelation, of a Quran 'that makes things clear' S.15:1.) This verse reveals the remarkable Muslim relationship with earth. Let us first ponder on the Divine words:

> 19. And the earth We have
> spread out
> (Like a carpet); set thereon
> Mountains firm and immovable;
> And produced therein all kinds
> Of things in due balance.
> 20. And We have provided therein
> Means of subsistence, – for you
> And for those whose sustenance
> Ye are not responsible.
> 21. And there is not a thing
> But its (sources and) treasures
> (inexhaustible) are with Us;
> But We only send down
> Thereof in due and ascertainable
> measures.

The above verse sums up the spirit on which Islamic principles of human relationships with each other, with nature and the principles of conservation of environment are based. Ibn Taymiyah, the medieval Muslim jurist, further explained the significance of these Divine words:

> In considering all these verses it must be remembered that Allah in His wisdom created these creatures for reasons other than serving man, for in these verses He only explains the benefits of these creatures.[7]

It is in this aspect of earth, as provider of sustenance, that Muslim scholars and Sufis discovered a reflection of women's role. Rumi, the most famous of the Sufi poets, wrote:

> In the view of the intellect, heaven is the man
> and earth the woman.
> Whatever the one throws down,
> the other nurtures.[8]

Similar to Rumi's poetical expression some other thirteenth-century Muslim Sufis, such as Nasafi[9] and Ibn Arabi[10] found a relationship between earth and women. Ibn Arabi in his work *al-Futuhat al-makkiya,* writing about fathers and mothers makes a similar point:

> God placed between heaven and earth a supra-formal conjunction and an attentiveness toward the children – the minerals, plants, and animals – which He desired to bring into existence in the earth. He made the earth like the wife and the heaven like the husband. The heaven casts something of the command that God revealed to it into the earth, just as the man casts water into the woman through intercourse. When the casting takes place, the earth brings out all the strata of the engendered things that God has concealed within it.[11]

Indeed Ibn al-Arabi, while commenting on the verses of the Quran that man is made out of earth (S.15:26), said: 'For it is the Mother from whom we emerged and to whom we will emerge once again. To her we are submitted and entrusted.'[12]

Representation of Women in Traditional Sources

Traditional sources, Quranic exegesis (*tafsir*), jurisprudence (*fiqh*), and scholastic theology (*kalam*) along with Sufi works (*malfuzat* and *tazkireh*) require to be treated with caution in regard to information about women and their status, as although all four draw their inspiration, as well as authority, from the Quran and the Hadith, they move away from both in a complex fashion. Out of the jumbled mass of this rhetoric, it is usually a semi-educated religious orator who addresses the crowd of men gathered on Fridays and annual congregational prayer times, choosing texts to suit his own viewpoint. Time and space, ethno-cultural influences, political and economic pressures, and above all human nature, as being 'unjust and foolish' (S.33:72) and prone to 'plot against their own souls' (S.6:123), have created a plethora of anti-women writings. These writings are an antithesis to Islam's concept that all human relationships are established on justice *(adl)* and equity (*ihsan*).

Muslim jurists (*faqih*) are credited with volumes luminous on a variety of religious themes, from defining punishments for disobedient women to polemics over divorce, marriages, and number of children that a woman should bear, and to types of fish prohibited or permissible for a Muslim, have circumvented the study of Islam's ethics of environment and ecological preservation. More tragic than this omission is that some of these studies have wrong-fully sided with the sham notion that women are not only non-active agents contributing little to their society's betterment but indeed are the cause of *fitna* (chaos) and must therefore be controlled and contained. In some philosophical treatises on Muslim ethics (*Akhlaqiat*), for example Nasir al-Din al-Tusi's (d.1274 CE) *Akhlaq-i Nasiri,* women's position is made subject to the fulfilment of men's needs. Tusi was not only read widely but his work *Akhlaq-i-Nasiri long* remained part of Muslim boys' syllabus. In *Akhlaq-i-Nasiri* he instructs his male readers that, 'Divine wisdom has decreed that every man should take a mate, who will both attend to the care of the household and its contents and through whom the work of procreation will be accomplished.' That to women alone God has bestowed the unique privilege of conceiving and giving birth so that the purpose of creation continues is not disputed as the Quran also refers to this (S.46:15). What shocks the sensibility of a Muslim is Tusi's further argument which apparently contradicts the spirit of Islam. He writes that 'women are moved by the jealousy rooted in their natures, together with the deficiency of their intelligence and ignominies'. He went further, to the extent of contradicting the *Sunna* of the Prophet, and warned husbands not to show excessive affection to their wives or to consult them on issues of major importance.[13] I assume that the significant role of the Prophet's first wife, Khadija, immediately after the First Revelation was known to him. I quote here the most important event of Islam to show how misleading and injurious Tusi's inference is. After the first encounter with Archangel Gabriel (Jibraeel of the Quran) at Mount Hira, the Prophet 'shaken' by the Majesty of the Divine Word returned home and confided it to his wife. Ibn Ishaq in his biography of the Prophet quotes this unusual incident in the very words of the Prophet:

> And I came to Khadija and sat by her thigh and drew close to her. She said, 'O Abu al-Qasim (that is Muhammad, here called 'Father of Qasim', his first son, who did not survive), where have you been? By God, I sent my messengers in search of you and they reached the high ground above Mecca and returned to me.' Then I told her what I had seen; and she said, 'Rejoice, O son of my uncle, and be of good heart. Verily, by Him in whose hand is Khadija's soul, I have hope that you will be the prophet of this people.'[14]

How historical evidence can be twisted to support issues of power and control is best illustrated by another example in the writings of Nizam al-Mulk. He makes woman responsible for Adam's suffering and later, referring to an incident when the Prophet, because of illness, could no longer lead the prayers and wished Abu Bakr to do so, attempts to prove that women should not be consulted as they are incapable of arriving at right decisions. Ayesha, the Prophet's wife, however, felt otherwise. She suggested that instead of Abu Bakr, Omer would be a better choice. The Prophet rejected her suggestions and the prayers were led by Abu Bakr. Showing an utter misunderstanding of the Mission of the Prophet, Nizam al-Mulk draws this inference: 'in spite of all the nobility, the learning, the devotion and piety of Ayisha (may Allah be pleased with her), the Prophet (upon him be peace) did the opposite of what she wanted. So imagine what the opinions of other women are worth.'[15] Thus, Nizam al-Mulk attempted to prove that women are incapable of making correct decisions. Long before the colonization of Muslim lands by Europeans took place, ideas about women, such as these, had already begun the 'colonization' of Muslim women by Muslim men. The patriarchal tendency in Muslim societies to elevate men and to degrade women has not yet ended. Curiously these exploitative ideas have surfaced in recent works on ethics in Iran. Hojatoleslam A. A. Akhtari, a religious leader, in his *Akhlaqeh Hamsardari Eslami (Ethics of Islamic Marriage)* referring to men said that their 'wisdom, judgement, integrity and farsightedness' enables them to 'control and curb the hiatus caused by the unruly passion of women'.[16] Muslim society, by subjugating women and taking away their rights, cannot function as a community 'justly balanced' and as 'witness over other nations' (S.21:143).

A study on the relationship of Muslim women and Earth, therefore, extends far beyond the mere environmental concerns. It studies, examines and interprets all aspects of life on earth. Indeed, to understand the relationship between women and Earth one has to study all aspects of development.

An inquiry into the Quranic view of the relationship between women and Earth is an urgent need in Muslim societies. The Message of the Quran is addressed to both men and women. Thus Islamic environmental ethics, explains Mawil Y. Izzi Deen, is based on the concept that all human relationships are established on justice (*adl*) and equity (*ihsan*): 'Lo! Allah enjoineth justice and kindness' (S.16:90).[17] Such a study will not only further enlarge religious scholarship, it will provide an agency to address the urgent need of millions of men, women, and children forced to exist without water, food, and shelter.

During my early childhood I was initiated into a sacred relationship with the Earth by my mother and other older women relatives. I am sure persons of my age, living in beehive-type houses of a small town in North India, where the end was the beginning and the beginning was the end, a circle within the circle, would recount similar childhood anecdotes. I was told not to 'hurt' the Earth by throwing things at her as the Earth has a tender heart, and when she gets hurt, she cries in pain, and God sitting above on his throne takes note of this appeal. The person causing this hurt will be punished. We were warned not to jump down from tree-tops on to the ground below as it would cause tremors in the Earth's heart. I also remember my mother instructing me not to waste water (water was not scarce at all, as there were several wells of sweet water and one handpump drilled into one of these wells), and throw food crumbs around while eating our meals. On the Day of Judgement we will be answerable for all that we have 'consumed' and wasted. In fact I was careful to collect bits of bread as I was made to believe that on the Day of Judgement we would have to pick up all the bits of food that we had thrown away and wasted with our eyelashes. These anecdotes should not be regarded as mere women's tales. They emanate from an ideology which I would recognize as grounded in Quranic culture. Later, on reading the *Sura Zilzal* I could understand what my warnings of childhood meant. The *Sura* describing the tremendous tumultuous convulsions of the Earth on the Last Day says that on that Day, the Earth will 'declare her tidings' and on that Day all human beings will 'proceed in companies sorted out to be shown the deeds that they had done' (S.99:4,6). My mother warned me that I should be extra careful lest I trample on little ants hurrying hither and thither because when they get hurt or killed they shriek and their cries reach the skies. As a young child watching the troop of ants marching out of tiny cracks of earth swollen by monsoon rains I was never able to catch any sound made, but I remained very scared of my mother's warning that on the Day of Judgement these ants will stand up and will charge me of causing them harm. These childhood anecdotes may have a marked local stamp, however they emerge from the Quran and the Hadith and have, therefore, a universal message. Let us turn to the *Sura Anam* and see what wisdom is there:

There is not an animal
(That lives) on the earth,

Nor a being that flies
On its wings, but (forms
Part of) communities like you.
Nothing have we omitted
From the Book, and they (all)
Shall be gathered to their Lord
In the end. (S.6:38)

The Prophet Muhammad, known to Muslims as *Rahmat al-alameen* (God's Mercy on planets), considered all living things worthy of protection (*hurmah*) and kind treatment. He discouraged cruelty towards animals: 'For (charity shown to) each creature which has a wet heart there is reward.'[18] The Quran warns that 'Allah loveth not the wasters' (S.6:141).

Women in Muslim societies have lost touch with their traditions. The reasons for this are complex: the majority of Muslim women are victims of illiteracy. Thus they are inadequately prepared even for an effective role of parenting, a role which is publicized as the only role befitting a Muslim woman. Lack of knowledge and awareness about their own potential has dwarfed their personalities so that the majority of them have little understanding of the purpose of their lives. It is my basic premise that the widespread illiteracy among Muslim women around the globe has made it difficult for them to assert their natural (human) and even their legal rights and has limited their access to the world outside. It has also 'de-linked' any sacred connection between them and the Earth. By this severing Muslim societies have suffered an insurmountable loss, spiritually as well as materially.

Today Muslim societies are plagued by three afflictions: wastefulness of their natural resources, destruction of the environment, and under-utilization of their human resources. All three are rooted in one single factor: an imbalance in the social structure, which creates and sustains unnatural distribution of resources. A search for the causes of this affliction should begin by a self-assessment. The Quran has already declared:

Whatever misfortune
Happens to you, is because
Of the things your hands
Have wrought, and for many
(of them) He grants forgiveness (S.42:30).

What are these misfortunes to which God refers in this verse? It is not self-injury. The verses following verse 30 quoted above refer to 'evil which men have earned', to 'greater crimes and shameful deeds'. In verse 42 of the same Sura we find a connection between wrongdoing, exploitation of the earth and human misery:

> The blame is only
> Against those who oppress
> Men (annas) with wrong-doing (yazlemmoon)
> And insolence transgress
> Beyond bounds through the land [ard],
> Defying right and justice:
> For such there will be
> A Penalty grievous. (S.42:42)

The essence of the verse, which is also the spirit of Islam, is to warn against wrongdoing and causing harm to people on this Earth. One meaning of the very word 'Islam' (or Salam = submission) is peace. Can there be a peace on earth if people are not allowed to survive, if life, in all its forms, is threatened? Izutsu, a Japanese scholar of Quranic studies, explains the inherent meaning of the two terms, wrongdoing and transgression, as follows: 'In the sphere of ethics it seems to mean primarily "to act in such a way as to transgress the proper limit and encroach upon the right of some other person". Briefly and generally speaking, *zulm* is to do injustice in the sense of going beyond one's own bounds and doing what one has no right to.'[19]

Among the most deprived and exploited of human beings are women in all societies. This ill-treatment of women, a common factor in all Muslim societies, is a total repudiation in action of the Divine Command:

> O ye who believe!
> Ye are forbidden to inherit
> Women against their will.
> Nor should ye treat them
> With harshness.(S.4:19)

Women and land have become items of possession within Muslim societies. Both women and land can be controlled, disputed, exchanged and gifted to settle discords and to create alliances. Some even disparage them as the source of all feuds and fights.[20] In Sindh, Pakistan, 'sangawatti' or the politics of marriage may determine the fate of a woman long before her birth. In exchange marriages, if women of productive age are not available, pledges are made in a custom called *paith likhi diyan* – to pledge a pregnancy – in which a woman not yet born is pledged into marriage in the exchange. In Upper Sindh, especially Larkana, the father who makes the transactions prefers to charge half the money for his daughter in bride-price and the other half is charged as a *sangh* (Sindhi: marriage contract). The same daughter will return a daughter, born to her, to the father who would then pass on the girl to his agnates (paternal relatives) in the exchange deal.[21] Here one may draw a tragic connection between women and exploitation of nature and Earth. As Shaheen Sardar Ali writes, women in some parts of Pakistan 'are by and large excluded from inheritance in general and landed property in general. The major reason is that since descent and recognition is reckoned through male ascendants, a woman inheriting her father's land is seen as snatching it away from the rightful owners and passing it to her husband's alien family.'[22]

Water scarcity today is a nightmare in most Muslim countries. This scarcity is both natural and man-made. Bad management and misappropriation of natural resources by those who are in power has often caused the drying-up of water resources. Women and girls are, therefore, forced to spend long hours in fetching water, while the local administration, overlooking the needs of water supply, spends money on construction of roads and other 'high-tech' projects. One would agree with Murata when she wrote about man's position as viceregent and as servant to God: 'Without servanthood, the urge to viceregency becomes what we see before our eyes: the rape of the environment and the destruction of all those values and institutions that help human beings achieve servanthood and peace.'[23]

Earth is not a mute entity. It moves, grows, and dies. It lives a life of its own. Earth is not a mere geological occurrence. It was created with a purpose. It moves within a set pattern. It has the power and the potential to mould others. More importantly Earth is to be respected.[24] It is to be respected as God has blessed it (S.41:10):

He set on the (earth)
Mountains standing firm,
High above it,
And bestowed blessings on
The earth, and measured therein
All things to give them
Nourishment in due proportion,
In four Days, in accordance
With (the needs of)
Those who seek (sustenance).

To preserve and protect a blessed creation of God is, therefore, a meritorious act.

Women and Earth: The Development Discourse

It was perhaps Esther Boserup's ground-breaking work in which she stressed that 'women not only collected and consumed what grew in nature but they made things grow' that a new area of investigation into women's exploitation gained ground. Out of this emerged concerns for women and ecology.[25]

With the debate on ecofeminism, women's issues are now increasingly discussed as emerging out of the 'rape of the earth'. Millions of women around the world are poor and resourceless. Women who manage households, particularly in rural areas, experience soil erosion, deforestation, contaminated water supplies, and shortage of food and fuel. It is from the herbs and plants that a woman still treats her family's illnesses. As mothers and as family carers, women are probably now more burdened with work as they toil to provide for the well-being and comfort of their families. Research into the causes of dwindling resources reveals that the growing market economy, with capitalist concerns as the main focus, have displaced women as traditional custodians and conservators of the Earth and the environment.

This research has also revealed that the development paradigms, set in the main by the experts from the First World (a World which in the recent past, benefited from the plunder of the resources of the countries for whom the development programmes are now created) have been too little concerned with gender needs and sustainable resource use. Thus women who were already victims of double discrimination by their own men, and through exploitation during centuries of colonization of their lands, are now experiencing the third phase of their misery. Women researchers, in particular, Merchant[26] and Shiva,[27] taking a radical stance on the relationship between gender, environment, and Earth, have presented new 'ecofeminist' theories critiquing the development paradigms marketed aggressively by the West. The ecofeminists argue that in new development planning and techniques, the domination of nature and the domination of women run in parallel. This chapter, dealing with the themes in the light of the Quran, finds itself echoing Shiva's statement. She writes: 'Industrialism created a limitless appetite for resource exploitation, and modern science provided the ethical and cognitive license to make such exploitation possible, acceptable – and desirable. The new relationship of man's domination and mastery over nature was, thus, also associated with new patterns of domination and mastery over women and their exclusion from participation *as partners* in both science and development.'[28] The idea that development strategies, such as those described by Shiva, are halting the pace of development, is gaining support in countries where development is urgently needed. Many women in the so-called Third World societies are sceptical of development agendas which fail to consider them and their link with the land. In fact many women are convinced that development strategies are indeed instruments of vandalization and brutalization of both Earth and women.[29]

Colonization of the major Muslim societies in Asia and Africa in the past was not limited to the mere occupation of their land or to the plundering of their resources. It went far beyond it. Wande Abimbola, an African scholar, writes aptly of the colonization of 'the minds of the nations'.[30] Recognizing women's natural links with Earth and Nature will be one effective strategy of reversing this process. Thus true freedom, which is the freedom of mind and soul, will occur only when women's access to Nature is no longer hindered.

Signs of Change: Women's Self-Empowerment

How long will Muslim women remain de-linked from the Earth? Are they capable of bringing about a change for a better life? There can be no easy, direct answers to these questions. But it is not the answer which is important here. It is the question itself, as it opens the possibilities for researching, thinking, speculating, and dreaming. It is in raising this question that an iota of optimism rests.

Evidence confirms that women given access to opportunities make profitable use of them. In the chronicles of Muslim empires and kingdoms there are many records of men who ravaged the Earth by pillaging its resources, while there are more examples of women who invested their energies in harbouring and protecting Earth's resources than plundering them. Zubayda (d.831), the wife of the Abbasid Caliph, Harun al-Rashid (r.786–809), to redress the drought, constructed an aqueduct in 805 to carry water from the spring of Hunain to the city of Makkah (Mecca) some twelve miles away.[31] She also had wells and caravaserais built along the nine

155

hundred miles road, from Makka to Kufa. The road is now known as Darb-i-Zubayda.[32] Similarly, Mughal women of sixteenth-century Hindustan continuously searched for new and fresh ways for the expression of their love for Nature. Their strong relationship with Nature was very explicitly reflected in the superb gardens, canals, waterways and monuments of public utility which they created. Through their activism they displayed how well they understood the message of the Prophet when he is reported to have said: 'All creatures are God's dependents and the best among them is the one who is most useful to God's dependents.'[33]

Some noticeable changes are taking place in Muslim societies. Today women are awakening to realize that God created them as active and not as passive human beings to fulfill His Will. In the slums of Karachi, in Pakistan, 265 women and girls aged 11 and over were interviewed about self-employment. All these women related amazing tales of courage and determination. Instead of accepting a life of servitude and misery they discovered means of gainful employment, thus making this Earth a better abode for their children, their families, and themselves. Some of these resourceful women learnt on their own the art of recycling the waste and make a living out of it.[34] Umm Ali, a woman living far from Pakistan in a village near Beirut, a village school drop-out, married with five children, has made her own way as an entrepreneur. Umm Ali says: 'To me there is no difference between boys and girls. They are equal and all must attend school because education is the ground for everything. . . Girls are capable of doing what boys can do.'[35] This awareness has led women like Gihan in Egypt to form a network called *Bint-el-ard,* Daughter of the Earth.[36]

Notes

1 A. Y. Ali, *The Holy Quran, Arabic Text with and English Translation and Commentary* (Lahore: Muhammad Ashraf, 1937–38), p. 292.
2 F. Rahman, *Major Themes of the Quran* (Minneapolis, Minn: Biblioteca Islamica, 1980), p. 28.
3 Ibid. pp. 29, 56.
4 A. Wadud, 'Woman and Islam: Beyond the Stereotypes', *Pakistan Journal of Women's Studies: Alam-e-Miswan,* 4 (2), 1997, pp. 1–14.
5 S. Murata, *The Tao of Islam: A Source Book of Gender Relationships in Islamic Thought* (Albany: State University of New York, 1992), p. 119.
6 Ibid.
7 A. Ibn Taymiyah, M. Fatawa (Rabat: Saudi Educational Attache, n.d). quoted by Mawil Y. Izzi Deen in 'Islamic Environmental Ethics, Law, and Society', in *Ethics*

of Environment and Development: Global Challenges, International Response, eds J. R. Engel and J. G. Engel (London: Belhaven, 1990), p. 150.

8 Maulana Jalal-al-Din Rumi, *The Mathnawi-i-manawi of Jalaliu'ddin Rumi*, ed. and trans. Reynold A. Nicholson (Leiden: E. J. Brill, 1925–40), vol. III.

9 Nasafi, Aziz ud-Din. (d.695/1295)

10 Ibn Arabi, Muhay ud-Din. (d.638/1240)

11 Ibn Arabi, *Futuhat*, 1. 131.23, quoted in Murata, p. 143.

12 Ibid., p. 140.

13 Nasir al-Din al-Tusi, *Akhlaq-i-Nasiri*, English trans. G. M. Wickens, *The Nasirean Ethics* (London: Allen and Unwin, 1964), pp. 163–64, 185. al Dawwani's (d.1501) *Akhlaq-i-Jalali* carries the same theme. For details see Majid Fakhry, *Ethical Theories in Islam* (Leiden: Brill, 1991), pp. 143–47.

14 M. Ibn Ishaq, *The Life of Muhammad: A Translation of Ishaq's 'Sirat Rasul Allah'*, trans. with intro. and notes by A. Guillaume (London: Oxford University Press, 1955), pp. 106–07, quoted in F. E. Peters, *A Reader on Classical Islam* (Princeton: Princeton University Press, 1994), pp. 52–53.

15 N. al-Mulk, *The Book of Government: or, The Rule of Kings: The Siy-astanama, or Siyar al-Muluk*, trans. from the Persian by H. Darke (London: Routledge & Kegan Paul, 1960), pp. 185, 188–89.

16 Quoted by H. Afshar in 'Women, Marriage and the State in Iran', in *The Women, Gender & Development Reader*, eds. N. Visvanathan *et al* (London: Zed Books, 1997), pp. 318–19.

17 M. Y. Izzi Deen, "Islamic Environmental Ethics, Law, and Society', in *Ethics of Environment*, eds, Engel and Engel, p. 190.

18 Quoted in ibid.

19 T. Izutsu, The *Structure of the Ethical Terms in the Quran: A Study in Semantics* (Montreal: McGill (1st edn, Tokyo, 1959), 1966), pp. 164–65.

20 One of the many disparaging proverbs is, 'women, wealth, and land (*zan, zar, zameen*) are the source of all miseries'.

21 N. Shah, 'A Woman's Sexual Space: Control and Deviance', *Pakistan Journal of Women's Studies*, 4 (2), 1997, p. 34.

22 S. Sardar Ali, 'Are Women also Human? Women's Rights and Human Rights in Tribal Areas: A Case Study of Provincially Administrated Tribal Areas of Pakistan', *Pakistan Journal of Women's Studies*, I (1) 1994, p. 22.

23 Murata, *Tao of Islam*, p. 323.

24 See for more details Fakhr ud-Din Razi's (d.606/1209) discourse on the excellence of heaven and earth in his *al-Tafsir al-kabir*, 1, pp. 324–25. See also Murata, *Tao of Islam*, pp. 139–40.

25 E. Boserup, *Women's Role in Economic Development* (London: George Allen & Unwin, 1970).

26 C. Merchant, *The Death of Nature: Women Ecology and the Scientific Revolution* (London: Wildwoodhouse, 1980).

27 V. Shiva, *Staying Alive: Women, Ecology and Development* (London: Zed Press, 1989), p. xvii.

28 Ibid., p. xvii.

29 For more details on these arguments see J. L. Collins, 'Women and the Environment: Social Reproduction and Sustainable Development', in *The Women and International Development Annual*, vol. 2, eds R. S. Allen and A. Ferguson, (Boulder: Westview Press, 1991), pp. 33–58.

30 W. Abimbola, *Decolonizing African Thought in Tradition and Development in Africa Today* (Paris: UNESCO, 1990), pp. 15–22.

31 N. Abbott, *Two Queens of Baghdad: Mother and Wife of Harun al-Rashid* (Chicago: University of Chicago Press, 1946), pp. 242–44.
32 For more details see, E. Atil, 'Islamic Women as Rulers and Patrons', *Asian Art*, 6(2), 1993. This is a special issue of the journal *Asian Art* on Muslim women and their patronage of art and architecture.
33 Izzi Deen, in 'Islamic Environmental Ethics', p. 196.
34 N. Ayub, *The Self-Employed Women in Pakistan: A Case Study of the Self-Employed Women of the Urban Informal Sector in Karachi* (Karachi: Pakistan Association for Women's Studies, Noor Jahan Memorial Educational and Welfare Society, 1994).
35 B. Jabre *et al*, eds, *Arab Women Speak Out: Profits of Self-Empowerment*, (Baltimore: Johns Hopkins School of Public Health, 1997), p. 87.
36 Ibid, p. 23.

10

Soil as the Goddess Bhudevi in a Tamil Women's Ritual: The Kolam in India

Vijaya Rettakudi Nagarajan

What we separate as art, economics, and religion appear intermeshed as aspects of the same performance. The aesthetics, ethos, and world-view of a person are shaped in childhood and throughout early life, and reinforced later, by these verbal and nonverbal environments.

A. K. Ramanujan, *Folk Tales from India: A Selection of Oral Tales from Twenty-two Languages*

[W]e draw the *kolam* as our first ritual act in the morning to remind ourselves to remember *Bhudevi*. We walk on her. We spit on her; we poke her; we burden her. We expect her to hear us and all the activities we do on her with endless patience. So, we do the *kolam*.

Jaya Mami, Thanjavur District

Jaya Mami answered my question: Why do you draw the *kolam* on the threshold of your house every day at dawn?[1] We were sitting in the cool and open rectangular space in the centre of her house, the sun streaming through the red-tiled roofs, the centre of the room opening to the sky. Even though it was December in Tamil Nadu, it was hot in the noonday sun, hot enough that people still used umbrellas to brace themselves against the searing heat and light. I had arrived in India during the month of *Margaii*, falling between mid-December and mid-January, the most important ritual month for the cultural practice of the *kolam*.[2]

This chapter deals with the notion of 'embedded ecologies' in the Hindu folk religious practice, the *kolam*, a women's ritual art performed at dawn on the thresholds of houses, temples, and

159

streets throughout Tamil Nadu. An exploratory meditation ranging from 'embedded ecologies' to the idea of 'intermittent sacrality', the thread linking the various 'beads' of this chapter, is the assumption that notions of ecology are culturally constructed and maintained in what we can call 'embedded ecologies', whether in the West or non-West. The West has eagerly desired to understand the 'ecological' beliefs of non-Westerners, especially more recently with the increasing environmental pollution and the breakdown of a community sense of moral order and restraint in the West.[3] The West's curiosity has centred on religious notions of respect and even worship towards natural landscapes such as rivers, mountains, forests and even the earth itself. Although non-Western religions may have a reverence towards landscapes, I contend they do not necessarily lead to an attitude of 'ecological' practices that resemble 'ecological' in the sense that the West has come to know it. I suggest that scholars and activists who would study Hindu 'ecological' beliefs and practices will need some understanding of how 'ecology' has come to be formed as a concept and practice in the modern West.[4] For while ecology is integral to modern Western history, there are dangers in deploying it as a normalizing concept when translating Hindu traditions into the 'modern' notion of ecology. Furthermore, Western notions of ecology are steeped in embeddedness as well. The institutional structures that frame ecological beliefs are themselves embedded with assumptions, histories, and contestations. Simon Schama has shown this brilliantly in his *Landscapes of Memory*.[5].

Sacrality

Hindus view the Ganges as sacred and worship the river. Yet, at the same time, the prevalent lack of care and protectiveness towards the Ganges in everyday practice within popular Hinduism is also clear.

Natural objects are shot through with the notions of sacrality embedded within and through them. Sacrality is both a force and a substance. It moves around; it has volition; it is characterized by ritual hospitality. Sometimes the object itself, whether natural or human, previously not sacred, becomes sacred during a specific time period.

Throughout my experience in working in and on India, I have found as much disjunction as correlation between the perception of the natural world as sacred and the consequent 'ecological' and 'non-ecological' actions that result from this perception.

The first half of this chapter is a theoretical exploration of what I call 'embedded' notions of ecology, where cultural and religious frameworks orient perceptions of 'ecological' spaces. The concept of 'embedded ecologies' is partly taken from Karl Polanyi and partly my own coinage. I will look at embedded ecologies in Hinduism. How has Hinduism as an ecological reality been specifically shaped, understood, and interpreted? One task is to look more closely at how the notion of sacrality, when applied to a natural object, has been necessarily and automatically understood to be 'ecological', especially recently by Indian environmentalists such as Vandana Shiva.[6] Furthermore, how is it that this understanding has not been precise enough in terms of illuminating the contradictions between the imagined ideal behaviour and what actually happens in everyday life?

Embedded Ecologies

The idea of 'embedded ecologies' opens up a theoretical and ethnographic space for reflection on the cultural construction of nature in India. This notion could serve to explain some of the difficulty of conceptualizing categories of nature and culture, whether in the South Asian context or outside of it. Why use the term 'embedded ecologies'? Karl Polanyi, the economic anthropologist, formulated the notion of embeddedness, in the context of understanding non-Western economies in relation to Western economies. Polanyi asserts, 'The prime reason for the absence of any concept of the economy is the difficulty of identifying the economic process under conditions where it is embedded in non-economic institutions.'[7] Polanyi refers to the larger cultural forces, understandings and ideas in which the economy as a cultural concept is embedded. It is embedded in ritual practices or organizational strategies at the kinship and clan level, which serve to organize production and consumption activities. The notion of 'economic' is itself subsumed under other cultural categories, bound together inseparably. Another aspect of Polanyi's contention is that any attempt to separate economics from the rest of life is itself an artificial construct based on Western categories.

I extend Polanyi's understanding of embedded economies to the notion of 'embedded ecologies' – 'the difficulty of identifying *ecological* processes under conditions where it is *embedded* in *non-ecological* institutions' is the prime reason for the confusion of our reading contemporary ecological notions about conservation into religious and gendered ideological frameworks. In other words, underlying our thought and understanding of religion and environment is the proposition that 'sacrality' when attached to a natural object makes that object a bounded religiously endowed entity and that object is automatically, therefore, assumed to become more protected. The 'sacrality' itself creates a context where people surrounding that natural object are more careful, more resource-conscious, and more 'ecologically' sensitive to the consequences of using that natural resource. As economy is embedded in culture, so too is ecology embedded in culture. Another layer of complexity is that landscape is gendered, male and female. Trees are male and female; so are mountains and bodies of water.

Building on Polanyi's articulation of embedded economies and Schama's detailed investigations of specific variations of cultural notions of 'landscape', I argue that whether the location is South Asia or elsewhere, notions of ecology, ecological substances, practices and beliefs are situated in a complex matrix of larger cultural ideas and practices and, therefore, have a much more nuanced meaning that we have given these notions credit for. Furthermore, it is difficult to untangle the ecological from the non-ecological when it is embedded within other cultural practices.

The notion of 'embedded ecologies' does not refer to an idealized or romanticized notion of the past in India, where people are depicted as living in a relatively benign and unchanging relationship with the natural world. It does not refer to a cultural construction of the environment as 'everything is related to everything else', a grossly holistic view and explanation. It does not, furthermore, allude to an ever-harmonious cultural relationship with the natural world. In fact, I intend to propose a notion of 'embedded ecologies' that at the very outset is contested, historicized, and culturally specific. It is contested in the sense that there are multiple points of view within the Hindu tradition, an embedded ecological belief could at one moment refer to a practice that is 'ecological' and the next moment 'unecological', in the sense of non-conservation oriented. A belief or practice that is labelled or believed to be 'ecological' will have to be scrutinized much more carefully to see if it does fit a conservation-based framework. 'Embedded ecologies', moreover, does not refer to an 'embedded' world that is automatically enrolled in a project of ecology (environmentalism) in the sense that we understand it in the Euro-American conservation sense. I would like to use the term to refer to the complex intertwining of the natural world and the cultural perception of it in a specifically framed exploration. It is based on the implicit understanding that each culture has its own myths, memories, associations and, to use Simon Schama's word, cultural 'obsessions' about the natural world. As Schama has said, *'Instead of assuming the mutually exclusive character of Western culture and nature, I want to suggest the strength of the links that have bound them together.'*[8] [italics added]

One of the specific, obvious and logical 'embedded ecological' sites within the Indian context, where one could look for a cultural understanding of ecological substances, beliefs and practices, is within Hinduism. More precisely, I suggest that one of the key locations within Hinduism where these embedded ecological substances, beliefs and practices could be found, are the various kinds of 'spaces' where the notion of sacrality is applied. Specifically, one can point to sacred geographies, where sacrality is imbued in particular places, that is, in rivers, groves and mountains.

Sacred Landscape as Ecological

We have, I believe, come to misunderstand the notion of the sacred landscape as intrinsically ecological. I too linked the two for a long time. Because of the sacrality of a grove, there exists prohibitions in the cutting of trees in that specific grove. Because of the sacrality of a river, there exists a ritual of 'purification' of a river that sometimes accompanies the use of a river for bathing. Because rocks, mountains and the earth themselves are considered to be sacred, there is invested in them a special kind of awareness. We have come realize that the implications for the conservation ecology of the grove, river, and mountain are similar to the Western understanding of ecological conservation and preservation. It seemed not to surprise us that the individual person or community's perception of the place made sacred through ritual actions, whether grove, river, or mountain, would be necessarily conserved and kept free from pollution. This correspondence between ritual care, acknowledgement, and offerings to a place and the concomitant protection of a place may be accurate in some instances, but not necessarily so in all.

One of the environmental writers and scholars who has

expounded this type of understanding is Vandana Shiva, who trained as a physicist in the 1970s in Canada, and subsequently returned to India. In her best known text, *Staying Alive: Women, Ecology and Development*, Shiva articulates an interpretation of the Hindu perception of the sacred as intrinsically ecologically protective. Although much of this text is devoted to arguing against the paradigm of Western development and its concomitant ideological grid of dams, mechanized agriculture, pesticides, and misguided commercial forestry schemes, a subtle but pervasive assumption laces the text, the assumption that Hindu women have been, and continue to be, naturally 'culturally' ecological. One of the examples she uses is the *tulsi* plant, the basil, that is worshipped daily. She argues, 'Tulsi is a little herb planted in every home, and worshipped daily . . . The tulsi is sacred not merely as a plant with beneficial properties but as Brindavan, the symbol of the cosmos. In their daily watering and worship women renew the relationship of the home with the cosmos and with the world process . . . Ontologically there is no divide between man and nature.'[9] She continues with an analysis of the contrast between the Cartesian mechanized view of the post-Enlightenment period in the West and the lack of division between humanity and nature in India, because in India both are perceived to be sacred. It is true, to a certain extent, that the infusion of the natural world with notions of sacrality affect the behaviour of people towards the natural world. Yet I have some misgivings about the implications of such a view of Indian culture, that it intrinsically has some internal checks and balances that keep the rapaciousness of human greed in check.

Shiva's work in generating environmental thought and action in India and elsewhere has been remarkable. Although her work on understanding the Chipko women's movement as well as her current work on recovering native seed varieties in India is a courageous voice of resistance to the 'monoculturalization' of the mind, I find myself uneasy with her subtext of claiming a general 'ecological virtueness' that applies generally to Indian women daily watering their *tulsi* plants. The cosmological referent of the *tulsi* plant may indeed be true, but how it relates to the conservation-oriented Hinduism is left unspecified. Shiva argues unconvincingly that a Hindu woman who, as part of her religious practice, waters her *tulsi* as a daily ritual in her own garden is automatically enrolled in an ecological project of conservation and protection of natural resources in general. Not long ago, I too believed this to be true. Although Shiva roots the practice in Hindu mythology and notions of sacrality, her judgement of the effect of these rituals, myths and notions of sacredness is, I think, too broad and generalized. Furthermore, Shiva argues that women intuitively understand the limits of the natural world's capacity to provide an endless supply of resources. In a context where the scale is the community, village, or neighbourhood, this may indeed have been true, but in an increasingly large mass-oriented culture and religion, it is hard to imagine a set of limits deriving from a religious sense of bounds holding firm within the context of modernity. Here I should point to the elision that we sometimes make within the environmental discourse between identifying a belief or a way of life as ecological and the concomitant belief that is conservation-oriented. We tend to assume a cultural lifestyle as ecological when it is also conserving of the environment, creating less waste and pollution.

The trope of the traditional Hindu woman who performs her *tulsi* rites in her household is presumed to carry around a vision of the conservation and environmental ethics that seem to derive as much from Hinduism as from origins far from Hinduism; that is to say, from Western notions of ecology and environment. This conceptualization, rather, seems to reflect more of a projected Western-type of conservation ethic on to Hindu women that may be completely unwarranted. Just as Yosemite National Park in California was created through a cultural imagination of a 'pure' place, that is without any of the previous local inhabitants, so, too, the care that women impart to a local *tulsi* plant is assumed, and not only symbolically, to connect to other mythical plants, but in addition to have real 'ecological' consequences. In other words, Hindu women are presumed to reflect about the environment in the same way that a modern Western-trained environmentalist is supposed to; this calls to mind Schama's reference to earlier American conservation movements reading into the landscape a desire for it to be emptied of humans: to be pure and preserved. The *tulsi* plant itself may be the only plant that is conserved in the vicinity of the household, but it does not necessarily reflect on the conservation of the natural world outside the village boundaries. Therefore, the assumptions of Shiva and others (including my earlier ones) that worshipping the *tulsi* plant leads to a concomitant and parallel preservation of both the *tulsi* plant and non-*tulsi* natural world is unfounded. I would argue, therefore, that the assumption that 'sacrality = ecological' is a highly problematic assumption. Rather the perception of the natural world as sacred does not *necessarily* lead to a more 'environmental' or ecological attitude

towards nature. Having a religious attitude towards a plant such as
tulsi may be a kind of 'embedded ecology', but it does not necessarily mean an ecological frame of mind that has goals similar to the
history of Western conservation movements; in other words, to
preserve and conserve natural environments. 'Embedded Ecologies' are, therefore, *not* intrinsically conservation-oriented.

The *Kolam* Ethnography

I will examine the cultural construction of nature in Hinduism from
a particular vantage point: the *kolam*, a women's popular ritual art
form in Tamil Nadu that binds together conceptions of sacrality,
nature, and culture. How do we better understand the implications
of 'ecological' subtexts in a religious ideology such as Hinduism
that centres on the sacralization of the 'natural'? It is necessary to
look more closely at popular cultural and religious practices to
scrutinize these two questions more carefully.

I have chosen to limit the discussion to the following three questions: (1) How does the *kolam* reflect notions of the natural world
in Tamil Nadu? (2) How do women talking about the *kolam* refer
to aspects of the natural world? (3) What are the links between
these explicit references to the natural world and the broader attitudes towards the natural world? To begin to answer these three
questions I have chosen to introduce, first the *kolam* itself, and second to analyse the *kolam* as a cultural expression that, though
containing evidence of an 'embedded ecology', does not necessarily lead to a conservation/preservation environmental ethic as
we would have hypothesized from Shiva's argument in an earlier
section. I will also explore the paradoxes of assuming an embedded
ecology that is considered to be 'sacred' and the category 'sacred',
whether associated with time or space. Third, I introduce an
expression I have coined to help describe, analyse and understand
some of the contradictions between the conceptual and pragmatic
levels of Hinduism; the expression is called '*intermittent sacrality*'.
I would like to conclude with a call towards probing the dialectic
between vernacular environmental and cultural ethical formations
and the pragmatic, experiential practices of those formations.

What is the *kolam*, and what is its relationship to women's perception of the natural world in Tamil Nadu? At first the *kolam*
appears to be a simple and beautiful ritual performed by women
that has little consequence for understanding Tamil culture either

as a whole, or as embodied in particular, localized contexts. With the help of more than a hundred women in Tamil Nadu with whom I discussed the *kolam* at length, and who shared with me how they saw and understood their world through *kolam*, I believe that the importance of the *kolam* to Tamil culture, especially in women's oral and visual culture, cannot be overestimated. The irony is that the *kolam*, though dense with meaning, in appearance is very light, ephemeral, almost weightless; it appears as shadowy bodily gestures and handstrokes in the early morning light. Physically located on the boundary of the household/street, that is, on the threshold, and because of its ephemeral nature, the *kolam* disappears onto people's feet and into the soil.

The kolam

The creation of the *kolam* is one of the first rituals done by millions of women in the misty light of pre-dawn; it is performed on the threshold space in front of the house, at the feet of the image in the main domestic shrine, and on the temple grounds. Before the *kolam* is made, a mixture of cow dung and water is ritually splashed on the floor, ground, or soil, creating a darkened wet 'canvas'. Often signalling the first step towards creating a sense of sacred space in domestic household or public rituals, the *kolam* can be simple or elaborate, made from wet or dry rice flour or, more recently, from ground stone powder and bright bazaar-bought colours. Drawn most elaborately to mark a woman's marriage and childbirth, and significantly absent during menstruation and mourning times, it is an important ritual that visually celebrates states of transition in time and space. Although the *kolam* is a vital sign of the social circulation of women's energies, it is located at the edge of women's spatial world, the threshold between home and street, between the inside and outside of the household, and all the charged friction that that space implies. It is an identity marker of gender, bearing the traces of a woman's presence in the vicinity.

The *kolam* plays an equally important role during festival days for women and various goddesses. Thought to be a seat for welcoming the goddesses Lakshmi and Mariyamman, it deflects the ill effects of the evil eye. Attracting auspiciousness and well-being, the *kolam* is associated with bringing prosperity and good health. Four goddesses constantly circulate in the women's *kolam* narratives: they are Bhumadevi, the earth goddess, Lakshmi, the goddess of wealth, good fortune, prosperity, and rice, Mudevi, the goddess of laziness, sleepiness and poverty, and Tulasi Devi, the goddess of the Indian basil. (Lakshmi and Mudevi are a pair of natural opposites, laziness and sleepiness as opposed to activeness (*shurushuruppu*), poverty to wealth, ill-luck to good fortune, an empty bowl to an overflowing bowl of rice; the two opposing goddesses are constantly at war with each other; they cannot be found in the same room. Where Mudevi is found, there Lakshmi will not come, it is said. Tulasi Devi is another wife of Vishnu; like Lakshmi, she is one who brings good fortune and protection from evil. Bhudevi is also another wife of Vishnu, flanking him along with Lakshmi in iconographic representations.)

What does it mean then 'ecologically' to have a religious belief that imputes sacrality to a natural object, whether it is the earth, basil, or water? An example of how an 'embedded ecology' works within a cultural practice is the way *Bhudevi* is represented and understood within the context of the *kolam* practice.

The Goddess Bhudevi

The goddess Bhudevi is the mythic, iconic and metonymic personification of the earth in Hinduism. The specific belief of the earth, a natural object, as an earth goddess, Bhudevi, is woven partly through ritual actions. Three questions arise: Who is Bhudevi, the Hindu earth goddess? How does the cultural and religious construction of 'Bhudevi as earth' become a subtext of explanation for everyday life habits and cultural practices, especially in the *kolam*? And, in turn, how do these articulations of religious practices reflect an ontological division in Hinduism between what is said and what is done? (Furthermore, in a broader context, I will also discuss the problem of attributing the earth as a divine goddess, a figurative metaphoric device that I argue later enables mythic narratives, iconic and metonymic understandings to be misread as 'ecologically' beneficial in an automatic kind of way.)

In Hindu mythology, Bhudevi's call for help initiates many of Vishnu's incarnations. For example, in Vishnu's Varaha avatar myth, Bhudevi is carried off by Asuras and submerged in the ocean, and she cries for help to Vishnu. Varaha, Vishnu's Boar avatar, comes and rescues Bhudevi. One of the most common iconographic representations of Bhudevi is Varaha carrying her aloft on his nose; the image of Bhudevi is small, fragile, and feminine, in contrast to Varaha, who is portrayed as large, virile, and masculine. There is an underlying concern for the soil and the earth, as the vulnerable one, and the effect of her weakening is perceived as disastrous to the countryside. It is the vulnerability of the soil and the earth that is emphasized. The earth, the soil, is fragile. Just as the earth goddess is fragile, so, too, is the soil. They both need protection. This kind of linking was common in women's everyday language. Here, in this instance, an explicit language of protection and vulnerability runs alongside the mythologization of the earth as goddess.

One of the reasons for doing the *kolam* the first thing in the morning is to exercise the memory of the debt felt to the earth goddess, who bears all of the human and non-human actions on her. Whether this consciously has any relation to women's actions during the rest of the day, I am not sure. I would suggest that every woman who makes a *kolam* also makes a conscious effort to think of Bhumadevi. In my conversations with Tamil women, Bhudevi or Bhumadevi was referenced both as the physical earth, as a large, alive being with a soul, as well as the particular soil at women's feet in that particular village, town, or city. I am particularly interested in this *simultaneity* of belief and daily practice and when the belief is and is not practised in everyday life.

Jaya Mami, a woman in her fifties, a grandmother, from the village of Thilaisthanan, which lies along the Cauvery River in Thanjavur District, explained *Bhuma-devi* in this way. Her words were echoed and re-echoed in many other narratives. '*Bhuma-devi* is our mother. She is everyone's source of existence. Nothing would exist without her. The entire world depends on her for sustenance and life.' Her articulation of the earth goddess's plight: 'We walk on her. We spit on her; we poke her; we burden her', and a daily offering of the *kolam* as a way of paying attention to the ground that people daily walk on, certainly brings to a more conscious level our own embeddedness and dependence on the earth. In everyday life this could be useful in remembering to take care of that or this particular piece of earth or ground. There are many proverbs, folktales, mythologies, and stories linked to how people should care for the earth and the specific ground that people step on throughout the day; there are equally widely existing references to how people should respect Bhudevi and, above all, not take her for granted. Yet I would add the caveat that these attitudes are not necessarily linked to a more 'ecological' way of life.

A subtext within the *kolam* narratives of the material earth is that of Bhudevi, on whom we stand and by whom we are supported. What does this 'embedded' subtext mean ecologically, to have a recognition of the earth not only as Goddess Bhudevi, but also of the burden we humans place on her, by 'poking her', 'spitting on her', etc.? Could it be that this ritual to Bhudevi, as other rituals to Bhudevi, is more of a symbolic gesture? By acknowledging her contribution through a ritual, it does not really imply that the actions carried out during the rest of the day need to incorporate the notion of the earth as a goddess. Therefore, the notion that the earth needs to be 'conserved' or 'preserved' in the sense that we understand it in the environmental movement, whether in the United States, Europe or India, should not really be expected in the everyday context. The ritual of the *kolam* similar to other rituals to Bhudevi could be compensatory rituals that do not imply a change of behaviour during the rest of the non-ritual time and space. Other parallel gestural movements include the first gesture a Bharatha Natyam dancer will make before she begins her performance; the first prayer includes a gesture to Bhudevi, to forgive the dancer for stamping on her, and yet, the dance performance does not itself stop. Although keeping in mind that the word ecology is a modern word, it is interesting to see how the patience of Bhudevi, here a willingness to bear the world, is constantly invoked in the *kolam* narrative; the making of the *kolam* is a set of gestures directly compensatory for 'thanking Bhudevi in bearing us'. As one woman, Chitra, commented from the town of Thanjavur, 'Bhudevi must be one of our first thoughts in the morning'. But, my question, then, is what happens after the morning rituals are over?

Throwing Waste on Bhudevi

In India there is a common daily practice of throwing waste on the house's front or back threshold. The threshold itself, dividing the familial from the community space, becomes the invisible line beyond which familial responsibility is but a shadow of what it is within the threshold of the household. It is common practice to throw rubbish just beyond the confines of the family property line. Spaces exterior to the household are cared for differently from those interior to the household, with few exceptions. One might argue that in the past household waste used to be organic material and now it often is not, and that is why the soil is polluted with toxic chemicals from pesticides, and so on. Yet, despite this, people are aware that plastics and other household products do not disintegrate as quickly as bamboo and other natural materials. Even within the practice of the *kolam*, the switch from rice flour to plastic stick-on transfers is commented on but not invoked as disturbing the soils of Bhudevi. What puzzled me was the lack of feeling of contradiction amongst the women who would espouse the ideas of how to treat Bhudevi, or the earth goddess, with great care and reverence, but then, throughout the day, throw rubbish on the very same substance that they consider to be sacred. This is as true for the soil goddess as it is for the river goddess, Ganga, where dirt, waste and pollution are collapsed into a category that is seen to be absorbable by both Bhudevi and Ganga; the goddesses are so large, indeterminate, and infinite that the waste of humanity is seen as just a speck in the large expanse of sky, earth, or water.

Perhaps part of the answer lies in the vast cosmological connections that Shiva refers to, that the *tulsi* plant, by being connected to the larger cosmological self, attains the powers of purification, not just as a symbolic gesture of purification, but as connected to the vast, broader powers of 'purification' that is part and parcel of the larger cosmological self. For Bhudevi, she, too, as much as the *tulsi* plant, is connected to the larger cosmological self, and, therefore, holds intrinsically the powers of purification, regardless of man's, or in this case woman's actions, on her. Moreover, the earth goddess Bhudevi, as much as the goddess Ganga, has the power to absorb, purify and cleanse the pollutants, regardless of size and scale. Perhaps it acts as a metonymic referencing to ecological understandings. One might argue that in the particular examples of Ganga and Bhudevi as goddesses, it is this very quality of the nature of 'sacrality' that precludes a sense of power of the actions of men and women that could destroy the soils or the waters. It seems odd to me that paradoxically it could be the very belief of a cosmological relationship that prevents the seeing of the *tulsi*, or, for that matter, Ganga, or Bhudevi, as needing protection from human beings. In other words, it is at times the very act of sacralization that prevents the seeing of the necessity of conservation, in the Western sense. We need to re-understand, re-invent and re-imagine the specific ways cultural notions of 'conservation', 'preservation' and 'ecology' are constituted and framed within everyday discourse; there are embedded ecologies culturally bound whether located in the West or non-West.

Intermittent Sacrality or Sacrality that Expires

If perceptions of natural objects are steeped through with notions of sacrality, will not that naturally lead to a heightened sense of protection and care of that natural object? It seems obvious that a heightened sense of natural objects would then lead to a protection or conservation of those natural objects. Within the category of 'embedded ecologies in Hinduism' I propose the idea of 'intermittent sacrality' or 'sacrality that expires'. From conversations with women as well as men, when I would point out what seemed to me to be a contradiction between belief and action, both women and men would laugh and repeatedly tell me, 'Oh, what we believe does not have to rule at all times and in all places. Just because one place is made sacred at one particular time does not mean that it remains sacred throughout the day, necessarily'. This comment came up again and again in the *kolam* narratives. I call this idea, 'intermittent sacrality'. Intermittent sacrality *occurs* when the divine is invited at a specific moment to come and be in a place, a site, or substance, and then, at a later moment, the divine is asked to leave or is believed to leave that locus. In many rituals the divine is hosted and 'dehosted' by women and men; the divine is invited as a guest and then the divine departs.

The *kolam*, a 'painted prayer' for women to acknowledge the goddess Bhudevi, also, participates in this hosting and dehosting of the divine. As a result, the sacrality that is attached to that locus is temporary, not permanent. Therefore, there seems to be no apparent contradiction between the sacrality, ritually created or not, attached to a particular site at one particular moment in time and then, the act of waste/rubbish being dumped on the same site. The sacrality attached to a particular space when the *kolam* is made is indeed a call to Bhudevi to forgive mankind's intransigence, and it implies a care of that space for that particular period of time, but it does not then carry over as a space to conserve or preserve in the sense that the Western environmental movement has understood it. For the *kolam*, then, soon after it is made, that is, soon after Bhudevi is acknowledged, recognized, decorated and hosted into being, Bhudevi is dehosted from that space by the gradual dispersal of the rice flour patterns. The idea of intermittent sacrality explains what on the surface appears to be a contradictory move – 'to trash the commons', in a manner of speaking, and therefore causing a 'tragedy of the commons' – but on reflection fits in with another aspect of the Hindu ideological construction of sacred space.

I take the final insight from A. K. Ramanujan in his classic essay, 'Is there an Indian way of thinking? An informal essay'. Ramanujan says:

> I think cultures (may be said to) have overall tendencies (for whatever complex reasons) – tendencies to idealise, and think in terms of, either the context-free or the context-sensitive kind of rules. Actual behaviour may be more complex, though the rules . . . are a crucial factor in guiding the behaviour. In cultures like India's, the context-sensitive kind of rule is the preferred formulation.[10]

'Context-sensitive thinking', as Ramanujan points out, is also another way of understanding the seeming contradiction between a belief and the way it is carried out in everyday life. It is the context that determines the regime of a belief, a rule, or a ritual. If it is a context-sensitive attitude that engages the making of embedded ecologies, then it should not be a surprise to us if Hindu beliefs about the sacrality of the natural environment do not always lead to a more conservation-oriented religious practice.

Notes

1 This ethnographic research is based on conversations with women, men, and *alis* (hermaphrodites) and was primarily conducted in Tamil Nadu during four consecutive winter seasons from 1987–1991.

2 For a brief introduction to the *kolam* in Tamil women's everyday lives see, V. Nagarajan, 'Hosting the Divine', in *Mud, Mirror and Thread: Folk Traditions of Rural India*, ed. N. Fisher (Albuquerque: Museum of New Mexico Press, 1993).

3 R. K. Nelson, *Make Prayers to the Raven* (Chicago: University of Chicago Press, 1983); W. Sax, *Mountain Goddess: Gender and Politics in a Himalayan Pilgrimage* (Oxford: Oxford University Press, 1991); V. Shiva, *Staying Alive: Women, Ecology and Development* (London: Zed Books, 1989); F. Zimmerman, *The Jungle and the Aroma of Meats: An Ecological Theme in Hindu Medicine* (Berkeley: University of California Press, 1987 [1982]). Interestingly, this is not necessarily limited to environmentalists looking at Hinduism, but it can also be extended to other belief systems, especially Native American. See Nelson, *Make Prayers* for extensive indigenous points of view towards the natural world. It is not that environmentalists articulate this belief explicitly; it is implicitly believed and understood to be true, but rarely discussed.

4 D. Worster, *Nature's Economy: A History of Ecological Ideas* (Cambridge: Cambridge University Press, 1977).

5 S. Schama, *Landscape and Memory* (New York: Knopf, 1995).

6 Shiva, *Staying Alive*, pp. 39–40.

7 K. Polanyi, *Trade and Market in Early Empires* (Boston: Beacon Press, 1957), p. 71.

8 Schama, *Landscape and Memory*, pp. 13–14.
9 Shiva, *Staying Alive*, pp. 39–40.
10 A. K. Ramanujan, 'Is there an Indian Way of Thinking? An Informal Essay', in *India through Hindu Categories*, ed. M. McKim (New Delhi: Sage Publications, 1990).

11

Nature and Gender in Theravada Buddhism

Sandra Bell

Based on a survey of ethnographic research, this chapter considers the role of rural women in two Buddhist countries – Thailand and Sri Lanka. It explores recent debates about the causes and degree of women's religious disadvantage brought about through their exclusion from the order of monks known as the Sangha. Questions arise about how women's exclusion is culturally validated in spite of the vital contribution that they make to the maintenance and continuity of the Sangha. Exploring these issues leads to an examination of protective sacred power in Theravada Buddhism, its connections with male celibacy and the threatening effects of female sexuality.

While women, as inheritors of land and as primary agricultural producers, possess a high degree of economic and social independence relative to their sisters in other parts of Asia,[1] perceptions of femininity as polluting and dangerous impede women's association with the sacred. Furthermore, women are not identified with nature. Ethnographic evidence suggests that women require protection from the fearsome forces of the wild represented by the forests, which are only safe for the most ascetic monks, and that the binary oppositions between female/male and nature/culture advocated by structuralist anthropology do not apply to Theravada Buddhist societies.

Before launching upon a discussion specific to the topic of gender, it would be helpful to provide a brief sketch of the background to Theravada Buddhist belief and practice. To begin with, there is a great deal of discussion in the literature about the relationship between the canonical stream of Buddhism – the religion of the scriptures and commentaries – and a host of associated, and sometimes contradictory, beliefs and practices. One useful analytical device that is frequently deployed to understand the multifarious forms of religious expression in Theravada Buddhism as a systematic whole draws on a theory of peasant culture expounded by the American anthropologist Robert Redfield. In the 1960s the Sri Lankan anthropologist, Gananath Obeyesekere, examined the utility of Redfield's two concepts of the great tradition and the little tradition,[2] whereby there is 'a great tradition of the reflective few, and a little tradition of the largely unreflective many'.[3] His examination of Sri Lankan Buddhism leads Obeyesekere to reject a clear cut division of Buddhist civilization into two related, but analytically separate, elements, and to conclude that 'peasant cultures or little traditions are linked with the great tradition through a common cultural idiom'.[4] The common idiom is made up of a 'core of shared meanings associated with the terminology which facilitates movement between the two traditions'. Moreover, the terminology 'not only links the little tradition with the great, but it also links the little traditions with one another. This represents an important aspect of the cultural unity of a civilization: a shared commonality of meanings which define the central values of the people and constitute their governing ethos'.[5]

The cultures of Sri Lanka and Thailand are both intrinsic to the composition of Theravada Buddhist civilization. They share certain major concepts that are attached to specific forms of expression within each distinct cultural complex.

These concepts include:

- The notion of magico-religious power that may adhere to supernatural beings such as gods, ghosts or demons or to persons such as monks; this power may be beneficial and protective, as is the case with the religious merit (Pali – *punna*) that accrues from making offerings to monks, or from rituals that propitiate the gods. Sacred power may also be a source of misfortune as is the case when gods are displeased or when demons descend into the human realm. The theory of sacred power in Theravada Buddhism tends towards notions concerning protection and the loss of protection.
- The notion of a hierarchy of relative status and power in which all beings, supernatural and otherwise, are placed, with the Buddha at the apex and creatures such as ghosts at the bottom.

Human beings rank somewhere in the middle and the celibate, mendicant Buddhist monk ranks highest among human beings. All beings are under the moral authority of the Buddha, who is thought to have delegated some of his authority to the inhabitants of the world of the gods (Pali – *devaloka*). Devotees will usually affirm the canonical doctrine that the Buddha has passed into *nibbana* and is no longer accessible to human agency – only his teachings (Pali – *dhamma*) remain in *samsara* (endless cycles of death and rebirth) – but their actions may sometimes appear to contradict this position.

• The notion of karma (Pali – *kamma*): the idea that the performance of deeds given a positive social sanction may bring fortune in this life and rebirth in fortuitous circumstances in the next. Actions that carry a negative sanction lead to baneful consequences in this life and the next. Buddhist salvation (Pali – *nibbana*) lies in escape from the suffering (Pali – *dukkha*) entailed in cycles of death and rebirth (Pali – *samsara*) by detaching oneself from desires that produce intentional acts bearing karmic consequences. The ideal conditions for cultivating detachment are encoded in the regulations and meditation practices of the Buddhist monastic order, the Sangha. Monks practice mendicancy and must be supported by lay people, they thus provide lay people with the opportunity to increase their stock of religious merit through making gifts to monks, an act which is associated with positive karma. Lay people can also ensure positive karma in abiding by five general precepts proscribing killing, stealing, untruth, sexual misbehaviour, and the use of mind-altering substances, including alcohol.

These key concepts inform the logic of rituals and beliefs surrounding phenomena such as spirit possession, exorcism and astrology, but they are equally seminal to the logic and goals of the most orthodox monks. They also shape the assumptions, expectations and categories that feature in everyday social life, including the fundamental categories of gender.

Women and the Sangha

There is only one formally constituted religious institution within Theravada Buddhism and that is the Sangha, or Order, of monks from which women are categorically excluded. Ample canonical and non-canonical evidence exists to prove that there once existed an Order of Nuns. The scriptures indicate that a nuns' order was founded by the Buddha himself, though some stories portray him as reluctant to permit his aunt Mahaprajapati and her five hundred companions to renounce lay life and become the original Buddhist nuns. The history of the women's order is shadowy and the cause for its decline and ultimate extinction remains undeterminated. Gombrich and Obeyesekere suggest that in Sri Lanka the nuns' order died out 'probably in the late tenth century'.[6] Falk maintains that in India the nuns' order 'virtually disappeared from the historian's view' by the end of the twelfth century CE.[7] According to Kabilsingh, the nuns' order never reached Thailand.[8]

The fact that women are debarred from participation as fully ordained members of the Sangha – and thus from the ideal conditions required for salvation – constitutes a primary element in the structure of religiosity and pervades the culture of gender in Theravada Buddhist societies. Since the nineteenth century there has been a number of attempts to reinvent the nuns' order. Gombrich explains that there are many women in Sri Lanka who lead 'nun-like' lives and 'would evidently wish to be real nuns if that were possible' but they are prevented from doing so because they would have to receive 'a double ordination: one by validly ordained monks, and the other by validly ordained nuns'.[9] The only available nuns belong to Mahayana schools of Buddhism and, though there is no reason within Theravada canonical law preventing them from participating in the ordination of Theravadin nuns, there is a widely held suspicion within the Sri Lankan Sangha, and among the public at large, that the Mahayana tradition may be lax in discipline.[10] In Thailand this debate is more muted as the movement to reinvent a nuns' order is less mature than that in Sri Lanka, but it is presently beginning to gain ground.

I do not intend to examine the nascent nuns' movement but to focus on the implications that underlie and stem from women's absolute exclusion from membership of the Sangha, and consequently from the sphere of sacred power. In spite – or perhaps even because – of their exclusion, women most often prepare and offer food to monks and thus support the prescribed mendicancy on which the Sangha's magico-religious power rests. The ubiquity of women in the provision of daily offerings to monks is viewed by some scholars as an indication of the greater need for women to accrue the religious merit (Pali – *punna*) generated by prestations to monks (Pali – *dana*). This perspective, which has been explored with particular reference to the ethnography of Thailand by

Thomas Kirsch, argues that in Theravada Buddhism women are perceived as more attached to the mundane world than are men because, in being debarred from the Sangha, women are denied the prescribed path to salvation through the realization of nirvana (Pali – *nibbana*).[11] Without recourse to joining the Sangha they have little option but to make religious merit through *dana*, and in this way women need merit more than men.

Charles Keyes takes issue with the proposition that Theravada Buddhist culture imposes the idea that men have a greater propensity to realize salvation than do women. Instead he postulates that the Buddhist worldview presents both males and females with the problem of seeking liberation from the attachments of *samsara*. He suggests rather that 'by "nature" males and females are inclined to be attached to the world in different ways'.[12] Keyes is concerned to challenge the analysis of feminist writers who propose that 'Buddhism serves as an ideology of oppression for women in Thai society'.[13] By analysing religious texts culled from the popular culture of the Khonmuang tradition of northern Thailand and the Thai-Lao tradition of north-eastern Thailand,[14] Keyes explores images of women that function as common currency in the moral economy of gender. The dominant image he finds to be that of woman as mother (*mae*).

The mother image is not restricted to women as 'the "natural" mother for while it might be in women's nature to bear children, what is marked in the texts is the relationship of woman as mother to that supremely cultural product, the Buddhist religion'.[15] Such a view is consistent with women's role in feeding monks. Keyes observes that the image of woman as mother/nurturer finds expression in the actual role that most women in Khonmuang and Thai-Lao villages play. The close relationship that women have with productive land is emphasized by an inheritance system whereby a valuable commodity such as rice land passes from parents to daughters and their husbands.

The nurturing role appears again in the activities of female traders (*mae kha*). Small-scale trading results from an extension of women's productivity in the fields, together with craftwork at home, and is recognized as providing extra resources to enhance the well-being of the trader's family,[16] including the benefits associated with *dana*. In the songs of lamentation, which are taught to young girls by monks, women's experience embedded in their reproductive role is treated as something that better enables them to realize the truth of the Buddha's teaching, whereas men must cultivate such experiential knowledge by becoming monks. For Keyes this is evidence that:

> In a real sense, an understanding of this teaching comes more 'naturally' for women than for men, for men have to break from their normal life routines before they can temper their passionate natures with the knowledge of religious truth gained through adherence to the discipline and the study of the texts.[17]

Kirsch's response to Keyes' argument is to repeat his assertion that women in Thailand are 'religiously disadvantaged' by their categorical exclusion from the Sangha. And though he agrees strongly with Keyes' view that 'the image of woman as 'mother/mother-nurturer' is a major one in Thai society',[18] he is keen to warn against regarding the concept of nurture as being 'distinctively and uniquely associated with women in general or with mothers in particular'.[19] For example, he points out that within the client-patron relations that pervade Thai society, the patron may take a paternalistic role in 'nurturing' the client, as illustrated by the fact that high ranking officials sometimes personally prepare and serve food to their clients.[20]

Among Thai Buddhists there is a common expectation that all males will enter the Sangha, at least for a temporary period, which amounts to a rite of passage whereby young men move from their role as dependent sons to become monks dependent on their teachers, eventually to return to the secular world as fully independent and marriageable men. The temporary ordination confers religious merit and status on the young man and, significantly, on his parents. As Kirsch points out, this expectation has often been more of an ideal than a reality, though the recent decline of the practice may account for part of the overall depletion of numbers of men becoming ordained as monks in Thailand.[21] He also points to the deep social meanings implicit in the ordination ceremony which signifies the 'highest importance' of perpetuating the Sangha, despite the 'onerous requirements' this places upon the individual. The ceremony also has marked implications for the life cycle of the family. 'In the ordination ritual the mother (and father) symbolically give up their claims on the son to enable him to enter the order, while the son also gives up his attachment to them and to a worldly style of life.'[22] The act has more resonance for the mother than the father, due to the greater social distance which typically occurs between fathers and their offspring in Thai Buddhist families compared with that which exists between mothers and their children.[23]

To have a son who becomes ordained as a monk is one means, other than the routine feeding of monks, that enables women to accrue great religious merit. Consequently, according to Kirsch, many young men who may otherwise avoid becoming monks are ordained because of their love for their mothers and their desire to provide them with the enormous religious rewards they can only receive in this way, because Buddhist sex role definitions deny a woman admission to the Sangha on her own.[24] It is worth noting that although the practice of temporary ordination does not occur in Sri Lanka, in families where there are several sons it is not uncommon for one to be selected by the parents to train for full membership of the Sangha from a young age.

The argument between Kirsch and Keyes is really about the extent to which the essentially patriarchal structure of the Sangha generates and buttresses an ideology of female oppression. Keyes thinks that women are somehow compensated for their exclusion from the only available religious institution in Theravada Buddhism by being considered more 'naturally' able to comprehend spiritual truths. Kirsch objects to Keyes attempts to minimize and ameliorate the degree of female subordination that emerges from women's exclusion from the Sangha. He also refutes Keyes' view that the undisguised image of women as sex objects, that has become enlarged alongside a recent marked increase in prostitution in Thailand, has no precedent in Buddhism and belongs to a secular genre. For Kirsch this is patently untrue, the blatant modern versions of women as sex objects that accompany prostitution are, in Kirsch's view, merely elements of a traditional image composed into new forms.

The Containment of Sexuality

The work of many other ethnographers in both Thailand and Sri Lanka certainly indicate that ideologies of gender in Buddhist civilization are generally informed by anxieties surrounding female sexuality and fertility. Such anxiety is clearly expressed in attitudes and rituals surrounding menstruation and childbirth. Terwiel for Thailand,[25] and Obeyesekere[26] and Winslow[27] for Sri Lanka, demonstrate how women are unequivocally divorced from any possibility of immersion into the sacred power attached to the Sangha. They also show how justification for women's exclusion centres on concepts of pollution and danger, embodied in female sexuality, that oppose and threaten the ritual purity and moral authority that are the source of the Sangha's sacred power.[28]

There is a strong tendency in Theravada Buddhist cultures for women of childbearing age to be represented as being possessed of voracious sexual appetites and as incarnations of intense carnal desire inimical to the kind of restrained behaviour required for the pursuit of salvation. Women's inherent seductiveness is viewed as especially threatening to the security of monks. Tierwal observes that 'one of the most important areas of controlled behaviour [for monks] centres around the avoidance of contact with females. No monk should touch a woman, a female animal or even an object that is held by a woman.'[29] He goes on to list the avoidance strategies monks and women are expected to follow. Women are not allowed to speak with a monk in private, a third person should always be within earshot. Monks must avoid inadvertently bumping into women and if a woman notices a yellow robe approaching along the path she must move aside. In Thailand monks are provided with special seats on buses so that they do not accidentally come into contact with women.[30] Another feature of life in Thailand is the 'offering cloth'. When a woman, even a close relative, wishes to present a monk with food or medicine that is not placed directly into his bowl, the monk has to provide a piece of cloth on which the woman places the gift, while he holds the edge of the cloth. The cloth acts as a kind of screen to preserve the beneficial power of the monk while permitting the prestation to bring some gain to the woman as 'a bit of the beneficial power flows from the fingertips of the monk, via the cloth, through the object to her fingers'.[31]

In the Sinhalese Buddhists village of Laggala, Obeyesekere found that men viewed women as 'inherently inferior, and incapable of idealism and fidelity'.[32] Birth as a female was thought to be the result of bad karma and it was the unanimous view of villagers that women could not be trusted. Amarasingham, in an analysis of nine myths that are commonly recited during rituals of exorcism, concludes: 'the central problem of Buddhism – desire and its relation to suffering – is imaged in women both in doctrinal material and in exorcist myths'.[33] The myths concern the origins of demons who are born of women and represent a threat to the human order brought about through the fruits of excessive and inappropriately directed desire. In these myths women are passive instruments of male desire. They rarely act to instigate the copulation that results in the birth of demons; rather they are portrayed as objects of desire whose existence passively provokes active masculine lust.

The myths echo the sentiments of canonical Buddhism where monks are exhorted to stay away from women and to strengthen their resistance to the superficiality of feminine charms by contemplating the impermanence of female sexual attraction. Amarasingham quotes a text where monks are bid to reflect on the eventual corruption of the entrancing beauty of a young girl:

> What now, ye monks, is the misery of the embodied? Only let us look upon this sister at a later time, in her eightieth, ninetieth or hundredth year; broken, crooked, shrunken, trembling, shuffling along, supported upon crutches, infirm, withered, toothless, with bleached wisps of hair, bare tottering head, wrinkled, the skin full of spots, what do you think monks; is it not what was once shining beauty, wholly departed, and misery now come in its place?[34]

Amarasingham's assertion that the quotation demonstrates how women can be particularly apt object lessons on the impermanence of all things, simply because they are among the most desired, is supported by Keyes' observations surrounding a text that is often read as a sermon at funerals, 'The Blessings of Disposing of Corpses'. In this text 'the image of a beautiful young maiden (i.e. one who is most likely to incite passion in others) is juxtaposed to the image of her putrid corpse to convey the truth of the Buddha's insight into human experience.'[35] On the whole though, Amarasingham's analysis tends to support Kirsch's argument that Buddhist cultures assign women, more than men, to a life of attachment because of women's intimate connection with the household life. She points out that as the ones who give birth, which is a metaphor for all becoming, women are 'more grossly implicated in the ensnarements of the world then men'. This idea is not restricted to the great tradition, but is equally apparent in the little tradition of village exorcism.[36]

We have seen from the example of the offering cloth that the monk's disassociation from women is premised on more than his need to resist carnal desires prompted by the temptation of women as sex objects. Here is also an allusion to another kind of power complex which, though not entirely distinct from the notion of women as sirens, refers to the directly polluting effects of female sexuality. Terwiel reports from his experience of several months spent as a Buddhist monk in central Thailand that 'menstrual blood is considered highly charged with dangerous magical power and even a casual contact may destroy some of the beneficial force of the members of the Sangha'.[37] Tannenbaum, in her ethnography of the Shan of north-western Thailand, expounds on the logic that informs such beliefs with a reminder that Buddhist magico-religious power generally refers to protection.[38] 'Power-protection does not cause good things to happen, it passively prevents bad things from happening.'[39]

However, there are beings that cancel power protection. These are the spirits of people who have had sudden or violent deaths and women. The genitalia and menstrual fluids of sexually mature women are destructive of power protection.

> Any object that has been in contact with women's genitals or genital excretions has the capacity to remove protective barriers. Women do not ride on the top of minibuses because that would place their genitals above men's heads and destroy their power or that of their amulets. Women's skirts, underwear and pants are hung up to dry in low places so that men will not be able to walk underneath them, thus destroying or weakening their power.[40]

Strict taboos associated with menstruation are also to be found in Sri Lanka where the power to cancel protection is known as *kili*.[41] Though, as Obeyesekere reports, *kili* does not prevent menstruating women from participating in Buddhist rites, few women of childbearing age take part in meditation and prayer on holy days (*poya*) anyway, and these activities are usually left to older village women. *Kili* is also associated with birth and with death. The connection between the ritual pollution associated with death and women in Sri Lanka chimes with that between bad death spirits and women noted by Amarasingham. The link with death prompts Obeyesekere to observe that 'men can be polluting only when they are no longer social beings; when they have moved for good out of the social structure. Women are polluting while they occupy certain definite positions in the social structure, between two phases in their life cycle – puberty at one end, and the menopause at the other.'[42] He also remarks that *kili* at childbirth is even more dangerous and polluting than at puberty, but this is contradicted by Winslow in her study of rituals surrounding first menstruation in Sri Lanka. She writes about how the pollution of first menstruation is said to be far greater than that of either birth or death.[43]

Winslow is instructive about the way in which pre-pubertal and post-menopausal females are treated, in stark contrast to those of childbearing age. For example, girl children are dressed in white, a colour associated with purity, and confer blessings on patients during curing exorcisms and also at weddings. Post-menopausal women also dress in white to participate in a ceremony to ensure the health of a child.[44] The role that these females, outside their childbearing years, fulfils is associated with the goddess Pattini, who is one of the Guardian Deities of Sri Lanka. Pattini is associated with the solving of family problems, but she also has a less benign aspect associated with the bringing of certain diseases. Winslow suggests that Pattini represents all the conflicting and diverse characteristics found in representations of Buddhist women. At certain stages of the life-cycle the female is 'infertile and pure with powers to bless and cure. At other times a woman is fecund and dangerous, possessed of unpredictable powers for a new life and for death.'[45] Women, nevertheless, remain constant in their important functions of providing subsistence for monks and sons for the perpetuation of the Sangha. So, by being both indispensable and threatening, women are rendered ambiguous and problematic.

Women, Reproduction and Production

It is obvious that fertile women can receive merit, otherwise they would have little or no investment in the day-to-day feeding of monks. Even so, the daily task of preparing and offering food to monks is not rated as highly in the economy of merit-making as is men's *dana*, which is more likely to take the form of offering other kinds of requisites to monks and in sponsoring the building of temples and founding of monasteries. Nevertheless, in line with their ambiguous status, fertile women can be recipients of protective merit as well as spoilers. Women can also generate some merit through moral deeds and can transfer merit to ancestors, either by thinking of them at the time of making *dana* or through a transference ritual. As has already been mentioned, most significantly women gain merit by producing sons for the Sangha.

Unlike men, including married men, women can never attain to the status of celibate monks, who are the generators and transmitters of merit *par excellence*. However, because of their crucial support for the material welfare of monks, the relationship between women and monks is not one of straightforward opposition at all levels. Classical structuralist analysis, based on the notion of binary opposition, indicates a universal tendency for women to be associated with the natural environment and the usually fearsome forces of nature, locating women in opposition to men who come to stand for the reassuring and civilizing forces of culture. But the analysis of gender in Buddhist societies is more complex than this. As Carol MacCormack warns: 'Neither the concept of nature nor that of culture is 'given' and they cannot be free from the biases of the culture in which the concepts were constructed.'[46]

One perspective on Buddhist concepts of nature in Sri Lanka and Thailand is provided through the long – though not entirely unbroken – historical tradition that the most meritorious and pure monks are those who dwell in the forest.[47] Taylor deals in depth with the symbolic relationship between contemporary meditating forest monks and their forest environment in the north-east of Thailand.[48] He characterizes the connection between the world renouncer and nature as 'polyphonous co-existence',[49] by which I take him to mean that the forest monks and the forest environment are not at one in the semantic sense, where through metaphorical extension one might stand for the other. Taylor's own choice of metaphor, 'polyphony', implies instead a harmony between distinct elements that are nevertheless in tune, so that for forest monks 'spirituality and the natural environment cannot be separated'. This is true even though the forest is commonly and pervasively figured as a fearsome place, inhabited by uncivilized tribal peoples, dangerous wild animals and malevolent spirits. The proper and secure place for ordinary civilized people is within the domesticated sphere of human settlement, but forest monks are protected from dangers by their mental attitudes of moral purity and goodwill.[50] It is instructive to note that during the early period of Buddhist history when the nuns' order remained extant, nuns were not permitted to become forest dwellers.[51] Is this because, though themselves renouncers, they remained open to the pollution attached to menstruation and could not achieve the extreme degree of purity attested to in stories of forest monks taming wild animals, even teaching them *dhamma*?

In mythology women are victims of men's uncontrolled lust that leads to them conceiving demons. In the lay people's practice of exorcism, women are also considered to be the prey of demons. This implies that they must be protected from wildness because they are more susceptible to it, just as they are passively susceptible to men's desires. Despite the surface appearance of women's sexuality leading to devious and deviant behaviour, it turns out that male sexual passion is the true source of disorder and a pre-eminent threat to purity. In its unrestrained form, male sexuality gives issue to demons and brings defeat to monks.

Male sexuality is also a factor in the breaking of the lay precept against sexual misconduct and in the breach of strong sexual taboos against adultery and incest. In the story of the Buddha's enlightenment his final heroic act is to deny sexual desire. This occurs when the devil-figure Mara, having tried all manner of tricks to defeat the Buddha, summons his daughters as temptation. Male sexuality, which is given an active orientation in relation to passive female sexuality, may, therefore, be construed as even more potent and dangerous. Such an interpretation goes some way to explaining the containment and subsequent transformation of male sexuality into protective power within a celibate order of monks. But there is also an inherent contradiction to be overcome, because the continuation of the Sangha, that incomparable field for the planting of merit by lay people of either gender, is dependent on women giving birth to sons. However, as the earlier discussion of the debate between Keyes and Kirsch reveals, this bald fact of life is masked and manipulated by a patriarchal discourse to produce the effect that it is women who need monks – particularly sons who become monks – as a source of religious gratification.

In addition, the degree of dependence that the Sangha has upon women in the economic sphere is also very great, though portions of their contribution are hidden and unacknowledged. Women's participation in the day-to-day feeding of monks is quite apparent, but their further contribution to monastic resources is indirect. Monastery buildings for example are usually sponsored by men, but their gifts are derived from income that has been generated by a household economy in which women are extremely productive. Within many sectors of both Thai and Sri Lankan society women of child-bearing age play an enormous part in economic production,[52] though they play far less a part than men in the political sphere, including involvement with monastic affairs.[53] Women's labour is, however, crucial to agriculture and other non-domestic economic spheres. After surveying a number of studies Winslow concludes that in Sri Lanka rural working women have 'considerable economic importance, independence and autonomy',[54] even though this belies the ideological subordination of women that has been described in this chapter. In rural Thailand women are prominent in entrepreneurial activities and land is often passed from parents to daughters. In as much as it depends on donations generated by households, the Sangha relies for its continuing existence on women's productive capacities, as well as their reproductive function.[55]

Buddhism and Nature

The previous examination of the ideological aspects of the culture of gender in Theravada Buddhism reveals no trace of the idea that women are 'sacred custodians' of the environment or that women have a special beneficial relationship with the natural world. Women may be represented as more 'attached' to *samsara*, but *samsara* includes both nature and culture. In the samsaric realm women are represented as deeply implicated in culture through their involvement with the family and the domestic economy rather than with the natural order. As we have seen, where nature, in the shape of the forest, is opposed to culture, in the form of human settlement, women are viewed as being in need of protection from its inherent perils.

Ian Harris argues that Buddhist doctrinal views of nature do not provide the kind of foundation 'from which environmental concerns can easily be developed in the way that some other religions, notably the Semitic religions of Judaism, Christianity and Islam do'.[56] As an example he considers the case of a vanishing species, such as the black rhino. Environmentalists in the West are keen to protect endangered species and such thinking can be traced back to a strand of thought in Christianity which proposes that humankind are 'stewards' of God's creation. Buddhist doctrine, however, teaches that: 'the rise and fall of things, whether they be mountains or animals, is part of the inexorable process Buddhists call *samsara*. In a sense, contemplation of this fact brings home to us our own lack of substance and permanence.'[57] The radical pessimism of the doctrine of impermanence is not to be mistaken for nihilism, but serves to demonstrate that those who inhabit *samsara* share the same fate.

In the light of the doctrine as it appears in the scriptures Harris concludes:

In essence and theory, then, Buddhism cannot uphold an environmentalist ethic. The reason for this is straightforward. There is nothing within the sphere of nature which can be said to possess any meaning or purpose. There can be no Buddhist justification for the fight to preserve habitats and environments. Everything, without exception, is subject to decay. It is not at all clear that change, within the natural world, can be positively affected by human intervention.[58]

Despite these difficulties, however, contemporary concern for the environment in Buddhist countries is taking on a religious aspect, especially in the context of development programmes. Lily de Silva, professor in the Department of Buddhist Studies at the University of Sri Lanka, employs the Pali scriptures to arrive at a completely different interpretation of the canonical attitude to the environment. de Silva concludes that while Buddhism stresses that change is inherent in nature it also teaches that 'humanity's moral deterioration accelerates and shapes the changes, bringing about circumstances which are adverse to human well-being and happiness'.[59] For de Silva Buddhism offers a 'middle way' in the form of moderation 'eschewing both extremes of self-deprivation and self-indulgence'.[60] de Silva is writing in a style and context associated with what has come to be known as ecoBuddhism, which is a synthesis of Judeo-Christian elements with orthodox Buddhist ideas. Even Ian Harris does not regard ecoBuddhism as a serious rupture with Buddhist tradition. Rather he views it as an example of 'a vigorous tradition engaged in a healthy process of reflexive apologetics'.[61] But even if ecoBuddhism grows in influence in Theravada Buddhism in the future, it is most likely to do so initially among educated urbanites rather than among the rural population who most usually form the focus for development projects.

Conclusion

Penny Van Esterik asserts that in Thailand and other parts of South-East Asia 'development and modernization have not always benefited women, either as urban entrepreneurs or as village farmers'.[62] This is because 'development planning usually reinforced existing values, emphasizing women's household and childrearing tasks, and superimposed Western values regarding appropriate work for women'.[63] Development planners should understand indigenous concepts of work which are not overlaid with the same distinctions, between productive and reproductive labour or between public and private domains, that operate in North Atlantic and Anglophone societies. We have seen how the same foods that are prepared by a woman for her family's consumption may also be sold on a vending stall or translated into symbolic and spiritual capital through donations to monks.

The fact is that Thai village women, particularly those of childbearing age, are almost always hard at work, and it is clear that this is also true for rural Sri Lanka, especially in dry land farming areas where women undertake 65 percent of agricultural activities. Wickramasinghe calculated that in the dry zone of Sri Lanka the total number of hours devoted to work by women, both in agriculture and in the house, is considerably higher than that of men,[64] and suggests that in order to improve the living conditions of rural women and to integrate them into the developmental process it is important to widen their training and employment opportunities.[65] A major obstacle is the lack of time which women have to devote themselves to training. As it is, women with small children do not even have enough time for sufficient sleep – let alone leisure. In Wickramasinghe's assessment the contemporary situation reflects a worsening one for many mothers, who do not nowadays receive as much help from their older children who are encouraged to attend school.

Development projects which do not recognize women's commitment to a packed schedule of farming, cooking, housekeeping and marketing, caring for the sick, the elderly and the young, as well as the production of extra resources for the routine feeding of monks, are therefore unlikely to succeed. As Elizabeth Harris has pointed out, in Asian societies, where disparities between urban rich and rural poor continue to increase, the search for reassurances through protective blessings is unlikely to diminish. In these circumstances the Sangha's role 'will not easily be displaced',[66] together with its implications for women.

Notes

1 A. T. Kirsch, 'Buddhism Sex Roles and the Thai Economy', in *Women of South East Asia*, ed. P. van Esterik (Illinois: Northern Illinois University Centre for South East Asian Studies, 1982), p. 28; D. Winslow, 'Status and Context: Sri Lankan Potter Women Reconsidered After Fieldwork in India', *Comparative Studies in Society and History*, 36 (1), 1994, pp. 3–35.

2 G. Obeyesekere, 'The Great Tradition and the Little in the Perspective of Sinhalese Buddhism', *Journal of Asian Studies*, 22 (2), 1963, pp. 139–53.

3 Ibid., p. 139.

4 Ibid., p. 153.

5 Ibid.

6 R. Gombrich and G. Obeyesekere, *Buddhism Transformed: Religious Change in Sri Lanka* (Princeton: Princeton University Press, 1989), p. 274.

7 N. Falk, 'The Case of the Vanishing Nuns: The Fruits of Ambivalence in Ancient Indian Buddhism', in *Unspoken Worlds: Women's Religious Lives in Non-Western Cultures*, eds N. Falk and R. Gross (San Francisco: Harper and Row, 1980), p. 207.

8 C. Kabilsingh, 'The Future of the Bhikkhuni Samgha in Thailand', in *Speaking of Faith: Cross Cultural Perspectives on Women*, eds D. L. Eck and D. Jain (London: The Women's Press, 1986), p. 142.

9 R. Gombrich, *Theravada Buddhism: A Social History from Ancient Benares to Modern Colombo* (London: Routledge and Kegan Paul, 1988), p. 16.

10 Ibid.

11 A. T. Kirsch, 'Economy, Polity and Religion in Thailand', in *Change and Persistence in Thai Society*, eds A. T. Kirsch and G. Skinner (Ithaca: Cornell University Press, 1975).

12 C. Keyes, 'Mothers or Mistresses but Never a Monk: Buddhist Notions of Female Gender in Rural Thailand', *American Ethnologist*, 11 (2), 1984, p. 226.

13 Ibid., p. 224.

14 Keyes, 'Mothers or Mistresses', p. 227, claims that these rural areas provide 'the cultural contexts from which come the majority of those women (and men) who are entering new economic roles in contemporary Thailand'. Keyes also believes that his argument can be sustained 'if constructed with reference to rural Siamese or central Thai culture, and probably even with reference to Khmer and Burmese culture'.

15 Ibid., p. 227.

16 Ibid., p. 229.

17 Ibid., p. 232.

18 A. T. Kirsch, 'Text and Context: Buddhist Sex Roles/Culture of Gender Revisited', *American Ethnologist*, 12 (2), 1985, pp. 302–20.

19 Ibid., p. 309.

20 Ibid., p. 310.

21 Ibid., p. 308.

22 Ibid.

23 Ibid., footnote 11.

24 Ibid., p. 308.

25 B. J. Terwiel, *Monks and Magic: An Analysis of Religious Ceremonies in Central Thailand*, revised edn. (London and Malmo: Curzon Press, 1979). Terwiel's fieldwork was carried out in Ratburi in the south-west corner of the central rice-growing area of Thailand. He was able to experience the avoidance practices of monks towards women first hand when he joined the Sangha.

26 G. Obeyesekere, 'Pregnancy Cravings (Dola-Duka) in Relation to Social Structure and Personality in a Sinhalese Village', *Journal of Asian Studies*, 65 (2), 1963, pp. 323–42. Obeyesekere was assisted in his research among Laggala women on topics usually considered too sensitive to discuss with men by Ms Sumana Saparamadu.

27 D. Winslow, 'Rituals of First Menstruation in Sri Lanka', *Man*, n.s.,15 (4), 1980, pp. 603–25.

28 A monk who confesses to having intercourse with a woman, or is proved to have done so, is *ipso facto* no longer a member of the Sangha. Even if he does not confess, the monk is in any case said to be 'defeated' in his efforts towards salvation and is no longer actually a monk. If he conceals his offence and takes part in the twice monthly recitation of the 227 rules of the monastic code he compromises the 'purity' that is the charismatic source of the Sangha's magico-religious power. In this case his influence comes to resemble that of female fertility in its propensity to diminish the protective power derived from the ascetic practices of male celibates.

29 Terwiel, *Monks and Magic*, p. 114.
30 A fellow anthropologist reported to me that while on holiday in Bangkok she saw a monk sitting on one of the reserved seats of a bus reading a 'girlie' magazine.
31 Terwiel, *Monks and Magic*, p. 114.
32 Obeyesekere, 'The Great Tradition', p. 326.
33 L. Amarasingham, 'The Misery of the Embodied: Representations of Women in Sinhalese Myth', in *Women in Ritual and Symbolic Roles*, eds J. Hoch-Smith and A. Spring (New York: Plenum Press, 1978), pp. 101–26.
34 P. Dahlke, *Buddhist Essays* (New York: Macmillan, 1908), quoted by Amarasingham, 'Misery of the Embodied', p. 103.
35 Keyes, 'Mothers or Mistresses', p. 231.
36 Amarasingham, 'Misery of the Embodied', p. 104.
37 Terwiel, *Monks and Magic*, p. 115.
38 N. Tannenbaum, 'Witches, Fortune, and Misfortune Among the Shan of Northwest Thailand', in *Understanding Witchcraft and Sorcery in Southeast Asia*, eds C. W. Watson and R. Elder (Honolulu: University of Hawaii Press, 1993) pp. 67–80.
39 Ibid., p. 70.
40 Ibid., p. 75.
41 Obeyesekere, 'Pregnancy Cravings'.
42 Ibid., p. 330.
43 Winslow, 'Rituals of First Menstruation in Sri Lanka', p. 617.
44 Ibid., pp. 616–17.
45 Ibid., p. 620.
46 C. MacCormack, 'Nature, Culture and Gender: A Critique', in *Nature Culture and Gender*, eds C. MacCormack and M. Strathern (Cambridge: Cambridge University Press, 1980), p. 6.
47 M. Carrithers, *The Forest Monks of Sri Lanka* (Delhi: Oxford University Press, 1983); S. J. Tambiah, *The Buddhist Saints of the Forest and the Cult of Amulets* (Cambridge: Cambridge University Press, 1984).
48 J. L.Taylor, *Forest Monks and the Nation-State* (Singapore: Institute of Southeast Asian Studies, 1993). Taylor draws comparisons and support for some of his own findings from Carrithers, 1983.
49 Ibid., p. 236.
50 Ibid., p. 237.
51 I. Harris, 'Buddhism', in *Attitudes to Nature*, eds J. Holm and J. W. Bowker (London: Pinter Publishers, 1994), p. 22.
52 For Sri Lanka see Winslow, 'Status and Context', pp. 2–36; A. Wickramasinghe, 'Women's Roles in Rural Sri Lanka', in *Different Places, Different Voices*, eds J. H. Momsem and V. Kinnard (London: Routledge, 1993). For Thailand see Kirsch, 'Buddhism Sex Roles', pp. 16–40.
53 Bunnag, for example, reports that in Thailand women play a negligible part in the monastery committees that provide a link between the monastery and its supporters - 'as they tend to be less highly educated, and, allegedly, more naturally stupid than their male counterparts, they are felt to be unfitted for the "paperwork" which committee membership may entail'. J. Bunnag, *Buddhist Monk, Buddhist Layman: A Study of Urban Monastic Organization in Central Thailand* (Cambridge: Cambridge University Press, 1973), p. 135.
54 D. Winslow, 'Status and Context: Sri Lankan Potter Women Reconsidered After Fieldwork in India', *Comparative Studies in Society and History*, 36 (1), 1994.

55 This point is also made regarding Theravada Buddhism in Laos by M. Ngaosy-vathn, 'Buddhism, Merit Making and Gender: The Competition for Salvation in Laos', in *'Male' and 'Female' in Developing Southeast Asia*, ed. W. J. Karim (Oxford: Berg Publishers, 1995).

56 I. Harris, 'Buddhism', in *Attitudes to Nature*, eds Holm and Bowker, p. 16.

57 Ibid.

58 Ibid., p. 25.

59 L. de Silva, 'The Hills Wherein My Soul Delights: Exploring the Stories and Teachings', in *Buddhism and Ecology*, eds M. Batchelor and K. Brown (London: Cassell Publishers, 1992), p. 20.

60 Ibid., p. 29.

61 I. Harris, 'Buddhist Environmental Ethics and Detraditionalization: The Case of EcoBuddhism', *Religion*, 25, 1995, pp. 199–211.

62 P. van Esterik, 'Rewriting Gender and Development Anthropology in South East Asia', in *'Male' and 'Female'*, ed. W. J. Karim, p. 249.

63 Ibid.

64 Wickramasinghe, 'Women's Roles in Rural Sri Lanka', p. 169.

65 Ibid, p. 174.

66 E. Harris, 1980. 'Internal and External Authority Among Lay Buddhist Women in Contemporary Sri Lanka', *Scottish Journal of Religious Studies*, 18 (1), p. 73.

12

Nature, Holism and Ecofeminism: A Chinese Worldview

Stewart McFarlane

When environmental issues are discussed in a cross-cultural or religious context, it has become almost commonplace to cite ancient Chinese values as providing a model for a balanced understanding of human interdependence with the natural and cosmic order. The traditional Chinese concern with harmonizing the personal, social, natural and cosmic, in terms of yin-yang and the notion of a universal energy, are frequently elaborated as contributing to a deeper ecological understanding. Sophisticated traditional techniques for establishing harmony, such as Chinese medicine, feng shui (geomancy), ch'i kung and T'ai chi ch'uan /Tai ji quan and use of the Yi Ching as a book of wisdom, combine to form a compelling picture of an alternative to Western methods of dominance and technical dependence.

The Main Features of the Traditional Chinese Worldview

An important feature of the fundamental categories of Chinese naturalistic thought is that they are describing the functions of things, events and processes rather than their ultimate metaphysical natures. Spirituality is not the concern. Chinese thought tends to deal with processes in concrete and functional terms rather than abstract ones. It also tends to avoid fragmenting characteristics, and instead emphasizes their fluidity, interdependence and relationship.

All these features are apparent in the notion of ch'i. The traditional way of drawing the character illustrates vapour rising from rice. This illustrates how the material or substantial rice gives rise to the non-material or insubstantial vapour. Both are involved in generating the kind of energizing force that constitutes ch'i. Without the rice there would be no vapour. Many accounts of ch'i confuse people because they deal with the concept in a too abstract and metaphysical way. It is necessary to specify the type of ch'i being referred to by specifying its functions, and describing the context in which it is being used. In a medical context, specific types of ch'i are usually being referred to. Manfred Porkert's monumental study of the basic concepts and systems of Chinese medicine refers to thirty-two types of ch'i which are commonly described in Chinese medicine. He compares the concept of ch'i in traditional Chinese thought, to the concept of electrical energy in modern Western thought. Just as electrical energy is a general term for a phenomenon which has different specific forms, such as high and low voltage, or high and low amperage, so ch'i is a general term for a phenomenon with a wide range of aspects and functions.[1] On the other hand, ch'i is a frequently occurring concept in ordinary conversation, and may mean anything from kind – he ch'i (literally 'harmonious spirit'), to brave – yong ch'i, and the weather – t'ien ch'i (literally 'sky vapours').

It is apparent that the term 'ch'i' is extremely common in the Chinese language, with a wide range of apparently quite unrelated meanings. Unless the context provides a clear indication of what meaning of ch'i is being used, then it is necessary to specify the type of ch'i in question. This is most easily achieved by specifying its function.

Taoism and the Natural

Taoism, like Confucianism, incorporates the fundamental assumptions of Chinese thought, but developed them in different directions and towards different skills. The Taoist mystics, sages and poets valued the primitive and natural as models of spontaneity (tzu jan) and non-volitional action (wu wei). They saw Confucian prescriptions and policies as harmful because they imposed inappropriate and artificial standards on people, and did not allow Heaven and nature their role as the ultimate models, arbitrators and illuminators of the Way (Tao).

Heaven is long lasting and earth is enduring.
Why is this so? Because they do not live for themselves.
Therefore they endure.

The highest good is like water;
Water benefits the ten thousand things but does not compete with
   them.
It dwells in the places that people disdain.
Therefore it is close to Tao.

In dwelling, the good thing is the land;
In the mind, the good thing is depth;
In giving, the good thing is to be like Heaven;
In speaking, the good thing is sincerity;
In governing, the good thing is order;
In affairs, the good thing is ability;
In action, the good thing is timing.

In not competing it is without error.
Tao Te Ching – 4th century BCD (own trans.)

The early Taoists elevated the feminine as the creative and nurturing Mother, and saw her as the highest expression of harmony
with Tao, and the key to ordering life (see Tao Te Ching, chap. 25).
Many chapters in the Tao Te Ching recommend taking the 'female'
or 'infant' or yin role in one's actions (chaps 10, 22, 25, 52, 61). This
involves taking a passive, yielding, non-intrusive role. It could be
argued that this still represents a patriarchal projection of the idealized feminine, rather than a realistic model for women. Furthermore, the advice in the Tao Te Ching is specifically directed to the
Sage Ruler, and, indirectly, to anyone who would rule himself. No
real guidance is given to women as to what role they should take.[2]
If male sages are taking the female, yin, role, it raises the question
what role female sages should take? The text seems to suggest that
they become even more yin in quality. That greater strength will be
derived from greater submissivness and apparent passivity.

   The great Taoist sage Chuang tzu (fourth century BCE) develops
his message more systematically than the Tao Te Ching. With a
combination of clever argument and poetic skill, he criticizes pre-
scriptive teachings which fail to recognize epistemological, linguistic, cultural, natural, and developmental diversity, and which
rigidly impose partial and limited views both in theory and in policy. His main contemporary targets were the Confucian officials,
and their rivals the Legalists. His arguments and illustrations,

while primarily concerned with linguistic and epistemic relativity, have clear behavioural and environmental implications. In chapter seven he tells the tragic but revealing story of Hun-tun. The ruler of primordial, creative chaos, Hun-tun is primal simplicity, in one sense, pre-ordered nature or wilderness. The rulers of the North and South were visiting Hun-tun at the central region. In discussing how to repay Hun-tun's kindness they noticed that he lacked the seven openings which all men have. So they decided to bore some openings for him. Each day they drilled a new hole in him. On the seventh day he died. Here Chuang tzu is criticizing a rigid mind-set which takes its own categories, values and judgements and imposes them unreflectively on others, and upon nature. The tendency to dominate and impose was evident in patriarchal, bureaucratic culture. Chuang tzu is warning of the dangers of such attitudes.

On the issue of gender and role reversal mentioned above the story prior to Hun-tun in chapter seven, describing Lieh tzu's process of illumination at the hands of his Taoist teacher Hu tzu, throws a little more light on the subject, but still illustrates role reversal as a male procedure. After witnessing a dramatic encounter between Hu tzu and a shamanic face reader, Lieh tzu realizes that he knows nothing, because from the standpoint of the Tao nothing is knowable, in formal propositional or descriptive terms. Consequently he stays at home for three years, replaces his wife at the stove, feeds the pigs as though feeding people, shows no discriminatory preferences in his attitudes, and returns to plainness and simplicity, 'In the midst of entanglement he remained sealed, and in this oneness he ended his life'.[3]

There is a strongly utopian, anarchistic and primitivist strand within the early Taoist texts, which appears to reverse the conventional Confucian ideal of the ordered state. The Taoists commend decentralization, and low technology agricultural communities where people live out their lives in rural contentment, forming a deep attachment to the land, without aspiring to the trappings of civilization. (Tao Te Ching, chap. 80).

Though rarely given the chance to be implemented, this primitivist vision did influence the Taoist religious communities and rebel states which briefly flourished during the period of disunity towards the end of the Han dynasty (2nd century CE). Under the leadership of charismatic and visionary Taoist leaders, the Heavenly Masters sect in Szechwan, and the Way of Great Peace or Yellow Turbans in eastern China, controlled large areas and operated independently of the Han government. They were administered as village-based communities under the leadership of trained Taoist ritual and administrative leaders.[4] The Taoist respect for nature, and the ideal of balance and harmony, articulated in the earliest Taoist texts, continued to be expressed through Taoist-influenced painting, calligraphy and poetry. These ideas and images exert a powerful appeal to some Deep Ecologists, and environmental activists.[5]

Yin-Yang Classification and its Environmental Implications

In Chinese medical diagnosis ch'i is often classified in functional terms as either yin or yang in quality. Again, these terms carry with them a wide range of associations and meanings. Some of these are suggested in the pictographic elements used to write the characters. It is worth looking into these more closely. The character yin includes an element meaning hill, another meaning time and another meaning cloud or shade. The basic meaning is therefore understood as the shaded side of a hill. It extends in meaning to refer to the following qualities of things, phenomena and states of affairs: cold, rest, responsiveness, passivity, darkness, inwardness and decrease. The character for yang also has the element for hill, along with an element depicting the sun and an element depicting a waving flag. This is traditionally understood as the sunny side of a hill. It refers to the qualities of heat, brightness, stimulation, movement, vigour, light, and increase. It is clear from the way these concepts are used in Chinese thought, both in specialist areas and in general usage, that they are not metaphysical categories or irreducible entities. They do not describe the inner nature of things in the way that ancient Greek metaphysics sought to do. They are simply ways of characterizing things and how they relate to each other and to other phenomena.

By noting early references to yin and yang in ancient texts such as the Yi Ching (Classic of Change) and the Tao Te Ching, it is clear that these concepts were first developed on the basis of observing natural processes, the progression of time and the seasons, as the following passage from an ancient part of the Yi Ching illustrates.

When the sun goes the moon comes; when the moon goes the sun comes. The sun and moon give way to each other and their brightness is produced. When the cold goes the heat comes; when the heat goes the cold comes. The cold and the heat give way to each other and the round of the year is completed. That which goes wanes, and that which comes waxes. The waning and waxing affect each other and benefits are produced.

(Yi Ching 'Hsi Tz'u, 2 ll).[6]

This passage also suggests the idea of complementarity and mutual entailment that is always implicit in the identification of yin and yang qualities. This idea was developed in chapter 2 of the Tao Te Ching.

It is because everyone under Heaven recognises beauty as beauty that the idea of ugliness exists.
It is because everyone under Heaven recognises good as good that the idea of bad exists.
Being and non-being produce each other.

The simplified T'ai chi symbol (developed by the philosopher Chou Tun-yi (1017–1073 CE) perfectly illustrates this notion of mutual entailment and interdependence of yin and yang qualities. They gracefully interweave in the curve shaped like a reverse 'S'. Each quality contains within the seed or potential of its opposite, represented by the dot of the opposite shade in each segment. The curve which represents the boundary between yin and yang suggests movement, and a constantly changing relationship. Another passage in the Tao Te Ching emphasizes the creative and cosmological side of this relationship.

Tao gave birth to one,
One gave birth to two,
Two gave birth to the ten thousand things.
The ten thousand things carry yin on their backs and embrace yang in their arms.
Through blending ch'i they achieve harmony. (chap. 42).

This passage became very important in the development of religious Taoist liturgy, which ritually reproduces the conditions of the emergence of all phenomena in the universe.[7] Saso has shown in detail how family altars in the home, public temples and, in theory, the plan of a traditional Chinese city, are set out according to yin-yang five element principles.[8] He concludes:

the Yin-yang five element theory acts as a 'deep' (subconscious) structure, which determines how a city, temple, and altar are built and decorated, how ritual is initiated, and the cosmos is conceived in its macro (nature) and micro (body) environments. Whether recognized by the casual informant, or hidden in the memory banks of the expert Taoist priest, the structure of Chinese religious architecture, festivals and meditation, is operative everywhere in China.[9]

Because yin-yang classifications are expressing the qualities of things in relation to each other, then obviously what counts as yin and yang will vary according to the context. This is confusing to people who insist on thinking in an 'absolute fragmented way' of yin and yang as irreducible, dualistic opposites. What counts as yin depends on what it is being compared to, and under what circumstances. Ice is yin in relation to rock, but yang in relation to water. Water is yang in relation to steam. Similarly a man is yang in relation to a woman, but may be yin in relation to another man. It is clear from these examples that yin-yang thinking tends to refer to the relational and functional qualities of things and processes. It is consequently a great mistake to treat these terms as referring to fixed, absolute characteristics of things. In relation to most natural phenomena, yin describes the concretizing functions in nature, while yang describes the dynamizing tendencies in nature.

The basic classification into two tendencies was further refined by the introduction of the five phases or elements. These describe more the specific phases or qualities of ch'i as they transform and interweave, by relating them to the characteristics of five natural phenomena. The movement and constantly changing pattern of ch'i is strongly suggested in five phases (wu hsing) theory. What is important in traditional five phase thinking is how each phase gives way to or gives rise to the succeeding one. Thus, wood if heated becomes fire, which in turn becomes earth (ashes).

Chinese Geomancy (Feng shui)

The ch'i, yin-yang and five phases classificatory systems help to underpin and explain the force of the perceived correspondence between human affairs, our psycho-physical states and processes in nature and the cosmos. The feng shui or geomancy system of traditional China focuses on the flow and patterns of ch'i in the landscape, and claims to show how the position, and alignment of internal features, of buildings and tombs, crucially affect the flow of ch'i, hence the health and welfare of the occupants. The feng shui system is complex and highly adaptable. It flourishes in Hong Kong and Taiwan and is being revived in mainland China. In urban and controlled environments, where most people have little control over siting of buildings, considerable emphasis is placed on the location and alignment of doors, windows, mirrors and interior features such as furniture.[10]

While reflecting a sensitivity to the environment and an awareness of the subtle relationship between environment, structure and psycho-physical well-being, the feng shui system of traditional China is not the same as scientific ecological theory or even an environmental ethic. It does, however, reflect an indigenous knowledge system which appears to have anticipated and resolved problems with which the modern West is only just able to identify. The modern Western phenomenon of sick-building syndrome seems to have been anticipated and solved by the Chinese. Similarly the pragmatic effectiveness of many methods of Chinese medicine, which operate along the lines of the theories outlined, continue to impress Western patients and practitioners, as well as confound sceptics.

Confucian Expressions of Natural, Social and Personal Harmony

Such a system or way of thinking presupposes, and has its historical roots in, a naturalistic worldview and a deep appreciation of the interdependence of human and natural processes. From the Han dynasty (202 BCE – 220 CE) onwards, the role of the Emperor and the Confucian bureaucracy which supported him, was to ensure the harmony between Heaven, Earth and Humanity.

> The ruler of men uses his love and hate, his joy and anger to change and reform the customs of men, as Heaven employs warm and cool, cold and hot weather to transform the grass and trees. If joy and anger are seasonally applied, then the year will be prosperous, but if they are used wrongly and out of season then the year will fail. Heaven, earth and man are one, and therefore the passions of man are one with the seasons of Heaven. So the time and place for each must be considered. If Heaven produces heat in the time for cold, or cold in the time for heat, then the year must be bad, while if the ruler manifests anger when joy would be appropriate, or joy where anger is needed, then the age must fall into chaos.
>
> (Tung Chung-shu, 179–104 BCE)[11]

The centralized Han state was concerned with the controlled exploiting of the natural environment, and the careful monitoring of climatic, environmental and social change, as the means of confirming Heaven's approval of the Emperor's conduct and policies. The interactive correspondence between Heaven, Earth and Humanity and the high value placed on harmony is very clear in the above passage from the Confucian scholar Tung Chung-shu, the main formulator of Han cosmology and ideology. The Chinese Imperial state tended to take a long-term view, and recognized the importance of sustainable agricultural methods. Such views can be traced back to the authoritative Confucian teachings of Mencius (371–289 BCE) and Hsun tzu (300–230 BCE). Their teachings helped to shape Han and all subsequent Chinese Imperial cosmology, ideology and ethics. They repeatedly illustrate their ethical teachings and arguments with examples of sound sustainable agricultural practices. While placing human interests and sustainable agricultural methods at the centre of their theory, they emphasize the need to preserve species, and their environments. Mencius comments on the unnaturalness of the deforestation and over-grazing of Ox Mountain near the city (Book 6, Part A, v.8). Hsun tzu reminds ministers and rulers of the need to preserve habitats and animals in the breeding season:

> When shrubs and trees are in bloom and leaf, the axe must not enter the forest, people must not cut short the life of the trees or shrubs when young . . . when sea tortoises, water lizards, fish turtles, eels, and sturgeons, are full of roe or have spawned, nets or poison must not enter the marshes or pools, people must not cut short the life of these water creatures when young . . .'[12]

These injunctions also illustrate the fact that the Chinese environment, while vast, was not seen as inexhaustible, and that potential problems of deforestation, soil erosion and species depletion were recognized in ancient China.

Worldview and Practice: The Problem of China's Environmental Record

While acknowledging that the Chinese naturalisitic worldview valued nature, both as a sustainable resource and aesthetic inspiration for artistic and poetic creativity, the Chinese geographer Tuan Yi-Fu pointed out that, in some regions and periods, China's treatment of its environment has had disastrous consequences. He cites cases where officials criticized the action of local people in deforesting and over-grazing, resulting in soil erosion and dangerous flooding as water courses change.[13] Tuan also acknowledges the Chinese tradition of reforestation, which was frequently implemented by Confucian officials. What needs to be remembered is that as the Empire expanded even a benign administration, which endorsed the values outlined above, was incapable of monitoring and preventing destruction. This situation applied to China through most of the nineteenth and the first half of the twentieth century. The Japanese occupation, the civil war, and the Communist takeover in 1949, all contributed to the acceleration of environmentally destructive processes. These events also contributed to the collapse of the traditional Chinese worldview.

The policies of Mao and the early phases of the Chinese revolution, accelerated the damage. In a desperate attempt to increase agricultural production the Communist leadership opened up vast areas of unsuitable land, encouraged a population explosion, and forced agriculturally unskilled city dwellers onto the land, and developed heavy industry based around iron and coal production, with no apparent concern for their environmental impact or long-term economic value. These disastrous policies had to be reversed during the 1970s. Since the death of Mao in 1976, China has slowly attempted to liberalize economically, is now embracing capitalism and free enterprise with a vengeance. Despite some concessions to environmental considerations, including attempts to reforest and protect watersheds and reverse soil erosion, the post-Mao Chinese government's commitment to economic and agricultural expansion means that China's environmental prospects look bleak.[14]

Setting aside the contemporary situation, since China no longer operates under the influence of a traditional Chinese worldview, there is the fundamental issue raised by Tuan, which is that of the relationship between worldview, policy and actual behaviour. This is his major objection to the central argument of Lynn White's influential paper, that the early medieval Christian theology of human dominance over nature, and of the radical separation of humanity from creation, is directly responsible for the modern ecological crisis.[15] Tuan makes the point that even under administrations and systems which did value the environment, the failure to identify long-term consequences of actions was sometimes an issue. One ironic case may serve to illustrate this. In T'ang China, increasing literacy, and the expanding Confucian bureaucracy, which had to be trained through extensive written examination, required soot made from pine trees to make their ink for their writing brushes. So in order to be examined in the Confucian Classics, which as we have seen, attempted to harmonize Heaven, Earth and Humanity, and included injunctions against environmental destruction, and of course to compose beautiful poetry and landscape paintings which celebrate nature, as well as to print large runs of Buddhist ethical teachings and sutras which include injunctions to avoid meat-eating and avoid unnecessary damage to living things, large tracts of forest were destroyed between Shansi and Hebei.[16] Similarly, although Chinese Buddhist temples preserved groves of trees around the temple, in south-east China they encouraged deforestation by popularizing cremation ceremonies from the tenth to the fourteenth centuries.

Tuan considers the issue in terms of conflicting forces in Chinese culture, worldview and history. He employs the traditional classification, yang qualities of male dominance perpetuated by patriarchal Confucian values, and the neglect of Taoist-based yin qualities. One manifestation of this was the adoption of Heavenly (yang) based astronomical modelling in favour of the yin-based, earth-oriented feng shui system, in the construction of the city of Ch'ang An during the early seventh century. This notion of a tension in the Chinese worldview, producing different and opposite effects, is implicit in yin-yang polarity theory. It is an integral part of the theory to apply it to policies and phases of Chinese history. One of the strengths of traditional Chinese worldview is that it includes an account of the factors behind environmental, social and political disintegration. I shall return to this in the next section. It should not be thought that the Confucian methods of dominance and technological mastery (yang in character) are necessarily environmentally destructive and exploitative. Governor Li Bing's ambitious flood control and irrigation system at Dujiangyan on the Chengdu plain, which was constructed in 250 BCE, and which still functions today, protected the population from devastating floods, increased grain production, and prevented soil erosion and livestock losses. Similar flood control, canal and irrigation projects were undertaken during this period.[17]

Relevance Today

For modern activists and environmental campaigners, Taoism does have much to say. Taoist texts offer a model of harmony and simplicity and a traditional acknowledgement of human, natural and cosmic interdependence. They celebrate natural processes and emphasize the value of according with them rather than trying to control them. They have much to say on issues of conflict avoidance strategy, indirect means of achieving one's ends, the use of passivity as a source of strength and resilience, when to concede territory and when to avoid head on conflict, an enemy's weaknesses and when to push home an advantage. There are now many examples of Eco-Warriors employing Tibetan, Chinese and Native American ritual practices, meditational skills and rhetorical motifs, in support of their activism.[18]

The environmental group Earth First run camps in Wales which include training in effective resistance strategies to protect trees and land. They employ self-defence training based on tai chi methods which proved extremely useful at environmental protest sites such as Newbury, Fairmile and the Manchester Airport second runway protest.

In tactical terms it appears that a non-confrontational Taoist approach, often adopted by women's only direct action campaigns such as the women's peace camp at Menwith Hill in North Yorkshire, is frequently the most successful. One response would be to encourage and facilitate women's only non-violent direct action. Another would be to encourage male activists to adopt a less confrontational, more 'female' role. This is exactly what Lao Tzu recommends to the sage ruler in the Tao Te Ching. Non-confrontational Taoist-style self-defence methods based on T'ai chi ch'uan principles are effective both in terms of limiting injuries to both sides, and reducing aggression levels in direct action protests. Women in particular rapidly absorb these skills and find great internal strength and resilience in their application. There is a 'Taoist' quality about the approach to non-violent direct action adopted by women activists. The exemplars of such methods in Britain were the peace campaigners of Greenham Common. Their successors we the Women's Peace Camp at Menwith Hill surveillance facility, and the 'Ploughshares' campaigners against the export of Hawk warplanes to the Indonesian military, for use against the civilian population of Indonesian-occupied East Timor. All these provide challenging examples of the possibilities of non-confrontational, non-violent methods of resisting injustice.

The women of the Ploughshares campaign patiently exhausted all the legal methods of protest against such exports, including writing to the Government, petitioning MPs and writing to Defence, and

Trade and Industry officials. In January 1996 four of the campaigners illegally entered the British Aerospace facility at Warton and disarmed a Hawk aircraft which was ready for shipment. They then waited several hours for security officials and police to arrest them. They accepted the consequences of their action and did not resist arrest, but argued in court that their 'offences' of breaking and entering and criminal damage were justified in order to prevent the genocidal use of these planes in East Timor.[19] Ploughshares campaigners and eco-warriors, in their readiness to accept long-term imprisonment and their resistance to injustice, are a tribute to inner resilience, discipline and strength, as well as to the effectiveness of non-violent, but radical methods, just as the peaceful inhabitants of the Taoist utopia of the Tao Te Ching.[20] They were not prepared to use weapons of war, and were prepared to suffer extreme punishment or even death to resist an unjust system. Passages in the Tao Te Ching make it clear that military engagements should be taken reluctantly and as a last resort, and that military action which is defensive is superior to that which is offensive. Such passages are in effect outlining a strategy which is yin or female rather than yang or male, in quality. The action of the Ploughshares women who employed direct action to prevent greater violence, and were acquitted on that basis, brilliantly demonstrated a Taoist strategic response to the problem of violence and armed force.

The relevant chapters of the Tao Te Ching are translated here:

A good warrior is not violent.
A good fighter is not angry.
A good winner is not competitive.
A good employer of men is humble before them.
This is called the virtue of non contention,
Or employing the strength of others,
This is called conforming with the ultimate, heaven. (chap. 68)

The strategists say.
'I do not take the offensive but the defensive.
I do not advance an inch but retreat a foot.'
This is called advancing without advancing
Rolling up one's sleeve when there is no arm,
Attacking without an army,
Engaging without weapons.
There is no greater mistake than to undertake military action lightly.
To do so almost destroys my treasures.
So when two armies oppose each other,
The one with sympathy wins. (chap. 69)

When people are born they are supple and soft;
When they die, they are hard and rigid.
In life the ten thousand creatures, plants and trees are supple and
pliant;
In death they are brittle and dry.
So it is said that the hard and rigid are the companions of death, while
the supple and soft are the companions of life.
So if a fighter is rigid, he will not win,
If a tree is rigid it will come to an end.
The rigid and powerful are inferior,
The supple and soft are superior. (chap. 76)

The message in these texts is that conflict can be handled according to Taoist principles by employing the more yin aspects of the
Tao. It seems to be women activists such as the Ploughshares campaigners who have recognized and followed these principles. They
are following a tradition of Eastern-influenced civil disobedience
campaigns, and in particular the notion of 'moral jiujitsu' developed by Richard Gregg. Gregg's views were shaped by his experience of Gandhi's *satyagraha* (truth force) campaigns for Indian
Independence in the 1920s and 1930s.[21]

Holbrook on Paradigm and Practice

Bruce Holbrook whose book *The Stone Monkey* (1981)[22] was written as a result of his apprenticeship to a traditional Chinese doctor
in Taiwan, and his attempt to understand the theories and assumptions underlying Chinese medicine, internal arts and culture. His
project is much more ambitious than that of Tuan. He set out the
paradigm underlying Chinese ethical, social, scientific, medical,
and religious thought. He contrasts this with the paradigm underlying Western science, religion and thought. In his view, the Chinese paradigm and its applications are greatly superior in terms of
offering a genuine scientific, humanistic and ecological way of
engaging with the world. His critique of Western thought, science
and technology is wide and uncompromising.

Holbrook argues that traditional Chinese thought is founded
upon a 'polar complete' model or paradigm, in which apparently
opposite qualities and functions of things constitute a complementary, mutually supportive whole. He sees yin-yang theory as simply
the formalized expression of this type of thinking. The polar complete way of thinking identifies the mutuality and interdependence

of apparent opposites, it acknowledges that theorizing about and classifying phenomena is a human activity, and that theory and its applications should serve human interests. Decision-making, including the pursuit of scientific and technological research and development, must be made to serve humanity or human empathy, the Confucian concept of jen.

Holbrook argues that modern Western scientific thought is founded on an 'absolute fragmented paradigm', which sees the mental and material as absolute opposites, attempts to classify reality according to an abstract, mental or ideal scheme. Such a paradigm insists that scientific inquiry is only valid when it is objective, that is, when human considerations are removed from the inquiry. Holbrook sees the struggle between materialism and idealism in classical Greek thought, which still persists in various forms in the contemporary West, as simply different expressions of the Western absolute fragmented paradigm. He sees Western thought as seriously flawed in its attempt to explain ultimate reality as either material or mental/spiritual in nature. More seriously, he sees the failure to anticipate or acknowledge the seriousness of many of the 'side effects' of Western science and technology, such as pollution, bacterial immunity, radiation poisoning and ozone depletion, as attributable to the misguided pursuit of knowledge in the interests of scientific objectivity and neutrality, without regard for human considerations. Such knowledge, he argues, is always fragmented and partial, and the systematic failure to acknowledge human subjectivity in the pursuit of such knowledge means that it will always fail us. Quoting his teacher of traditional Chinese medicine and thought:

> One must fully realise that one is human, that humans are an aspect of the living whole, before one can reflect about what is true or false, right or wrong. It is because humans exist that we are here asking these questions. They are humans' reflections. To forget that disqualifies one from making any reflections at all. As soon is there is even a little misunderstanding about this, one has to invent a God of one kind or another to make up the difference.[23]

Dynastic Collapse and the Chinese View of History: Implications for Women and the Environment

Many of Holbrook's points are valid, but there is, however, a tendency in his argument to present an idealized and rather abstract version of the main features of Chinese naturalistic thought. He tends to dismiss the less admirable features of Chinese history and traditional culture, such as foot-binding, female infanticide, concubinage, judicial torture and extreme conservatism in legal and administrative matters, as unrepresentative aberrations, which only occurred at times of dynastic collapse and external influence. There is also a tendency for some Western observers to regard institutions and practices which were evident in nineteenth- and early twentieth-century China, as present throughout the whole of Chinese history.

There is evidence in the dynastic histories and other documents, that women's roles in the period up to the early Sung dynasty (960–1279) were more flexible, and were respected. There are cases of educated women being moral guides and exemplars, giving wise advice to their husbands, sometimes on official matters of state and politics, as well as taking the lead in resolving family crises.[24] There are also records of women Taoist adepts in respected positions in the Religious Taoist hierarchy.[25] The development of Sung Neo-Confucian thought, and perhaps economic factors, seem to have led to a downgrading of women and the restriction of their participation in society and public life. Neo-Confucianism appears to have adopted a dualistic ethic and an increasing ambivalence to the body and sexuality. The Chinese male had always feared depletion of the ching essence through excessive or unskilful sexual indulgence. This always had the potential to be expressed through fear of women's sexuality.[26] Ironically, under the influence of Sung Neo-Confucianism, instructional manuals on sexual alchemy and bedroom arts, which teach how to enjoy sex and nurture and supplement the ching essences without suffering depletion, were suppressed and removed from state libraries and bibliographies. By the Ming Dynasty (1368–1644 CE) this official censorship was complete.[27] Some of these texts survived in private libraries and many were preserved in Japan. Neo-Confucianism, possibly under the influence of Buddhism, became ambivalent about the distractions of family life, as a restriction on personal moral and spiritual cultivation.[28] The traditional Confucian view was that it was within the family that virtue, benevolence, deference and restraint were cultivated. In Neo-Confucianism, doubts about the value of family life seem to have emerged, partly because it distracted the aspiring Sage from his inward quest and personal cultivation. This had an effect on elite social attitudes. Similarly, foot-binding was not widely adopted for most classes of women until the eighteenth century, and it was unknown before the Sung dynasty (960–1279 CE).[29] In support of Holbrook, aberrations in later Chinese history should not be seen as typical for all China's past.

It can be agreed that in their classical or traditional formulations, fundamentally different paradigms dominated Western thought and Chinese thought. These paradigms certainly affected the respective worldviews, and must have had some influence on behaviour and policy. But they cannot be said to have been wholly determinative of behaviour. Local, historical and regional variables and individual acts of ecological vandalism, as well as the failure to predict long-term effects are apparent in both East and West. Though not made explicit, Holbrook's dynastic collapse argument is a reworking of the traditional Chinese integrated view of history, policy, and nature. It is the notion of the Heavenly Mandate, that the moral failure and oppressive policies of the ruler will lead to social, environmental and cosmic disorder.

The Global Village and the Paradigm Shift

What of the situation now? It is clear that China and much of East Asia in terms of public policy and economic orientation, has capitulated to Western capitalist economic values. From Holbrook's point of view, that pursuit of 'absolute fragmented' Western-style capitalist goals and methods means that it is doomed. In support of his case we could emphasize that recent assessments of China's environmental prospects are extremely pessimistic.[30] Ironically, judging by the number of Western intellectuals endorsing holism, interdependence, harmonious ecological living and the rejection of patriarchal models of dominance and exploitation, then the West, or rather some sections of the Western elite, seem to have appropriated traditional 'Eastern values'. Does this, along with the widespread endorsement of Chinese medicine, feng shui and internal arts mean that in a significant sense the West has easternized and the East has westernized? Is a major paradigm shift underway? Or is it that the categories of the East and West are redundant. Now that we operate in a global village and we can hear the crow of the cocks from a yard in Guanzhou, perhaps we should reconsider our boundaries. Of course, employing selective therapeutic and technical skills does not necessarily involve a paradigm shift. The influence of traditional assumptions and values continues to crucially affect the ways large sections of the population lead their lives, in spite of technological and economic changes. When we consider public values and behaviour in general, in conjunction with political and economic practices, then the sense of a paradigm shift or a move to holism, interdependence and environmental concern becomes much less apparent. About half of the skills, concepts and practices demonstrated at the annual Festival of Mind, Body and Spirit in London, are ancient Chinese in origin. Such events considered in isolation suggest that Britain has 'gone East' and adopted holism, mind-body and environmental integration.

Against this we must contrast the assumed core values of mainstream British society, as projected by our power elites, the 'John Major' vision of Britain, a place of country pubs, television soap operas, cricket, and wives who make the sandwiches and cook dinner. Western governments and policy-makers still maintain dualistic or absolute fragmented assumptions about the world, and generally operate under the influence of nineteenth-century political notions, re-worked versions of utilitarianism and quasi-Darwinian notions of progress. Their views reflect little exposure to holistic notions of interdependence or an inherent respect for nature and the environment. The discontinuities and cultural variables in the way different groups adapt to cross-cultural appropriation and change, is an important and fascinating study, but most of the issues involved will have to be addressed on another occasion.

In a sense, the problem which Holbrook has of generalizing on a global and historical scale, and the mismatch between ideal, policy and practice, was exactly anticipated by the Taoists, who in their utopian phases advocated small-scale, decentralized, village-based agricultural societies. That emphasis appeals to many modern day environmental activists and anarchists. Some of the rhetoric associated with communes resembles, and often draws on, Taoism for spiritual guidance and inspiration. In my view, the rhetorical value of Taoist images and motifs within Western environmental movements, and among individual activists, is considerable. Scientific environmentalists and orientalists may be critical of the adoption of Eastern models and rhetoric to support an environmental outlook. Tuan is clearly cautious in this respect. Harris takes such a position in relation to the invocation of Buddhism in support of a modern environmental outlook.[31] But these criticisms are largely misplaced. I do not subscribe to the view that modern environmentalism is only about weighing up scientific evidence, predicting outcomes and determining policies. The response to environmental crises particularly on a personal and local level is as much an emotional and spiritual process as it is a pragmatic or scientific one. Many peoples' environmental concerns and values are internalized and articulated in spiritual and religious ways. They are issues of 'ultimate concern' and religious language is an appropriate vehicle for that concern. An emotional or mystical response to powerful manifestations of nature are to be expected and valued. They could be said to be part of our global heritage since most traditional cultures express some versions of this. The contemporary emergence of whale-watching or swimming with dolphins or other methods of communing with nature, as implicitly religious experiences which are highly valued by the participants, is not at all surprising. The fact that they have largely supplanted hunting as an activity for the economically privileged, could be welcomed as indicating a major change of values, even if not going as far as a global paradigm shift.

Is the Western Appropriation of Chinese Concepts and Skills Problematic?

It does not strike me that Western appropriation of Chinese concepts and skills are illegitimate. For two thousand years or more, Chinese scholars, disenchanted officials, and poets invoked Taoist ideas and images to express their own protest, or disaffection with policy, or found inspiration in the natural images and models provided in the Taoist texts. These ideas became part of the intellectual and spiritual heritage of cultures which were not ethnically Chinese, for example: Japan, Korea, Vietnam, and large tracts of Central Asia. China developed worldviews and values which reflected considerable environmental sophistication.

In the West there is a reaction against dualism, against both mechanistic and idealist models of reality, and against a Christian theology domination of nature and alienation from creation, and of course a powerful reaction against patriarchy. Simultaneously, increasing Western exposure to traditional Chinese skills, knowledge systems and to the holistic assumptions on which they rest, is contributing towards this conceptual re-orientation.[32] Western appropriations of Eastern knowledge and skills, are not, of course, going to duplicate their Eastern antecedents; there never was a single Chinese model which could be duplicated in terms of detailed policy, since the paradigm itself incorporates a notion of change and adaptation.

Since the environmental crisis itself is global, the conceptual, ethical, behavioural, and political changes needed to address it are also going to be found globally, in the sense of drawing on traditions, knowledge, skills and values from a global rather than a specific group, culture or knowledge system.

Notes

1 M. Porkert, *The Theoretical Systems of Chinese Medicine* (Boston, Mass: MIT Press, 1974), pp. 166–96.
2 S. McFarlane (1994) 'Chinese Religions' in *Women in Religion*, ed. J. Holm (London: Pinter Publishers) pp. 65–166.
3 *The Complete Works of Chuang Tzu*, trans. B. Watson (New York: Columbia University Press, 1968), p. 97.
4 S. McFarlane,'Taoism' in *World Encyclopedia of Peace*, vol. 2, eds Ervin Laszlo and Jong Youl Yoo (Oxford: Pergamon Press, 1986), pp. 447–9.
5 Hwa, Yol Jung, 'The Way of Ecopiety: An Essay in Deep Ecology from a Sinitic Perspective', *Asian Philosophy*, 1/2, 1991, pp. 127–40.
6 Quoted in L. G. Thompson, *Chinese Religion: An Introduction* (5th edn., Belmont, Calif.: Wandsworth Inc. California, 1979), p. 4.
7 M. Saso, *Taoism and the Rite of Cosmic Renewal* (Honolulu: University of Hawaii Press, 1972), chaps. 1–3.
8 M. Saso, *Blue Dragon, White Tiger. Taoist Rites of Passage* (Honolulu: University of Hawaii Press, 1990), chaps. 1–3.
9 Ibid. p. 15.
10 For an excellent account of the general theory and the social implications of feng shui see, Ole Bruun, 'Fengshui and the Chinese Perception of Nature', in *Asian Perception of Nature. A Critical Approach*, eds Ole Bruun & Arnie Kalland (London: Curzon Press, 1995), pp. 172–88..
11 Quoted in W. Th. De Bary, *Sources of Chinese Tradition*, vol. 1 (New York: Columbia University Press, 1960), p. 165.
12 D. C. Lau, trans., *Mencius* (London: Penguin, 1970), pp. 164–5. Homer H. Dubs, trans. *The Works of Hsun Tzu* (London: A. Probsthain, 1977), p. 138.
13 Yi-fu Tuan, 'Discrepancies between Environmental Attitude and Behaviour: Example from Europe and China', *Canadian Geographer*, 12 (3), 1968, pp. 176–91 esp. p. 183.
14 V. Smil, *China's Environmental Crisis*, (Armonk, New York: M.E. Sharpe, 1993); V. Smil, 'Environmental Problems in China: Estimates of Economic Costs', *East-West Center Special Report*, no. 5, April 1996 (Honolulu: University of Hawaii).
15 L.White, 'The Historical Roots of our Ecological Crisis', *Science*, 155, March 1967, pp. 1203–07. (Reprinted in Roger S. Gottlieb, ed., *This Sacred Earth: Religion, Nature, Environment* (London: Routledge, 1996).
16 Tuan, 'Discrepancies', p. 188.
17 J. Merson, *Roads to Xanadu* (London: Weidenfeld and Nicolson, 1989), pp. 18–28.
18 R. Fields, *The Code of the Warrior* (New York: Harper Perennial, 1991), chap. 14.
19 *Guardian*, 1 Aug. 1996; *Red Pepper*, no. 28, Sept. 1996.
20 Chap. 80.

21 R. B. Gregg, *The Power of Non-Violence* (London: Routledge, 1935); M. Randle, *Civil Resistance* (London: Fontana, 1994), chap. 4.

22 B. Holbrook, *The Stone Monkey. An Alternative Chinese-Scientific Reality* (New York: William Morrow Inc., 1981).

23 Ibid., p. 128.

24 T. Kelleher, 'Confucianism', in *Women in World Religions*, ed. A. Sharma (Albany, New York: State University of New York Press, 1987), pp. 135–59.

25 B. E. Reed, 'Taoism', in ibid., pp. 161–81 esp. pp. 167–69.

26 McFarlane, 'Chinese Religions' p. 160.

27 R. H. van Gulick, *Sexual Life in Ancient China* (Leiden: E. J. Brill, 1974), p. 268.

28 Kelleher , 'Confucianism', 154–56.

29 van Gulick, *Sexual Life*, pp. 210–22. Lin, Yu-tang, *My People and My Country*, (London, Heinemann, 1939), pp. 158–61.

30 Smil, *China's Environmental Crisis*, and Smil, 'Environmental Problems'.

31 I. Harris, 'How Environmentalist is Buddhism?', *Religion*, 21, 1991, pp. 101–14.

32 H. D. Thoreau, *Walden* (Ware, Hertfordshire: Wordsworth Editions Ltd.); T. Gifford, ed. *John Muir: His Life and Letters and Other Writings* (London: Bâton Wicks Publications, 1996) and A. Leopold, *A Sand Country Almanac and Sketches Here and There* (New York: Oxford University Press, 1949).

Part IV

New Trends

13

Children of the Gods:
The Quest for Wholeness in
Contemporary Paganism

Amy Simes

The last line of a well-known invocation commonly used in modern Pagan ritual goes, 'For the earth is our mother, the sky our father, and we are the children of the gods.'[1] This invocation is traditionally said at the beginning of a ritual in order to establish one's relative position in the cosmos, and to remind those assembled of how all things are related – earth to sky, male to female, humans to nature, and humans to gods as well. It is also a typical example of one of contemporary Paganism's main tenets; that in all things, as in nature, there exists a polarity or complementary relationship between two extremes which, when balanced in combination with one another, results in a sacred and holistic creative force. Thus in Pagan ritual, as in Pagan lifestyles, both the masculine and feminine are honoured and held in equal esteem. This view of holism is commonly put into practice on a daily level in order to help restore and re-establish an ecological and social balance in the modern world.[2]

Paganism as a newly emerging (or re-emerging) religion in the twentieth century has been described simply as a religion of 'those who honour the earth'.[3] To most modern Pagans who have embraced the idea that the earth is a living organism, there has been an equal embracing of the notion that the earth is feminine. Thus to love the earth is to love the feminine, and all things of an earthly or feminine nature. Often this feminine association is expressed in terms of a goddess or goddesses, and thus the earth is frequently thought of as 'Mother Earth'. Even when the goddess is seen to be represented in the form of the moon, the earth is still revered as the ultimate 'mother' figure from whence all things come. The moon is beautiful but distant, cold and inconstant. The earth is solid, stable and steadfast, and she feeds us and gives us shelter. The earth is symbolic of fertility, and even more so of the female principle.

This approach is self-consciously acknowledged both within and without Pagan circles as a corrective to the patriarchal structure found in previously dominating Judeo-Christian views. Influences from the feminist movement of the 1960s and 1970s, the ecology movement, and older sources, such as medieval esoteric traditions, have all contributed to this widely held Pagan view.[4]

Equally, Pagans acknowledge and honour the masculine in their rituals and lifestyles, so that the Horned God holds as important a place in most modern Pagan pantheons as does the Triple Goddess.[5] In fact, the Horned God in his modern guise as lord and protector of nature is the acknowledged guardian of the forests. Following this lead, Pagan men often feel deeply connected to the earth, and sometimes extend this connection by consciously developing their inner 'feminine selves' – what Jung has termed the *anima*[6] – by taking part in 'traditionally female' activities, such as child-rearing, nursing, teaching and other service jobs.

Paganism, as it is re-emerging in the West, is such a diverse collection of traditions (Witchcraft, Druidry, Odinism, to name three) that it is difficult to generalize about beliefs or practices at all. However, Pagans do appear to hold one belief or philosophy in common, and that is that Mother Earth is a sacred entity which must be cared for. One expression of this care, which also characterizes most Pagan groups and individuals, is the celebration of the seasonal changes which occur at certain points during the 'wheel' of the year.[7]

Two contrasting examples of seasonal celebrations can be found in the Pagan rituals of Imbolc, traditionally a women's festival; and Lughnassadh, a festival to mourn the death of the male deity, Lugh. Imbolc is a winter celebration which corresponds to the Christian Candlemass, which takes place in early February and marks the first stirrings of the earth. It is often determined by the first appearance of snowdrops or the first indications that ewes are lambing. The festival honours the goddess Brigid, or Bride, the Irish goddess of milking, poetry, and smithcraft, and Pagans often make their own Bride dolls or *Brideog* images of the 'virgin' goddess. The corn or rag dolly is then 'put to bed' so that she can lie with the god and become fertile. Thus is the first stirring of the year suggested through ritual, and the image of Brigid, 'the radiant triple Muse-Goddess, who is also a fertility-bringer', is representative of the deeper understanding that 'the spirit is quickened as well as the body and the Earth'.[8]

Lughnassadh takes place in early August and marks the first harvest of corn, and thus the sacrifice of the corn spirit, or king. This ritual is viewed as a traditionally male festival because of the attention focused on the god-figure. Lughnassadh (which means 'the mourning of Lugh') also marks the end of growth, and the death of a vegetative god who must be sacrificed so that we may eat. As eating is also a form of fertility in that it maintains and encourages growth and life, this is also a celebration of the earth's fertility, but from the perspective of sacrifice and death.

Both Imbolc and Lughnassadh rituals, however, honour the male and female equally, and both are intimately tied to the seasonal changes of the earth, one marking the start of growth and fertility, the other its conclusion.

How We Became 'Un-whole': The Pagan View

A number of authors would argue that humanity has not always been so out of balance when it comes to equality of the genders.[9] Some authors hold that archæological and historical evidence points to an ancient goddess cult which existed globally, and which predominated systems of belief until the introduction of a patriarchal religion some 4,000 years ago.[10] Such a view often includes the opinion that modern patriarchal cultures evolved in tandem with Judeo-Christian religions, which saw women not only as naturally subordinate to men, but also as sexually immoral and unclean. They often point to figures such as the Virgin Mary as examples of survivals of this goddess cult, especially in areas where the Virgin is worshipped more actively than Jesus Christ, God, or any of the saints.[11]

Eliade goes even further to discuss the possibility of early cultures which held a belief in 'the myth of divine androgyny'. Most deities found in preliterate mythologies have a bisexual nature, whether they are called gods or goddesses, and some, as Eliade has found – usually the most powerful and ancient deities – are androgynous. He has discovered that androgyny is found 'in a great many religions', and is often also portrayed in concepts such as 'light' and 'darkness', 'for light and darkness are simply successive aspects of one and the same reality'.[12] Yet this unitary concept is contrary to the mythology of Christianity, where the god is seen as only male, only light, and is opposed by a dark twin who has 'fallen'.

As Judeo-Christian ideology developed in the West, so did concepts which favoured men over women. Ideas such as the subordination of women (who were seen by the clergy to be unclean), monogamy and legalized marriage, the virtue of chastity, and the natural sinfulness of human flesh flourished alongside Protestantism as it became a dominant religious view in the West during the sixteenth and seventeenth centuries. Eventually even the wholeness of the person was brought into question, and philosophers such as Descartes encouraged a view which divided the person into body and mind. Often in religious spheres this division linked the body with the female and the mind with the male. The view was that the process of thought validated the person, not actions associated with the flesh, which were seen to be somehow inferior, embarrassing, and encumbering to the advancement of humanity. There was certainly nothing spiritual or religious about the body or sexuality.

Such a notion is particularly important for women because the female principle is historically and mythologically tied to body and earth symbolism. As Levin notes, 'the character of the . . . earth, as our mythology repeatedly tells us, is . . . unmistakably feminine'.[13] Eliade reiterates this point, linking femininity with the earth and fertility.[14] Levin also quotes Jung, who insists that this archetype continues to persist cross-culturally. 'The soil of every country holds some . . . mystery. We have an unconscious reflection of this in the psyche.'[15]

This emphasis on 'mystery' and on the unconscious, the dark, the hidden, is the key to understanding the rationalist separation from all things related to the earth, the feminine and nature. The dark 'soil' of the fertile psyche, like the body, is often considered frightening, dangerous, and powerful. Jung referred to the 'power of the chthonic', and in mythology those beings which were the most horrible and terrifying originated below the earth, in the dark deepness. This is where we, as humans, are 'grounded', and such grounding, as Levin explains, directs us away from our patriarchal connection to 'higher' states of being, and separates us from our Creator.[16] And, as Davies points out, 'humankind often talks about itself as distinct from nature . . . because Christian men and women see themselves related to the world in a similarly separate way' to a transcendent God.[17] In the traditional Christian view, therefore, close association to nature is not a comfortable thought. Levin comments that: 'The "stay of mortals on the earth", . . . brings us back to the fact of our embodiment, and to the *truth* of that "medium", as that in which, and through which we become accustomed . . . to the earth of our dwelling.'[18] To become accustomed to the 'truth' of embodiment is an unpleasant task for the person who would prefer to identify with the *possibility* of a more lofty association. However, embodiment is an undeniable 'truth' expressed in its obvious material reality. It is verifiable and scientifically undeniable. Relationships with the spiritual plane are less certain.

Nonetheless, preferences for such relationships continue to be indicated amongst modern-day Judeo-Christian groups with the sometimes fundamentalist views that humans cannot possibly be related to the animal kingdom at all, despite Darwin's evidence to the contrary. So, as the Scopes trial of the 1920s argued, the desire to maintain a 'healthy' distance from nature continues for many in the West, and this distance also continues to encourage an historic gap between the genders.

The Way Back: Three Pagan Paths Towards 'Wholeness'

When Paganism began to emerge into the light of the twentieth century, its adherents saw themselves as neither establishing a new religion, nor as correcting an imbalance in modern society resulting from two thousand years of patriarchal influences in the West. In retrospect, however, it is possible to see that they were doing both.[19]

The second of these two unconscious decisions--this correcting movement away from patriarchy – is, for the purposes of this discussion, worth analysing in closer detail, for the modern Pagan quest for reunification of male and female, nature and culture, has taken a number of interesting turns in its efforts to re-establish a more fertile, unified and holistic approach to both spirituality and to secular orientation.

We shall look at three such paths separately: first, the use of experiential ritual and symbol as a means of acting out a social and spiritual transformation on a deep, somatic level, along with the revival of ancient folkways, customs, myths and beliefs in order to revive the belief in the sanctity of nature; and second, the resacralization of the feminine. Finally, the practical application of these rediscovered beliefs through individual care for the environment, personal ethics, support of environmental groups, direct action to prevent further destruction of the environment, the education of others, the use of sacred space and the support of local initiatives to maintain and repair the local countryside will be reviewed.

Making the Gods Real: The Embodiment of the Divine Through Experiential Ritual and Symbol

In much of modern religious ritual, myths are restricted to either being read out as scriptural stories, or portrayed pictorially in iconographic form in sacred buildings and areas.[20] In other words, the re-enactment of myths tends to be non-participatory. The dramatic re-enactment of myths is much less common.

In modern Paganism, participation in mythical re-enactment is almost essential. The use of mythology in ritual is most commonly found in the seasonal rituals, or the eight Sabbats, for here myth serves to touch upon the deeper esoteric meanings found behind the passing of one season into the next in nature's cyclic journey through the year.[21] Sometimes a myth is read or recited during a ritual, but more often it is acted out.

At Beltane (1 May) gatherings, for example, a man and woman will often dress as 'the Green Man' and 'the Lady,' two figures emerging out of folk customs but also connected to ancient myths of Herne, Persephone, Vivianne, Pan and others. The two characters will then act out the 'rites of Spring', which usually involves a chase and often incorporates symbols suggestive of fertility, such as the broom. Eventually they will lead the group in a dance around the Maypole, another fertility symbol. Finally, there might be a planting of some sort, or an earth healing meditation.

Victor Turner points out that 'through being shown a "mystery" in myth . . . one is transformed through deeper understanding'.[22] This transformation is often best accomplished within the context of ritual, as the deeper understanding which Turner writes about is likely to be spiritual in nature. It may, however, be a spiritual transformation which occurs as a result of understanding the meaning of one's own existence in relation to the natural world. This is something which Celtic authors appear to have implicitly understood, and which some Pagan authors may be discovering as well.

Modern Pagans appear to be re-establishing a connection to the natural world through an emphasis in religious ritual upon ancient myth and folk custom. Many ancient myths indicate that this connection once existed, but has now been lost as a result of the scientific and industrial revolutions, and through the Christian distrust of natural forms of embodiment. Ancient mythology is rich in drama and symbolism, and provides a refreshing change for many modern Westerners who have become disenchanted or bored with the banality which predominates much of modern religious and secular ritual. Eliade (1960) suggests that, rather than this change being a form of disenchantment or demythologizing, it is instead a 'revaluation, at the secular level, of the ancient sacred values'.[23] He further notes:

> This process is very well exemplified by the transformation of the values ascribed to Nature. We have not abolished the relationship of sympathy between man and Nature; nor was that possible. But this relationship has changed in value and in its orientation; for the magico-religious sympathy we have substituted emotion, either aesthetic or simply sentimental . . . while contemplation of Nature has been ousted by observation, experiment and calculation. It could not be said [that we no longer] 'love Nature'; but in this 'love' one could no longer find anything of the spiritual attitude of the man in the archaic societies.[24]

Yet Paganism is a modern attempt to reintroduce that 'spiritual attitude', to re-value the deeper connection between humankind and nature, by combining ancient myths with religious ritual.

By connecting mythology with the seasonal festivals, Pagans may be helping to remind themselves that once there was a time when humans had no choice but to live in harmony with nature, to work with it and to revere it. Even though most modern Pagans are not farmers or horticulturalists, they are likely to be well aware of the life-cycles of plants and animals through taking part in the yearly Sabbats. Also, because these festivals are normally held out of doors, Pagans are likely to experience greater awareness of the natural cycle. This cycle is referred to repeatedly in ancient myths, and it becomes necessary to be aware of the natural calendar in order to fully appreciate the storyline of most myths.

Often the acting out of myths through ritual drama requires dressing up as animals or as mythical characters or heroes. It may also include dancing, singing, playing musical instruments, or acting very humorously. When acting in this somewhat childlike (or even animal-like) manner, participants are often reminded that they are part of the natural world. At Lughnassadh, the song 'John Barleycorn' is often sung in a humorous style, and accompanied by much drinking and frivolity. Yet this is a folk song commemorating the 'death' of the corn spirit (or of the Celtic god, Lugh) as popularized over the centuries by the farming communities. Ancient Pagan mythology (and more recent Pagan folkways) are therefore revived in this seasonal celebration, and given new meaning through these modern uses.

Additionally, through the cross-cultural comparison of similar agricultural myths, it becomes apparent that celebrations like this one occur regularly throughout the world, often with similar symbolic meanings. Eliade notes dozens of such harvest festivals or ceremonies, and suggests that 'the "force" at work in vegetation is most completely personified when the harvesters make the last ears into an effigy as near to the human form as they can'.[25] In other words, it appears to be important cross-culturally to equate the connection between nature and humans with myth.

Most telling is the adaptation amongst Pagans of associating their deities with nature, a legacy perhaps derived from Sir James Frazer[26] and passed down through scholars such as Margaret Murray,[27] and through modern Pagans like Gerald Gardner.[28] The goddess is traditionally associated with the moon, the sea, or the earth, and the god is largely modelled on that of Pan or Herne, god of the natural world. Gaia, the Greek name for Mother Earth, mated with a sky god (Uranus), but she is easily adapted to also have as a consort the 'horned one', a figure derived from the Celtic god, Cernunnos, lord of animals and nature.

Eliade reminds us that: 'A great many beliefs, myths and rituals have come down to us which deal with the earth, with its divinities, with the Great Mother. As the foundation, in a sense, of the universe, the earth is endowed with manifold religious significance. It was adored because of its permanence, because all things came from it and all things returned to it.'[29] As was indicated earlier, even when the goddess is seen to be represented in the form of the moon, the earth is still revered as the ultimate 'mother' figure. As it was described by a Nottingham Druid, 'The earth is what holds us all together, while patriarchy is tearing us apart through the destruction of the earth. Yet the response to patriarchy is not matriarchy, but fertility.'

Making the Feminine Sacred Once Again

In an early 1990s edition of ITV's talk show, *The Time, The Place*, which focused on Paganism and Witchcraft, one of the members of the studio audience was Tony Grist, a former Anglican priest turned Witch. When asked to reveal the primary reason for his 'conversion', he replied that he had grown dissatisfied with the Church of England's doctrine because it provided no female expression of deity.

In general, Paganism supports doctrine in which the deity is seen to be both male and female. Witches and Druids, in particular, make mention of both a goddess and a god in many of their rites, although in some Druid rites the deity is more commonly referred to as a 'Great Spirit'.[30] Norse Pagans do not tend to adhere to a strictly duotheistic view, supporting instead a more polytheistic approach which acknowledges and reflects the pantheon of gods and goddesses portrayed in Norse mythology. Norse Wiccans, however, sometimes support a doctrine of duotheism, in which the god and goddess are alternatively represented by various deities from Norse mythology, 'with the Goddess having primary importance'.[31]

Specifically, Paganism is concerned with emphasizing the sacredness of the feminine, or perhaps with its 're-sacralizing'. According to Anderson and Hopkins:

> What is at issue here is not gender but historical imbalance. And today growing numbers of women feel that patriarchal traditions have alienated them from their deepest and truest understanding of God as Mother. For women who feel this way there is a conscious need to reclaim the holiness of female embodiment and recognize the sacredness of Mother Earth as well.[32]

In the West, Paganism appears to be the only religion 'which, according to its followers . . . recognises woman as divinity in her own right'.[33] This approach has sometimes been referred to as 'coven theology',[34] and its emergence in the form of modern Witchcraft and other forms of Paganism 'is linked to a process of retraditionalization using elements of the past, whilst they represent at the same time a religious innovation of the twentieth century'.[35]

The god, often portrayed as the horned hunter, or Lord of the Forest, is seen to be consort to the goddess. She is the Mother who gives birth to the god. The god matures, becomes her lover, and is then voluntarily sacrificed so that through his death he may again be reborn of the Mother.

Both men and women, then, are able to seek empowerment through the modern image of the goddess, who is often portrayed as a triple figure of virgin, mother and crone. Such an image, which portrays women of all ages in a positive light, serves as a defence for women who do not fit into the modern glossy image of what a woman should look and be like. Instead, this portrayal dignifies women from all walks of life, be they heterosexual, lesbian, single, married, old, young, ambitious or solitary. It is an encouraging image for women who must still interact within the confines of a traditionally male-oriented society. It also serves as a fulfilling image to Pagan males who do not agree with media portrayals of modern women.

York suggests that both Pagans and New Agers are drawn to the 'female idiom' found in both movements, but that this presence is more emphasized in Paganism through the unambiguous image of the goddess, than it is in New Age.[36] Whereas it is clear, as observed above, why women would find Paganism attractive, it is less clear what sense of sexual empowerment men receive from their involvement.

One suggestion is that the image of the 'Horned One', portrayed in the traditional form of the animal-god Pan, recognizes the dual nature of humanity, and especially men. In these somewhat sexually ambiguous times, men also appear to be searching for positive role models, and, it can be argued, such models are plentifully provided in the variety of mythical images portrayed in the form of animal-gods, vegetation-gods and heroic-gods. Through association with such images, men are re-connecting not only with the natural world, but with mythologies which are of ancient origin. The Druid who calls upon the solar god, Lugh, during the summer solstice, is invoking an image of strength, power, sovereignty, and life-giving qualities.[37]

A second explanation for the male attraction to Paganism is psychological in nature. With the imbalance experienced by both men and women from patriarchal divisions which emphasize the intellect over intuition, guilt over affection, and separation over fertility, it is not surprising to find that both sexes appear to be searching for a more feminine, more comforting and more balanced nature in divinity which does not suggest the sometimes cold, judgmental nature and one-sidedness of the Christian male god. Anderson and Hopkins note that this 'longing for wholeness is evident . . . [and] there is the express desire to gather together what has been fragmented and lost'.[38] Gadon states more specific-ally that 'The integration of the whole has never been achieved in monotheistic religions, rather they have led to an ever accelerating severance of nature from culture.'[39] But Jones and Matthews take this point to its logical conclusion when they assert that 'the absence of the Goddess, the Divine Feminine principle, from West-ern spirituality . . . has had dubious consequences for our society, for we are a people who have grown up without their mother.'[40]

This re-establishment of unity with a mother figure was also noted as an important theme by Sjoo and Moore,[41] who maintained that men, particularly, are encouraged in the West to sever ties with their mothers early in life, thus delaying and discouraging mature development. Eliade notes how in certain societies, male initiates usually experience, as part of the initiation process, a form of dramatic separation from their mothers, often associated with some form of death. 'The maternal universe was that of the pro-fane world', the earth, and must be left behind in order to become adult.[42] Could it be, therefore, that in modern complex societies, through the identification with a divine 'mother', men are some-how redressing this situation themselves by taking a positive, almost psychotherapeutic, step to reintegrate with their feminine 'selves' and to re-sanctify the feminine principle? Jones and Matthews suggest that 'The Goddess is of prime importance . . . as a corrective to the prevailing predominance in orthodox spirituali-ties of the Male Principle.'[43]

In reuniting with the feminine principle as symbolized by the goddess, both men and women are symbolically reuniting with the earth and with the natural world which has traditionally been associated with the female,[44] and therefore viewed as separate from humanity, which was made in the 'image' of a male god. Thus the associations continue to multiply, and to link both men and women more deeply with nature and the female principle.

In identifying with this truth of embodiment, and in re-examin-ing the relationships between the earth and the feminine, the body and the psyche, contemporary Pagans are, for the first time in many centuries, confronting the dark, deep aspects of existence and claiming them as the very heart of their religious symbolism. Ecology becomes 'deep' ecology, subjectivity through the practice of mysticism becomes 'deep' subjectivity, and the god comes out of the sky into the deepness of the earth and becomes the goddess.

Applying the Principle of 'Wholeness' in Daily Practice

Pagans are characterized by 'living their religion' to the point where Paganism can often be more accurately described as a life-style rather than just a religious practice. Pagan men and women both extol Pagan values on a daily basis, usually individually on a personal level, but also through group involvement. While not all Pagans demonstrate concern for environmental issues, most Pagans, when asked, will express strong opinions about such issues.

Many of the Pagans I met over the three years of my fieldwork emphasized the fact that they were Pagan '24 hours a day', and that their Paganism extended to all aspects of their lives. The reasoning for this was eloquently expressed in practical terms: 'I don't externalise my gods, so the respect for them goes into nature and the earth. I can penetrate it or it can penetrate me. I can achieve contact with that which I worship or believe in.'

Attitudes Towards the Environment

Such attitudes were often reflected in daily household practices of recycling, conserving energy, not owning a car, not smoking, picking up litter, using environmentally friendly products, replanting native trees and hedges, and educating others locally about environmental issues. Several people indicated that they would ideally prefer to work in an environmentally helpful occupation, such as nature conservation. There was also a growing awareness of the phenomenon known as 'green or eco-burial', which is concerned with the way in which human remains are interred. Several respondents indicated that they had changed their wills to reflect this awareness. Other practical applications included gardening and herb-lore, and the practice of astrology (which requires extensive knowledge of astronomy and earth cycles).

When asked whether being a Pagan had in any way influenced their ethical outlooks, many respondents indicated that it had, although some replied that very little had changed and that, in fact, it was their own 'moral and ethical outlook which made them Pagan' in the first place. Those who did feel that change had occurred pointed to such things as becoming more tolerant of others, becoming more aware of the environment, and becoming more sensitive to the 'karmic' nature of actions. Several had changed their attitudes towards animals, and a number of respondents had become vegetarian as a result of Pagan ethics.

The environment was viewed as 'very important', or 'extremely important', by every respondent. When asked to specify the single most important environmental issue, respondents found it difficult to choose one. Answers ranged from 'pollution/global warming' to 'trees' to 'overpopulation' to 'better transportation' and 'less short-sightedness on the part of elected officials involved in planning'. Others could not decide on one answer.

Social Symbols of Environmental Concerns

On a social level, Pagans appear very concerned about the symbols with which their organizations are identified. Perhaps more than any other symbol, modern Paganism refers to the tree as the most comprehensively reflective icon of its religious identity. The Pagan Federation,[45] in 1993, designed a logo which consisted primarily of a tree (probably an oak), combined with a sun and moon. This is one of the only nationally representative Pagan symbols which has been designed by modern Pagans, the other most notable one being the Dragon[46] rune, yet another tree symbol.

Tree symbolism is particularly interesting because it so success-fully reflects to outsiders the Pagan quest for wholeness. Pagans who believe in the concept of reincarnation often point to the tree as confirmation that such a system exists in nature. The tree loses its leaves each year, but it does not die. Each spring it is 'reborn'. As a magical symbol it is identified with the four elements, for trees grow from the earth, are fed upon water, and require air and sunshine (fire) for sustenance. Like the pentagram,[47] it is a comprehensive symbol, symbolic of a unified system of esoteric associations.

Many Pagans spend a year or more studying native trees of Britain and learning about their esoteric and biological associ-ations. Druids in particular point to the study of and knowledge about trees as a vital step to greater understanding of the natural world. A number of respondents owned a set of Ogham Tree Cards, consisting of 'twenty-five sacred trees' of Britain originally believed to be associated with Ogham runes (a form of symbolic language that early Druids are believed to have used).[48] Each card has a number of associations which are applied during a 'reading' – a form of divination – for the purposes of interpretation.

Sacred Space

Pagan attitudes towards nature are also reflected in their choices of sacred space. Much of modern Paganism is a reaction against cultural materialism and Western consumerism. Paganism, as has been shown, emphasizes a reverence for nature and a strong concern with the environment. As such, Pagan sacred spaces are designed to reflect this concern, and in fact, most sacred space is found within the environment. In common with Chinese, Japanese, and Hindu approaches, Paganism determines its 'prime sites' to be 'natural features, as in mountains, rivers and woodlands',[49] preferring to celebrate out of doors rather than inside.

On a social level, the conscious decision to designate natural features as sacred space has a levelling effect. Anyone can create ritual space, and the task is often already partially accomplished in nature anyway. Often groves of trees form a natural temple, or a stone circle exists as a natural site on a hilltop, ready for use. Nature is attractive to the Pagan because it is often private, it costs nothing to use, it is often very old, and, in most cases, it is open to the public all the time. Furthermore, it ideally belongs to everyone (a point which might be contested by English Heritage and the National Trust). Natural 'temples' are non-denominational and are incapable of excluding anyone who is physically able to access them.

Political Involvement

As a rule, Pagans do not seem overly eager to become involved with politics or with large groups that receive national attention. There is still considerable concern amongst some Pagans that public attention may threaten their family life and employment. Nonetheless, many of the respondents indicated an affiliation to the Green Party, and therefore felt politically impotent because, as one respondent pointed out, 'Greens don't have a political voice in this country'.

Modern concern with the environment began to receive special attention in Britain in the early 1970s after a long, slow build-up. The emergence of the Ecology Party (later the Green Party) in 1973 coincided with Arne Naess's introduction of the concept of 'deep ecology'.[50] Such a concept was very much a reaction against the predominant view of social ecology which concerned itself more with issues of class, race and gender identity than with issues relating to 'holism', the individual and the spiritual 'wisdom' of the Earth. Groups such as Friends of the Earth, Greenpeace and Worldwide Fund for Nature began to emerge as powerful political lobbies in support of environmental issues.

In the late 1980s in Britain, green politics began to merge quite unintentionally with modern Paganism.[51] Many Green Party members who followed a more socially ecological path resisted such a merger and remained true to a purely political path. But some joined proto-groups of Dragon, a direct-action environmental protest group founded by Wiccan, Adrian Harris, or the Woodland Trust, organized by Odinshof, a Norse Pagan group, and left the political arena largely behind. However, the vast majority of support for groups that attract media attention, such as Dragon, come either from urban dwellers who are primarily younger middle-class Pagans without families, or 'travellers'[52] who may or may not affiliate themselves with Paganism.

Local and Regional Environmental Activities

Most Pagans who live outside of London do something practical on a regional or grassroots level to help the environment, but only a small proportion of my respondents actually belonged to any sort of environmental organization (such as Greenpeace, Friends of the Earth, Woodland Trust, Dragon or local conservation groups), while even fewer indicated involvement in protest actions.

More popular, however, were local events, and usually (weather permitting) these would draw large crowds. Such events included Earth Healing Days, earth energy/mystery 'tours' which might include dowsing, picnics (which usually involved some form of earth healing, or some form of neo-shamanism which might be based upon earth energy-raising), or connecting with earth spirits. All such events were arranged to include a shared meal (or at least a shared drink) and usually supervision for children. There might also be a ritual attached to the activity, but this was not always the case.

Earth Healing Days were particularly well attended events, as these are nationally recognized days. These events either featured some form of planting (replacing hedges, reintroducing native trees to woodlands), or a clean-up operation designed to rid a local area of litter and household rubbish. Children were always encouraged to take part in such activities.

The Whole Picture

The contemporary Pagan answer to the question, 'Are women the sacred custodians of the earth?' would most likely be, 'Yes, just as are men'. In a world of division and post-modern fragmentation, Paganism ultimately strives to achieve reunion, not just of the body, mind and soul, but also of male and female, culture and nature, spirit and matter and, perhaps most importantly, of sacred and profane. For the typical Pagan, there is little difference between a walk in the woods and a ritual invocation. Picking up litter takes on a sacred meaning, just as inviting the gods into one's back garden allows a rare mingling of magic and mundane.

Through such attempts at re-enchantment, Pagan men and women both find ways to reconnect with the earth and with the archetypal and mysterious powers which are inherent in all earthly matter. What is more, they find ways to reconnect with each other in a mutual recognition of divinity which is as female as it is male. From this revelation emerges a new-found appreciation of the concept of fertility, a concept which, like a child, is representative of its heritage, yet profoundly greater than its creators.

Notes

1 From a personal 'Book of Shadows' which is a book handwritten by its author and based on the 'Book of Shadows' of others, normally coven members. It may include ritual scripts, magical workings, herb-lore, runic lore and foundational philosophies.

2 Some of this discussion of Pagan ritual, symbol, belief and practice is drawn from fieldwork carried out in the East Midlands of England between 1992–95, during which the author took part in a variety of Pagan rituals and secular activities with more than a dozen Pagan groups and more than 100 individuals. See A. Simes, 'Contemporary Paganism in the East Midlands' (Ph.D. thesis, University of Nottingham, 1995).

3 G. Harvey, *Speaking Earth, Listening People* (London: C. Hurst & Co., 1997), p. 16.

4 For further reading, see B. Devall and G. Sessions, *Deep Ecology* (Salt Lake City: Gibbs Smith, 1985); J. Porritt and D. Winner, *The Coming of the Greens* (London: Fontana, 1988); S. R. Anderson and P. Hopkins, *The Feminine Face of God: The Unfolding of the Sacred in Women* (New York: Bantam Books, 1992); Starhawk, *The Spiral Dance: A Rebirth of the Ancient Religion of the Great Goddess*, 10th Anniversary edn (San Francisco: Harper and Row, 1989); S. L. M. MacGregor, *The Key of Solomon the King* [trans. from the Latin, 1888] (London: Routledge & Kegan Paul, 1972) ; K. Grant, *The Magical Revival* (London: Skoob Books Publishing, 1991); J. Matthews and C. Matthews, *The Western Way: A Practical Guide to the Western Mystery Tradition* (London: Arkana, 1985).

5 The image of the triple goddess is often portrayed as maiden, mother and crone, or as the three phases of the moon. This is an ancient image dating back to a pre-Judaic period, and symbols of goddess-worship have been found throughout the Mediterranean, the Middle East and in North Africa in great numbers (see E. W. Gadon, *The Once and Future Goddess: A Symbol for Our Time* (San Francisco: Harper and Row, 1989).

6 C. G. Jung, *The Collected Works of C. G. Jung, Vol. 9, Part 2, Archetypes of the Collective Unconscious* (London: Routledge & Kegan Paul, 2nd edn 1968).

7 There are 8 seasonal festivals based largely on the Celtic calendar of cross-quarter days. See below, note 21.

8 J. Farrar and S. Farrar, *Eight Sabbats for Witches* [1981] (London: Robert Hale, 1992), p. 62.

9 For examples see M. Sjoo and B. Mor, *The Great Cosmic Mother: Rediscovering the Religion of the Earth*, 2nd edn (San Francisco: Harper and Row, 1991); D. M. Levin, *The Body's Recollection of Being* (London: Routledge & Kegan Paul, 1985); U. King, *Women and Spirituality: Voices of Protest and Promise*, 2nd edn (Basingstoke: Macmillan, 1993); M. Eliade, *Patterns in Comparative Religion* (London: Sheed & Ward, 1958); M. Stone, *When God Was a Woman* (San Diego: Harvest/HBJ, 1976); Gadon, *Once and Future Goddess*, and Anderson and Hopkins, *The Feminine Face of God*, to name only a few.

10 For further reading, see Gadon, *Once and Future Goddess*; Stone, *When God Was a Woman*.

11 Gadon, *Once and Future Goddess*, pp. 194–208; V. Crowley, *Wicca: The Old Religion in the New Age* (London: The Aquarian Press, 1989), p. 163.

12 Eliade, *Patterns in Comparative Religion*, p. 422.

13 D. M. Levin, *The Body's Recollection of Being* (London: Routledge & Kegan Paul, 1985), p. 283.

14 Eliade, *Patterns in Comparative Religion*, pp. 239ff.

15 Levin, *Body's Recollection of Being*, p. 284.

16 Ibid.

17 D. Davies, 'Christianity', in *Attitudes to Nature*, eds J. Holm and J. W. Bowker (London: Pinter Publishers, 1994) p. 36.

18 Levin, *Body's Recollection of Being*, p. 287.

19 For the development of modern Paganism in the West, see M. Adler, *Drawing Down the Moon: Witches, Druids, Goddess Worshippers, and Other Pagans in America Today* (Boston: Beacon Press, 1986); P. Carr-Gomm, *The Druid Way* (Shaftsbury, Dorset: Element, 1991); V. Crowley, *Phoenix From the Flame* (London: The Aquarian Press, 1994); S. Greenwood, G. Harvey, A. Simes and M. Nye, 'Current Research on Paganism and Witchcraft in Britain', *Journal of Contemporary Religion*, 10, 2 (May 1995), pp. 185–92; G. Harvey and C. Hardman, eds, *Paganism Today* (London: Thorsons, 1996); R. Hutton, *The Pagan Religions of the Ancient British Isles: Their Nature and Legacy* (Oxford: Blackwell, 1991); P. Jones and C. Matthews, eds, *Voices from the Circle: The Heritage of Western Paganism* (London: The Aquarian Press, 1991); A. Kelly, *Crafting the Art of Magic, Book I: A History of Modern Witchcraft, 1939–1964* (St Paul, Minnesota: Llewellyn, 1991); T. Luhrmann, *Persuasions of the Witch's Craft: Ritual Magic in Contemporary England* (Oxford: Blackwell, 1989); E. A. Tiryakian, ed., *On the Margin of the Visible: Sociology, the Esoteric, and the Occult* (New York: John Wiley & Sons, 1974).

20 M. Eliade, *Myths, Dreams and Mysteries: The Encounter Between Contemporary Faiths and Archaic Realities* (New York: Harper & Row Publishers, 1960), p. 34.

21 The 8 seasonal festivals include the summer and winter solstices (about 21 Dec. and 21 June), the spring and autumn equinoxes (about 21 March and 23 Sept.), and the four 'cross-quarter days' which fall in between these dates and mark the high point of each season: Imbolc (1 Feb.), Beltane (1 May), Lughnassadh (1 Aug.), and Samhain (31 Oct.). The cross-quarter days are thought to be Celtic in origin, and the agreed-upon names for each of the festivals are Irish Gaelic. The Celtic new year began at sundown on the 31 Oct., and was divided into a dark half (Oct.–May) and a light half (May–Oct.). All festivals began at sundown, therefore Beltane, for example, officially begins at sundown on 30 April.

22 V. Turner, ed., *Celebration: Studies in Festivity and Ritual* (Washington, DC: Smithsonian Institution Press, 1982) p. 211.

23 Eliade, *Myths, Dreams and Mysteries,* p. 28.

24 Ibid., p. 28n.

25 Eliade, *Patterns in Comparative Religion,* p. 339.

26 Sir James Frazer, who wrote the exhaustive series on world mythology and custom, *The Golden Bough* (first published 1922).

27 M. A. Murray, author of *The Witch Cult of Western Europe,* 1921, in which she proposed, amongst other things, that witchcraft had survived the Great Witch Hunt of the fifteenth-eighteenth centuries. Much of her evidence was later proved false.

28 G. Gardner, considered by many in Britain to be the 'father of modern Witchcraft', and author of several books on the subject.

29 Eliade, *Patterns in Comparative Religion,* p. 240.

30 Order of Bards, Ovates and Druids, '"Gwers" of the Order of Bards, Ovates and Druids' (printed material for the OBOD correspondence course) (Richmond, Surrey: OBOD, 1988), Nos. 1–24.

31 D. J. Conway, *Norse Magic* (St Paul, Minnesota: Llewellyn Publications, 1990), p. 39.

32 Anderson and Hopkins, *Feminine Face of God,* p. 128.

33 King, *Women and Spirituality,* p. 133.

34 Ibid., p. 127.

35 Ibid.

36 M. York, 'A Sociological Profile on the New Age and Neo-Pagan Movements' (Ph.D. thesis, King's College, London, 1991), p. 151.

37 Eliade, *Patterns in Comparative Religion,* p. 128.

38 Anderson and Hopkins, *Feminine Face of God,* p. 20.

39 Gadon, *Once and Future Goddess,* p. xiii.

40 Jones and Matthews, eds, *Voices From the Circle,* p. 14.

41 Sjoo and Mor, *Great Cosmic Mother,* p. 30.

42 Eliade, *Patterns in Comparative Religion,* p. 9.

43 Jones and Matthews, eds, *Voices From the Circle,* p. 30.

44 Eliade, *Patterns in Comparative Religion,* pp. 239ff.

45 The Pagan Federation was formed in 1971 and is a national secular organization designed to represent and support the views of Pagans in the UK.

46 Dragon is an eco-magical, direct-action organization which takes part in and organizes protests against environmental destruction, such as road-building in the UK.

47 The Pentagram is probably the most widely used symbol with which Pagans associate themselves. The symbol is sometimes thought to represent the goddess, Venus.

48 The Ogham Cards were originally designed and produced by Colin and Liz Murray in 1988.

49 D. Davies, 'Introduction: Raising the Issues' in *Sacred Place,* ed., J. Holm, (London: Pinter Publishers, 1994), pp. 1–7.

50 The phrase 'deep ecology' is credited to Norwegian philosopher, Arne Naess, in a conversation which took place with him in 1981, and was recorded in S. Bodlian's 'Simple in Means, Rich in Ends', essay in *The Ten Directions* (Zen Center of Los Angeles, Summer, 1981).

51 This is not so surprising a fact when one considers that one of modern Paganism's roots was the early conservation movement which began at the beginning of the twentieth century with groups such as the Woodcrafter's Guild.

52 Travellers are a loosely organized group of nomadic individuals in Britain, usually with no fixed address, who camp out on public land or live in caravans. Many become involved in road protests or other environmental protests designed to prevent the destruction of woodlands. The media have branded these people 'New Age Travellers'.

Select Bibliography

Abbott, N. 1946. *Two Queens of Baghdad: Mother and Wife of Harun al-Rashid.* Chicago, University of Chicago Press.

Abbott, W. M., ed. 1966. *Documents of Vatican II.* London, Geoffrey Chapman.

Abimbola, W. 1990. *Decolonizing African Thought in Tradition and Development in Africa Today.* Paris, UNESCO.

Abu-Lughod, L. 1986. *Veiled Sentiments: Honor and Poetry in a Bedouin Society.* Berkeley, Calif., University of California Press.

Adler, M. 1986. *Drawing Down the Moon: Witches, Druids, Goddess Worshippers, and Other Pagans in America Today.* Boston, Mass., Beacon Press.

Afkhami, A. and E. Friedl, eds. 1994. *In the Eye of the Storm: Women in the Post-Revolutionary Iran.* London; New York, I. B. Tauris Publishers.

Allen, D. E. 1978. *Naturalist in Britain: A Social History.* London, Pelican Books.

Allen, M. and S. Mukherjee, eds. 1982. *Women in India and Nepal.* Canberra, Australian National University Press.

Allen, R. and A. Ferguson, eds. 1991. *The Women and International Development Annual,* vol. 2. Boulder, Colo., Westview Press.

Anderson, S. R. and P. Hopkins 1992. *The Feminine Face of God: The Unfolding of the Sacred in Women.* New York, Bantam Books.

Ardener, S., ed. 1975. *Perceiving Women.* London, J. M. Dent and Son Ltd.

———, 1992. *Persons and Powers of Women in Diverse Cultures.* New York and Oxford, Berg Publishers Ltd.

———, 1993. *Women and Space: Ground Rules and Social Maps.* Oxford, Berg Publishers.

Arnold, D. and R. Guha. 1995. *Nature Culture Imperialism: Essays on the Environmental History of South Asia.* Oxford, Oxford University Press.

Aschwanden, H. 1990. *Karanga Mythology.* Gweru, Zimbabwe, Mambo Press.

Atkinson, J. M. & S. Errington, eds. 1990. *Power and Difference: Gender in Island Southeast Asia.* Stanford, Calif., Stanford University Press.

Balzer, M. M. 1996. 'Changing Images of the Shaman: Folklore and Politics in the Sakha Republic (Yakutia)', *Shaman,* 4, 1, pp. 5–16.

Bank Findly, E., ed. 1985. *Women, Religion and Social Change.* Albany, NY., State University of New York Press.

Banuri, T. and F. A. Marglin, eds. 1993. *Who Will Save the Forests?: Knowledge, Power and Environmental Destruction.* London, Zed Books.

Baring, A. and J. Cashford. 1993. *The Myth of the Goddess: Evolution of an Image.* London, Penguin Books.

Barker, J. H. 1994. *Always Getting Ready—Upterrlainarluta: Yup'ik Eskimo Subsistence in Southwest Alaska.* Seattle and London, University of Washington Press.

Batchelor, M. and K. Brown, eds. 1992. *Buddhism and Ecology.* London, Cassells.

Baviskar, A. 1995. *In the Belly of the River: Tribal Conflicts over Development in the Narmada Valley.* Delhi, Oxford University Press.

Bell, C. 1992. *Ritual Theory, Ritual Practice.* Oxford, Oxford University Press.

Bell, D. 1983. *Daughters of the Dreaming.* Sydney, McPhee Gribble/George Allen and Unwin.

Benjamin, W. 1973. *Illuminations.* London, Fontana Press.

Benton, T. 1993. *Natural Relations: Ecology, Animal Rights and Social Justice.* London and New York, Verso.

——————, and M. Redclift, eds. 1994. *Social Theory and the Global Environment.* London, Routledge.

Berleant, A. 1997. *Living in the Landscape: Toward an Aesthetics of Environment.* Lawrence, Kansas, University of Kansas Press.

Berry, T. 1988. *The Dream of the Earth.* San Francisco, Calif., Sierra Club Books.

Bharucha, R. 1993. *The Question of Faith.* Madras, Orient Longman.

Biehl, J. 1988. 'Ecofeminism and Deep Ecology: Unresolvable Conflict?', *Our Generation,* 192, pp. 18–32.

———, 1991. *Finding our Way: Rethinking Ecofeminist Politics.* Montreal, Black Rose Books.

Boddy, J. 1989. *Wombs and Alien Spirits: Women, Men and the Zar Cult in Northern Sudan.* Madison, Wisconsin University Press.

Bookchin, M. 1982. *The Ecology of Freedom: The Emergence and Disappearance of Hierarchy.* Palo Alto, Cheshire Books.

Boserup, E. 1970. *Women's Role in Economic Development.* London, George Allen & Unwin.

Bourgeaud, P. 1988. *The Cult of Pan in Ancient Greece,* trans. K. Atlass and J. Redfield. Chicago, University of Chicago Press.

Braidotti, R., E. Charkiewicz, S. Hausler, S. Wieringa, eds. 1994. *Women, the Environment and Sustainable Development: Towards a Theoretical Synthesis.* London, Zed Books with INSTRAW.

Braun, B. and N. Castree. 1998. *Remaking Reality: Nature at the Millenium.* London, Routledge.

Brody, H. 1981. *Maps and Dreams: Indians and the British Columbia Frontier.* Vancouver, Douglas and McIntyre.

Browne, K. 1998. *Divided Labours: An Evolutionary View of Women at Work.* London, Weidenfeld and Nicolson.

Brubaker, P. K. 1994. *Women Don't Count: The Challenge of Women's Poverty to Christian Ethics.* Atlanta, Ga., Scholars Press.

Bunnag, J. 1973. *Buddhist Monk, Buddhist Layman: A Study of Urban Monastic Organization in Central Thailand.* Cambridge, Cambridge University Press.

Bruun, O. & A. Kalland, eds. 1995. *Asian Perception of Nature: A Critical Approach.* London, Curzon Press.

Burkert, W. 1985. *Greek Religion,* trans. J. Raffan. Oxford, Blackwell.

Campbell, J. 1973. *The Masks of Gods,* 2 vols. London, Souvenir Press.

Carmichael, D., L. Hubert, J. Reeves Brian and S. Audhild. 1994. *Sacred Sites, Sacred Places.* London, Routledge.

Carr-Gomm, P. 1991. *The Druid Way*. Shaftsbury, Dorset, Element.

Carrithers, M. 1983. *The Forest Monks of Sri Lanka*. Delhi, Oxford University Press.

Carson, R. 1962 *Silent Spring*. Harmondsworth, Penguin.

Carsten J. and S. Hugh-Jones, eds. 1995. *About the House: Levi-Strauss and Beyond*. Cambridge, Cambridge University Press.

Cartledge, B., ed. 1998. *Mind, Brain and the Environment*. Oxford, Oxford University Press.

Cavarero, A. 1995. *In Spite of Plato: A Feminist Re-writing of Ancient Philosophy*. Oxford, Polity Press.

Cohen, Y. A., ed. 1974 [1952]. *Man in Adaptation: The Cultural Present*. Chicago, Aldine.

Collingwood, R. G. 1960. *The Idea of Nature*. Oxford, Oxford University Press.

Collins, P. 1995. *God's Earth: Religion as if It Really Mattered*. Dublin, Gill and Macmillan Ltd.

Conway, D. J. 1990. *Norse Magic*. St Paul, Minnesota, Llewellyn Publications.

Cooper, D. and J. Palmer, eds. 1998. *Milton in Spirit of the Environment*. London, Routledge.

Croll, E. and D. Parkin, eds. 1992. *Bush Base: Forest Farm, Culture, Environment and Development*. London, Routledge.

Crowley, V. 1989. *Wicca: The Old Religion in the New Age*. London, The Aquarian Press.

———, 1994. *Phoenix from the Flame*. London, The Aquarian Press.

Curthoys, J. 1997. *Feminist Amnesia: The Wake of Women's Liberation*. London, Routledge.

Dahlke, P. 1908. *Buddhist Essays*. New York, Macmillan.

Dalley, S. 1991. *Myths from Mesopotamia: 'Gilgamesh'*. Oxford, Oxford University Press.

Dalton, G., ed. 1968. *Primitive, Archaic and Modern Economies: Essays of Karl Polanyi*. Boston, Beacon Press.

Dankleman, I. and J. Davidson. 1988. *Women and Environment in the Third World: Alliance for the Future*. London, Earthscan Publication Ltd in association with IUCN.

Davis, R. 1991. *Ritual in an Oscillating Universe: Worshipping Siva in Medieval India*. Princeton, NJ, Princeton University Press.

Deane-Drummond, C. 1996. *A Handbook in Theology and Ecology*. London, SCM Press Ltd.

De Bary, W. T. 1960. *Sources of Chinese Tradition*, vol. I, New York, Columbia University Press.

Delaney, C. 1991. *The Seed and The Soil: Gender and Cosmology in Turkish Village Society*. Berkeley, Calif., University of California Press.

Devall, B. and G. Sessions. 1985. *Deep Ecology*. Salt Lake City, Gibbs Smith.

Dickens, P. 1992. *Society and Nature: Towards a Green Social Theory*. Brighton, Harvester Wheatsheaf.

———, 1996. *Reconstructing Nature: Alienation, Emancipation and the Division of Labour*. London, Routledge.

Dobson, A., ed. 1991. *The Green Reader*. San Francisco, California, Mercury House.

Douglas, M. 1975. *Implicit Meanings*. London, Routledge.

———, 1992. *Risk and Blame: Essays in Cultural Theory*. London, Routledge.

Duby, G. and M. Perrot. 1991. *Histoire des Femmes en Occident*. vol. 1. Paris, Plon.

Eade, J. and M. J. Sallnow, eds. 1991. *Contesting the Sacred: The Anthropology of Christian Pilgrimages*. London, Routledge.

Eastlea, B. 1981. *Science and Sexual Oppression: Patriarchy's Confrontation with Women and Nature*. London, Weidenfield and Nicholson.

Eck, D. L. and D. Jain. 1986. *Speaking of Faith: Cross-Cultural Perspectives on Women*. London, The Women's Press.

Eckersley, R. 1992. *Environmentalism and Political Theory: Towards an Ecocentric Approach*. London, UCL Press.

Eley, G. and S. B. Ortner, eds. 1994. *Culture/Power/History: A Reader in Contemporary Social Theory*. Princeton, NJ, Princeton University Press.

Eliade, M. 1958. *Patterns in Comparative Religion*. London, Sheed & Ward.

———, 1960. *Myths, Dreams and Mysteries: The Encounter between Contemporary Faiths and Archaic Realities*. New York, Harper & Row Publishers.

Ellen, R. 1986. 'What Black Elk Left Unsaid: On the Illusory Images of Green Primitivism', *Current Anthropology*, 6 (2) pp. 8–13.

———, and K. Fuki, eds. 1996. *Redefining Nature: Ecology, Culture and Domestication*. Oxford, Berg.

Ellis, G. and N. Murphy, 1996. *On the Moral Nature of the Universe: Theology, Cosmology and Ethics*. Philadelphia, Fortress.

Engel. J. R. and J. G. Engel, eds. 1990. *Ethics of Environment and Development: Global Challenge International Response*. London, Belhaven Press.

Evers, L. and F. S. Molina. 1987. *Yaqui Deer Songs: Maso Bwikam. A Native American Poetry*. Tucson, University of Arizona Press.

Fakhry, M. 1991. *Ethical Theories in Islam*. Leiden, E. H. Brill.

Falk, N. and R. Gross, eds. 1980. *Unspoken Worlds: Women's Religious Lives in Non-Western Cultures*. San Fransisco, Calif., Harper and Row.

Fardon, R., ed. 1995. *Counterwork: Managing Diverse Knowledges*. London, Routledge.

Farrar, J. and S. Farrar. 1992 [1981]. *Eight Sabbats for Witches*. London, Robert Hale.

Fawzi El-Solh, C. and J. Mabro, eds. 1994. *Muslim Women's Choices: Religious Belief and Social Reality*. Providence/Oxford, Berg Publishers Ltd.

Feldhaus, A. 1995. *Water and Womanhood: Religious Meaning of Rivers in Maharashtra*. Oxford, Oxford University Press.

Fields, R. 1991. *The Code of the Warrior*. New York, Harper Perennial.

Fisher, N., ed. 1993. *Mud, Mirror and Thread: Folk Traditions of Rural India*. Albuquerque, Museum of New Mexico Press.

Foucault, M. 1970. *The Order of Things: An Archaeology of the Human Sciences*. London, Routledge.

Fox, M. 1989. *The Coming of the Cosmic Christ: The Healing of Mother Earth and the Birth of a Global Renaissance*. Melbourne, Collins Drove.

Franzmann, M. 2000. *Women and Religion*. Oxford, Oxford University Press.

Frazer, Sir J. G. 1932 [1922]. *The Golden Bough*. Abridged Version, London, Macmillan.

French, R. K. 1994. *Ancient Natural History: Histories of Nature*. London, New York, Routledge.

Frietag, S. B., ed. 1989. *Culture and Power in Banaras: Community, Performance, and Environment, 1800–1980*. Berkeley, Calif. University of California Press.

Fukui, E. R. and K. Fukui, eds. 1996. *Redefining Nature: Ecology, Culture and Domestication*. Oxford, Berg.

Fuss, D. 1989. *Essentially Speaking*. London, Routledge.

Gadgil, M. and R. Guha. 1992. *This Fissured Land: An Ecological History of India.* Delhi, Oxford University Press.

Gadon, E. W. 1989. *The Once and Future Goddess: A Symbol for Our Time.* San Francisco, Harper and Row.

Gale, F., ed. 1970. *Women's Role in Aboriginal Society.* Canberra, Australian Institute of Aboriginal Studies.

Gnanakan, K. 1999. *God's World: Biblical Insights for a Theology of the Environment.* London, SPCK.

Geertz, C. 1980. *Negara. The Theatre State of Nineteenth-century Bali.* Princeton, NJ, Princeton University Press.

———, 1993. *The Interpretation of Cultures: Selected Essays.* London, Fontana.

———, 1993. *Local Knowledge: Further Essays in Interperative Anthropology.* London, Fontana.

Gimbutas, M. 1982. *The Gods and Goddesses of Old Europe.* London, Thames and Hudson.

Gold, A. 1989. *Fruitful Journeys.* Oxford, Oxford University Press.

Gombrich, R. 1988. *Theravada Buddhism: A Social History from Ancient Benares to Modern Colombo.* London, Routledge and Kegan Paul.

———, and G. Obeyesekere. 1989. *Buddhism Transformed: Religious Change in Sri Lanka.* Princeton, NJ, Princeton University Press.

Grant, K. 1991. *The Magical Revival.* London, Skoob Books Publishing.

Greenwood, S., G. Harvey, A. Simes and M. Nye. May 1995. 'Current Research on Paganism and Witchcraft in Britain', *Journal of Contemporary Religion*, 10 (2).

Gregg, R. B. 1935. *The Power of Non-Violence.* London, Routledge.

Griffin, S. 1979. *Women and Nature: The Roaring Inside Her.* San Francisco, Harper and Row.

Guha, R., ed. 1994. *Social Ecology.* New Delhi, Oxford University Press.

Gunther-Dietz, S. 1993. *Pastoral Deities in Western India.* Delhi, Oxford University Press.

Gupta, S. 1991. *Plant Myths and Tradition in India.* New Delhi, Munshiram Manoharlal Publishers.

Hamilton, L. S. 1993. *Ethics, Religion and Biodiversity: Relations Between Conservation and Cultural Values.* Cambridge, White Horse Press.

Haraway, D. 1989. *Primate Visions: Gender, Race and Nature in the World of Modern Science.* New York, Routledge.

Harris, I. 1991. ' How Environmentalist is Buddhism?', *Religion*, 21, pp. 101–14.

———, 1995. 'Buddhist Environmental Ethics and Detraditionalization: The Case of EcoBuddhism', *Religion*, 25, pp. 199–211.

Harris, E. J. 1980. 'Internal and External Authority Among Lay Buddhist Women in Contemporary Sri Lanka', *Scottish Journal of Religious Studies*, 18 (1).

———, 1998. *What Buddhists Believe.* Oxford, Oneworld.

Harrison, G., ed. 1993. *Human Adaptation.* Oxford, Clarendon Press.

Harvey, G. 1997. *Speaking Earth, Listening People.* London, C. Hurst & Co.

———, and C. Hardman, eds. 1996. *Paganism Today.* London, Thorsons.

Hawley, J. S. and D. M. Wulff, eds. 1995. *The Divine Consort: Radha and the Goddesses of India.* Boston, Mass., Beacon Press.

Hawley, R. and B. Levick, eds. 1995. *Women in Antiquity.* London, New York Routledge.

Hayward T. and J. O'Neill, eds. 1997. *Justice, Property and the Environment: Social and Legal Perspectives.* Aldershott, Ashgate.

Hayward, T. 1992. 'Ecology and Human Emancipation', *Radical Philosophy*, 62, pp. 3–13.

Hillman, D. C., ed. 1994. *Ecotheology: Voices from South and North*. Maryknoll, NY, Orbis Books.

Hoch-Smith, J. and A. Spring, eds. 1978. *Women in Ritual and Symbolic Roles*. New York, Plenum Press.

Holbrook, B. 1981. *The Stone Monkey: An Alternative Chinese-Scientific Reality*. New York, William Morrow Inc.

Holm, J. ed. 1994. *Women in Religion*. London, Pinter Publishers.

———, 1994. *Sacred Place*. London, Pinter Publishers.

Holm, J. and J. W. Bowker, eds. 1994. *Attitudes to Nature*, London, Pinter Publishers.

Holt, C. *et al.*, eds. 1972. *Culture and Politics in Indonesia*. Ithaca, NY, Cornell University Press.

Holthouse, H. 1973. *Australian Geographic Book of Cape York*. NSW, Australian Geographic.

Hook, R. H. and G. Devereux, eds. 1979. *Fantasy and Symbol: Studies in Anthropological Interpretation*. London, Academic Press.

Hoskins, J. 1996. *Headhunting and the Social Imagination in South East Asia*. Stanford, California, Stanford University Press.

Hove, C. and I. Trojanow. 1996. *Guardians of the Soil: Meeting Zimbabwe's Elders*. Harare, Baobab.

Hughes, J. D. 1994. *Pan's Travail: Environmental Problems of the Ancient Greeks and Romans*. Baltimore and London, Johns Hopkins University Press.

Hutton, R. 1991. *The Pagan Religions of the Ancient British Isles: Their Nature and Legacy*. Oxford, Blackwell.

Hwa, Y. J. 1991. 'The Way of Ecopiety: An Essay in Deep Ecology from a Sinitic Perspective', *Asian Philosophy*, 1, 2, pp. 127–40.

Illich, I. 1985. *H20 and the Waters of Forgetfulness: Reflections on the Historicity of 'Stuff'*. Dallas, Tex., Dallas Institute of Humanities and Culture.

Isaacs, J. 1987. *Bush Food: Aboriginal Food and Herbal Medicine*. Willoughby, NSW, Ure Smith Press.

Izutsu, T. 1966. [1959]. *The Structure of the Ethical Terms in the Koran: A Study in Semantics*. Tokyo, Keiv Institute of Philological Studies.

Jabre, B. *et al.*, eds. 1997. *Arab Women Speak Out: Profits of Self-Empowerment*, Baltimore, Johns Hopkins School of Public Health.

Jack, R. L. 1921. *Northmost Australia*. London, Simpkin, Marshall, Hamilton, Kent and Co.

Jackson, C. and R. Pearson, eds. 1998. *Feminist Visions of Development: Gender Analysis and Policy*. London, Routledge.

Jaggar, A., ed. 1994. *Living with Contradictions: Controversies in Feminist Social Ethics*. Boulder, Colo., Westview Press.

Jones, P. and C. Matthews, eds. 1991. *Voices From the Circle: The Heritage of Western Paganism*. London, The Aquarian Press.

Kapadia, K. 1994. 'Impure Women, Virtuous Men: Religion, Resistance and Gender', *South Asia Research*, 142, pp. 184–95.

Karim, W. J., ed. 1995. *'Male' and 'Female' in Developing Southeast Asia*. Oxford, Berg Publishers.

Keller, C. 1996. *Apocalypse Now and Then*. Boston, Mass., Beacon Press.

Kelly, A. 1991. *Crafting the Art of Magic, Book I: A History of Modern Witchcraft 1939–1964*. St Paul, Minnesota, Llewellyn.

Keyes, C. 1984. 'Mothers or Mistresses But Never a Monk: Buddhist Notions of Female Gender in Rural Thailand', *American Ethnologist*, 11 (2).

Khalid, F. M. and J. O'Brian, eds. 1992. *Islam and Ecology*. London, Cassells.

King, U. 1993. *Women and Spirituality: Voices of Protest and Promise*, 2nd edn. Basingstoke, Macmillan.

————, ed. 1995. *Religion and Gender*. Cambridge, Mass., and Oxford, Blackwell.

Kinsley, D. 1995. *Ecology and Religion: Ecological Spirituality in Cross-Cultural Perspective*. Englewood Cliffs, Prentice-Hall.

Kirsch, A. T. and G. Skinner, eds. 1975. *Change and Persistence in Thai Society*. Ithaca, NY, Cornell University Press.

Kohnert, D. 1966. 'Magic and Witchcraft: Implications for Democratization and Poverty Alleviating Aid in Africa', *World Development*, 24 (8), pp. 1347–55.

Kolig, E. 1987. *The Noonkanbah Story*. Dunedin, NZ, University of Otago Press.

Koonz, C. 1987. *Mothers in the Fatherland: Women, the Family and Nazi Politics*. London, Meuthen.

Krebs, C. J. 1994. *Ecology: The Experimental Analysis of Distribution and Abundance*. 4th edn. New York, Harper Collins.

Lan, D. 1985. *Guns and Rain. Guerrillas and Spirit Mediums in Zimbabwe*. London, James Currey.

Lansing, J. S. 1991. *Priests and Programmers: Technologies of Power in the Engineered Landscape of Bali*. Princeton, NJ, Princeton University Press.

Laszlo, E. and Jong Youl Yoo, eds. 1986. *World Encyclopedia of Peace*. vol. 2, Oxford, Pergamon Press.

Leslie, J., ed. 1992. *Roles and Rituals for Hindu Women*. New Delhi, Motilal Banarsidass.

Levin, D. M. 1985. *The Body's Recollection of Being*. London, Routledge & Kegan Paul.

Lin, Y. 1939. *My Country and My People*. (new and revised edn) London, William Heinemann Ltd.

Louth, A. 1990. *The Origins of the Christian Mystical Tradition: From Plato to Denys*. Oxford, Clarendon Press.

Lovelock, J. 1979. *Gaia: A New Look at Life on Earth*. Oxford, Oxford University Press.

————, 1989. *The Ages of Gaia*. Oxford, Oxford University Press.

Luhrmann, T. 1989. *Persuasions of the Witch's Craft: Ritual Magic in Contemporary England*. Oxford, Blackwell.

MacCormack, C. P. and M. Strathern, eds. 1980. *Nature, Culture and Gender*. Cambridge, Cambridge University Press.

MacGregor, S. L. Mathers. 1972 [1888]. *The Key of Solomon the King*. (trans. from the Latin) London, Routledge & Kegan Paul.

MacKinnon, M. H. and M. McIntyre, eds. 1995. *Readings in Ecology and Feminist Theology*. Kansas City: Sheed & Ward.

Mahapatra, S., ed. 1992. *The Realm of the Sacred: Verbal Symbolism and Ritual Structures*. New Delhi, Oxford University Press.

Marcus, G. E., ed. 1993. *Perilous States: Conversations on Culture, Politics, and Nation*. Chicago and London, University of Chicago Press.

Matthews, J. and C. Matthews. 1985. *The Western Way: A Practical Guide to the Western Mystery Tradition*. London, Arkana.

Maxwell, D. 1999. *Christians and Chiefs in Zimbabwe: A Social History of the Hwesa People, 1870s–1890s*. Edinburgh: Edinburgh University Press.

McConnel, U. 1935. *Myths of the Munkan*. London, New York, Melbourne University Press.

McGrath, A. 1987. *Born in the Cattle: Aborigines in Cattle Country*. Sydney, Allen and Unwin.

McKim, M., ed. 1990. *India through Hindu Categories*. New Delhi, Sage Publications.

Meeks, W. 1983. *The First Urban Christians*. New Haven, Conn., Yale University Press.

Merchant, C. 1982. *The Death of Nature: Women, Ecology and the Scientific Revolution*. London, New York, Harper and Row.

———, 1995. *Earthcare: Women and the Environment*. New York, Routledge.

———, ed. 1994. *Key Concepts in Critical Theory: Ecology*. New Jersey, Humanities Press.

Mernissi, F. 1975. *Beyond the Veil: Male-Female Dynamics in a Muslim Society* Cambridge, Mass., Schenkman Publishing Company, Inc.; New York, John Wiley.

Merson, J. 1989. *Roads to Xanadu*. London, Weidenfeld and Nicolson.

Mies, M. and V. Shiva. 1993. *Ecofeminism*. London, Zed Books.

Miller, B., ed. 1993. *Sex and Gender Hierarchies*. Cambridge, Cambridge University Press.

Miller, B. S., ed. 1985. *Exploring India's Sacred Art: Selected Writings of Stella Kramrisch*. Philadelphia, University of Pennsylvania Press.

Milton, K., ed. 1993. *Environmentalism: The View from Anthropology*. London, Routledge.

Moltmann, J. 1981. *Trinity and the Kingdom of God: The Doctrine of God*. London, SCM.

———, 1985. *God in Creation*. London, SCM.

Molyneaux, M. and D. Steinberg. 1995. 'Mies and Shiva's Ecofeminism: A New Testament?', *Feminist Review*, 49, pp. 86–107.

Momsem, J. H. and V. Kinnard, eds. 1993. *Different Places, Different Voices*. London, Routledge.

Moore, H. 1994. *A Passion for Difference*. Cambridge, Polity.

Morgan, P. and C. Lawton, eds. 1996. *Ethical Issues in Six Religious Traditions*. Edinburgh, Edinburgh University Press Ltd.

Morris, B. 1995. 'Woodland and Village: Reflections on the 'animal estate' in Rural Malawi', *Journal of the Royal Anthropological Institute,* 1 (2), pp. 301–15.

Morton, N. 1985. *The Journey is Home*. Boston, Beacon Press.

Mudenge, S. I. G. 1988. *A Political History of Munhumutapa, 1400–1902*. Harare, Zimbabwe Publishing House.

Murata, S. 1992. *The Tao of Islam: A Source Book of Gender Relationships in Islamic Thought*. Albany, State University of New York.

Murphy, P. 1988. 'Sex Typing the Planet: Gaia Imagery and the Problem of Subverting Patriarchy', *Environmental Ethics*. 10, 2, pp. 155–68.

Murray, L. and C. Murray. 1988. *The Celtic Tree Oracle*. London, Rider.

Murray, M. A. 1921. *The Witch-cult in Western Europe: A Study in Anthropology*. Oxford, Oxford University Press.

Nagar, S. L. 1993. *Varaha in Indian Art, Culture and Literature*. New Delhi, Aryan Books International.

Nanda, M. 1991. 'Is Modern Science a Western, Patriarchal Myth? A Critique of the Populist Orthodoxy', *South Asia Bulletin*, XI, Nos. 1 & 2, pp. 32–61.

Narayan, K. 1995. 'The Practice of Oral Literary Criticism', *Journal of American Folklore*, 108 (429), pp. 243–64.

Nash, J. A. 1991. *Loving Nature: Ecological Intergrity and Christian Responsibility.* Nashville, Tenn. Abingdon Press.

Nash, R. 1989. *The Rights of Nature: A History of Environmental Ethics.* Madison, Wisconsin, University of Wisconsin Press.

Nasr, S. H. 1981. *Knowledge and the Sacred* [Gifford lectures] Edinburgh, Edinburgh University Press.

———, ed. 1989. *Islamic Spirituality: Foundations.* vol. I, paperback edn. London, SCM Press Ltd.

Nelson, R. K. 1983. *Make Prayers to the Raven.* Chicago, University of Chicago Press.

———, 'Woman/Earth Speaking: Feminism and Ecology', *New Catalyst Quarterly,* 1987/8. No. 10.

Newport, J. P. 1998. *The New Age Movement and the Biblical Worldview.* Grand Rapids, Michigan, William B. Eerdmans Publishing Company.

Nicholls, D. 1994. *Deity and Domination: Image of God and the State in the Nineteenth and Twentieth Centuries.* London, Routledge.

Nizam al-Mulk, 1960. *The Book of Government or Rules for Kings. Siyasta-nama, Translated from the Persian by Hubert Darke.* London: Routledge & Keagan Paul.

Ohnuki-Tierney, E. 1993. *Rice as Self: Japanese Identities Through Time.* Princeton, NJ, Princeton University Press.

Order of Bards, Ovates and Druids. 1988. *'Gwers' of the Order of Bards, Ovates and Druids* (printed material for the OBOD correspondence course). Richmond, Surrey, OBOD, Nos. 1–24.

Osborne, R. 1982. *Classical Landscape with Figures: The Ancient City and its Countryside.* London, George Philip.

Padel, F. 1995. *The Sacrifice of Human Being.* New Delhi, Sage.

Peters, F. E. 1993. *A Reader on Classical Islam.* Princeton, NJ, Princeton University Press.

Peterson, I. 1989. *Poems to Siva: The Hymns of the Tamil Saints.* Princeton, NJ, Princeton University Press.

Phiri, I. 1997. *Women, Presbyterianism and Patriarchy: Religious Experience of Chewa Women in Central Malawi.* Blantyre, Kachere Books, n.d.

Plaskow, J. 1990. *Standing Again at Sinai: Judaism from a Feminist Perspective.* New York, Harper Collins.

Plumwood, V. 1993. *Feminism and the Mastery of Nature.* London, Routledge.

Porkert, M. 1974. *The Theoretical Systems of Chinese Medicine.* Boston, Mass. MIT Press.

Porritt, J. and D. Winner. 1988. *The Coming of the Greens.* London, Fontana.

Primavesi, A. 1991. *From Apocalypse to Genesis: Ecology, Feminism and Christianity.* Tunbridge Wells, Burns and Oates.

———, 2000. *Sacred Gaia: Holistic Theology and Earth System Science.* London, Routledge.

Prime, R. 1992. *Hinduism and Ecology.* London, Cassells.

Raheja, G. and A. Gold. 1994. *Listen to the Heron's Words: A Reimagination of Gender and Kinship in North India.* Berkeley, University of California Press.

Rahman, F. 1980. *Major Themes of the Quran.* Minneapolis, Mn: Biblioteca Islamica.

Randle, M. 1994. *Civil Resistance.* London, Fontana.

Ranger, T. O. 1999. *Voices From the Rocks. Nature, Culture and History in the Matopos.* Oxford, James Curry.

Reynolds, H. 1987. *The Law of the Land*. Victoria, London, New York, Penguin.

Richard, P. and B. E. Campbell. 1983. *The Idols of Death and the God of Life*. Maryknoll, New York, Orbis Books.

Robb, C. S. 1995. *Equal Value*. Boston, Beacon Press.

Rosaldo, M. 1980. *Knowledge and Passion: Ilongot Notions of Self and Society*. New York, Cambridge University Press.

Rosaldo, M. Z. and L. Lamphere. 1974. *Woman, Culture, and Society*. Stanford, Stanford University Press.

Rose, D. B., ed. 1991. *Nature and Gender*. London, Harwood Academic Publishers.

Ross, S. D. 1995. *Plenishment in the Earth: An Ethic of Inclusion*. Albany, State University of New York.

Ruether, R. R. 1983. *Sexism and God Talk: Toward a Feminist Theology* Boston, Beacon Press.

Rutland, V. 1998. *Imagining the Sacred: Soundings in World Religions*. Maryknoll, New York, Orbis.

Sabbatucci, D. 1988. *La Religione di Roma Antica: dal Calendario festivo all'Ordine cosmico*. Milan, Arnaldo Mondadori Editore.

Sachs, W., ed. 1993. *Global Ecology: A New Arena of Political Conflict*. London, Zed Books.

Saso, M. 1972. *Taoism and the Rite of Cosmic Renewal*. Honolulu, University of Hawaii Press.

———, 1990. *Blue Dragon, White Tiger. Taoist Rites of Passage*. Honolulu, University of Hawaii Press.

Sax, W. 1991. *Mountain Goddess: Gender and Politics in a Himalayan Pilgrimage*. Oxford, Oxford University Press.

Schama, S. 1995. *Landscape and Memory*. New York, Knopf.

Schleifer, A. 1986 *Motherhood in Islam*. Cambridge, Islamic Academy.

Schoffeleers, J. M., ed. 1979. *Guardians of the Land: Essays in Central African Territorial Cults*. Gwelo, Zimbabwe, Mambo Press.

Schoffeleers, J. M. 1992. *River of Blood: The Genesis of Martyr Cult in Southern Malawi c.ᴀᴅ 1600*. Madison, University of Wisconsin Press.

Schwartz, R. M. 1997. *The Curse of Cain: The Violent Legacy of Monotheism* Chicago, University of Chicago Press.

Sen, G., ed. 1992. *Indigenous Vision: Peoples of India Attitudes to the Environment*. New Delhi, Sage.

Sered, S. 1999. *Women of the Sacred Groves: Divine Priestesses of Okinawa*. New York, Oxford, Oxford University Press.

Sharma, A., ed. 1987. *Women in World Religions*, New York, State University of New York Press.

Sheldrake, P. 1998. *Spirituality and Religion: Christian Living and the Doctrine of God*. London, Darton, Longman and Todd.

Shipley, G. and J. Salmon, eds. 1996. *Human Landscapes in Classical Antiquity*. London, Routledge.

Shiva, V. 1989. *Staying Alive: Women, Ecology and Development*. London, Zed Books.

Shulman, D. 1985. *The King and the Clown in South Indian Myth and Poetry*. Princeton, NJ, Princeton University Press.

Sivaraman, K., ed. 1989. *Hindu Spirituality: I: Vedas through Vedanta*. London, SCM Press Ltd.

Sjoo, M. and B. Mor. 1991. *The Great Cosmic Mother: Rediscovering the Religion of the Earth*, 2nd edn. San Francisco, London, Harper and Row.

Slezkine, Y. 1994. *Arctic Mirrors: Russia and the Small Peoples of the North*. Ithaca and London, Cornell University Press.

Smil, V. 1993. *China's Environmental Crisis*. Armonk, New York, M.E. Sharpe.

———,1996. *Environmental Problems in China: Estimates of Economic Costs East-West Center Special Report*, No.5, April 1996. Honolulu, University of Hawaii.

Smith, G., ed. 1996. *The Nationalities Question in the post-Soviet States*. London and New York, Longman, 1996.

Soper, K. 1995. *What is Nature? Culture, Politics and the non-Human*. Oxford, Blackwell.

Starhawk. 1989. *The Spiral Dance: A Rebirth of the Ancient Religion of the Great Goddess*. 10th Anniversary edn. San Francisco, Harper.

Stevens, F. 1974. *Aborigines in the Northern Cattle Industry*. Canberra, Australian National University Press.

Stone, M. 1976. *When God Was a Woman*. San Diego, Harvest/HBJ.

Strang, V. 1997. *Uncommon Ground: Cultural Landscapes and Environmental Values*. Oxford, New York, Berg.

Strathern, M. 1992. *Reproducing the Future: Anthropology, Kinship and the New Reproductive Technologies*. Manchester, Manchester University Press.

——, 1992. *After Nature: English Kinship in the Late Twentieth Century*. Cambridge, Cambridge University Press.

Sturgeon, N. 1997. *Ecofeminist Natures: Race, Gender, Feminist Theory and Political Action*. New York, Routledge.

Tambiah, S. J. 1984. *The Buddhist Saints of the Forest and the Cult of Amulets*. Cambridge, Cambridge University Press.

Taylor, J. L. 1993. *Forest Monks and the Nation-State*. Singapore, Institute of Southeast Asian Studies.

Terwiel, B. J. 1979 [revised edn] *Monks and Magic: An Analysis of Religious Ceremonies in Central Thailand*. London and Malmo, Curzon Press.

Thompson, E. P. 1991. *Customs in Common*. New York, New Press.

Thompson, L. G. 1979. *Chinese Religion: An Introduction*. (5th edn.) Belmont, California, Wadsworth Inc.

Tiryakian, E. A., ed. 1974. *On the Margin of the Visible: Sociology, the Esoteric, and the Occult*. New York, John Wiley & Sons.

Trawick, M. 1900. *Notes on Love in a Tamil Family*. Berkeley, California, University of California Press.

Tuan, Y. 1968. 'Discrepancies between Environmental Attitude and Behaviour: Example from Europe and China.' *Canadian Geographer*, 12, No 3, pp. 176–91.

Turner, V. W., ed. 1982. *Celebration: Studies in Festivity and Ritual*. Washington, DC, Smithsonian Institution Press.

van Binsbergen, W. and M. Schoffeleers, eds. 1986. *Theoretical Explorations in African Religion*. London, RKP.

van Gulick , R. H. 1974. *Sexual Life in Ancient China*. Leiden, E. J. Brill.

van Esterik, P., ed. 1982. *Women of South East Asia*. Illinois, Northern Illinois University Centre for South East Asian Studies.

Vernant, J. P. 1983. *Myth and Thought Among the Greeks*. London, Routledge and Kegan Paul.

Versnel, H. S., ed. 1993. *Inconsistencies in Greek and Roman Religion II*. Leiden, E. J. Brill.

Visvanathan, N. *et al*. eds., 1997. *The Women, Gender and Development Reader*. London, Zed Books.

Waley, A. 1977. *The Way and the Power. The Tao Te Ching and Its Place in Chinese Thought*. London, Mendala Books, Union Paperbacks.

Walud, A. 1997. 'Woman and Islam: Beyond the Stereotypes', *Pakistan Journal of Women's Studies: Alam-e-Niswan*, 4 (2), pp. 1–14.

Watson, B. (trans.) 1968. *The Complete Works of Chuang Tzu*. New York, Columbia University Press.

Watson, C. W. and R. Elder, eds. 1993. *Understanding Witchcraft and Sorcery in Southeast Asia*. Honolulu, University of Hawaii Press.

Welbon, G. and G. E. Yocum. 1982. *Religious Festivals in South India and Sri Lanka*. New Delhi, Manohar Publications.

White, L. [Jnr] 1967, March. 'The Historical Roots of Our Ecological Crisis', *Science*, 155, pp. 1203–07. (Reprinted in Roger S. Gottlieb, ed. *This Sacred Earth Religion, Nature, Environment*. London, Routledge 1996, pp. 184–93.)

Williams, R. 1983 [1976]. *Keywords: A Vocabulary of Culture and Society*. New York, Oxford University Press.

Wilson, K. 1992. 'Cults of Violence and Counter-Violence in Mozambique', *Journal of Southern African Studies*, 18 (3), pp. 527–82.

Winkler, J. J. 1990. *The Constraints of Desire: The Anthropology of Sex and Gender in Ancient Greece*. London, Routledge.

Worster, D. 1977. *Nature's Economy: A History of Ecological Ideas*. Cambridge, Cambridge University Press.

Zimmerman, F. 1984. *Fluid Signs: Being a Person the Tamil Way*. Berkeley, California, University of California Press.

———, 1987 [1982]. *The Jungle and the Aroma of Meats: An Ecological Theme in Hindu Medicine*. Berkeley, California, University of California Press.

———, 1988. *Hindu Goddesses*. Berkeley, California, University of California Press.

Index

Major works cited in the text will be found in the bibliography.
Only authors whose work is treated at some length are indexed.

W

Wana people, 111, 112
waste, household, 170–1, 172
WED, 4
WEN, 4
West, Western, 1, 2, 4, 5, 6, 10, 11, 15,
    16, 123, 124, 195, 202
  and capitalist values, 211
  and Chinese concepts, 213
  consumerism, 232
  development models, 4, 164
  dominance, 195
  and dualism, 213
  and Eastern values, 211–2
  and environment, 171–2, 188, 212
  and holism, 211
  intellectuals, 211
  science, 208–9
  technology, 13, 77, 208–9
  thought, 196, 208–9, 211
  see also capitalism; development
white settlers, 13, 63
wholeness, 228, 230
Wiccan, Wiccans, 227, 233
wilderness, 15, 91, 198
wildlife reserve, 5
wildness, 186
witches; witchcraft, 1, 8, 14–15, 29, 95,
    96, 220, 227
wife, wives:
  of God, 98
  virgin, 99
Winslow, D., 181, 184–5, 187
womanhood, 39
women:
  adepts, 103, 210
  and agriculture, 95
  Aristotelian view of, 54, 175
  and botanical knowledge, 56, 57
  Brahmin, 39
  as carers, 69
  and chaos, 148
  and childbirth, 55, 148, 181
  concubines, and concubinage, 13,
    70, 210
  disparagement of, 9–10
  domination of, 3, 15
  economic activity of, 95, 187–8, 190
  and education, 9, 69, 74, 91, 156
  empowerment of, 228
  exploitation of, 154
  and environmental wisdom, 36
  European, 71
  exclusion of, 9
  and fertility, 56, 222
  and festivals, 55–9
  and illiteracy, 157
  and infanticide, 37, 210
  and land, 76, 91

and leadership, 17
and management, 3
as mediators, 10, 56, 70, 71, 76
as mediums, 96, 104
and menstruation, 28, 167, 181, 183,
    184
as men's partners, 12
as mothers, 26, 85, 92
and mystery, 222
and Nature, 104, 132
and non-violent campaigns, 206
ordination of, 27
and peace camp, 206
and pollution, 27–9, 39, 181, 184
and poverty, 154
as priestesses, 9, 47, 55
and property, 153
and religion, 8, 55, 98
reproductive roles, 9
as a resource, 3, 84
and rights, 142, 144, 148, 151, 152–3
and ritual, 9, 12, 55, 56–8, 59, 95,
    159, 164–5, 170
and the sacred, 6–7, 28
and sexual appetite, sexuality, 12,
    27, 28, 181–2, 221
and social inequality, 11, 28, 32
status, 8–9, 14
and subversion, 61n.39
as subordinate, subordination of, 3,
    11, 37, 57, 221, 222
subjugation, 77
in Western societies, 65
and 'wild femininity', 59
  see also cults; gender; rituals; *and
    under individual belief systems*
Woodland Trust, 233
worldviews, 212
World Wildlife Fund for Nature, 233
wu hsing, 201
wu wei, 196

X

Xaxa, 35

Y

yang, 199, 200, 201, 205, 207
Yatutsh (Siberia), 82
Yi Ching, 195, 199, 200
yin, 197, 199, 200, 201, 205, 207, 208
yin-yang, 10, 195, 199, 201, 208–9
Yir Yaront, 64
  rights to land, 13, 15
Yosemite National Park, 165

Z

Zambia, 97
zar, 39
Zimbabwe, 7, 38, 95–7, 98, 100

260